The Superman
From Nietzsche to Teilhard de Chardin

The Superman From Nietzsche to Teilhard de Chardin

JULES CHAIX-RUY

Translated by
MARINA SMYTH-KOK

UNIVERSITY OF NOTRE DAME PRESS
NOTRE DAME   LONDON

Grateful acknowledgment is made for excerpts from the following works:

The Complete Works of Friedrich Nietzsche, translated under the general editorship of Oscar Levy [1909–1911], New York: Russell & Russell, 1964, and London: George Allen & Unwin Ltd. Reprinted by permission of the publishers.

Pages 29, 31–32, 83–84, 73–74 in *The Divine Milieu*, by Pierre Teilhard de Chardin, translated by Bernard Wall. English translation copyright © 1960 by Wm. Collins Sons & Co., London, and Harper & Row, Publishers, Incorporated, New York. Originally published in French as "Le Milieu Divin," copyright 1957 by Editions du Seuil, Paris. Reprinted by permission of Harper & Row, Inc.

The poems "In Hospital" and "When It Clears Up" from *Pasternak Fifty Poems*, translated by Lydia Pasternak Slater, reprinted by permission of the publishers, George Allen & Unwin Ltd., London, and Barnes & Noble, Inc., New York.

The poems "Spring Rainstorm," "We Are Few," "The Tragic Story," and "Garden of Gethsemane" from *Poems*, by Boris Pasternak, translated by Eugene M. Kayden, reprinted by permission of the publishers, The Antioch Press, Yellow Springs, Ohio.

Report to Greco, by Nikos Kazantzakis, copyright © 1965, by Simon & Schuster, Inc. Reprinted by permission of Simon & Schuster, Inc., and Dr. Max Tau, Oslo, Norway.

Teilhard de Chardin, by Claude Cuénot, with permission of Helicon Press, Inc., Baltimore, Maryland, and Burns & Oates Ltd., London.

The Two Sources of Morality and Religion, by Henri Bergson. Translated by R. Ashley Audra and Cloudesley Brereton with the assistance of W. Horsfall Carter. Copyright 1935, © 1963 by Holt, Rinehart and Winston, Inc. Reprinted by permission of Holt, Rinehart and Winston, Inc.

Preface

*T*his book supplements rather than corrects the conclusions of a work that appeared more than thirty years ago. The century was then hardly beginning. At the very most one could sense that the tragic aspect of the human adventure would become more pronounced, that the gap between the unbounded ambition and the moral poverty of modern man would increase. The moving confession of our basic destitution which Jacques Rivière expressed in his *Carnets de captivité*[1] has become even more justified with the progress of technology. I know that it is now considered good form to cover up these horrors: We are supposed to forget that recent times have showed us to be ruthless beasts of prey, that fanaticism is still among us, that tyranny was born again, and we are expected to incense the irreversible process of "socialization" in the midst of a peaceful "noosphere"; I know that the technocrats, these new "Machiavellians" of which Burnham spoke, want us to build an artificial paradise. But where do we find the "bigger soul"[2] which would make it possible to avoid the imbalance created by progress?

We often hear that we are headed toward greater understanding and social justice. Is this not simply because the screen of lies hiding the lack of justice has become more dense? The efforts that were made during all the eighteenth century to subject politics to morality, or at least to soften its principles, were resumed after the First World War in the hope of founding what Maurice Blondel called "the civiliza-

[1] *De Renan à Jacques Rivière*, "Cahiers de la Nouvelle Journée," (Paris: Bloud et Gay, 1930).
[2] Bergson uses this expression ("supplément d'âme") in *The Two Sources of Morality and Religion*. Cf. passim.

tion of peace," but they too failed miserably. The confused debates of the U.N. hardly succeed in concealing with the emptiness of big words the sordid compromises between conflicting interests. The "reason of state" and the "state secret" have reappeared; the end is cynically invoked to justify the most atrocious means. Devious ways, traps, tricks, and the breach of promises in which the naive were foolish enough to believe are all in the rules of the game. Kant used to say that if peace is to be established and consolidated, one must no longer sow division, hatred, and mistrust. These are the very methods power is using today, without concern for the resulting irremediable destruction; communities that arose from ancient and steady affinities are now falling apart because of this.[3] This "Superman" whose imminent coming is everywhere announced might well turn out to be the perfected robot against which Bernanos has warned us, La Mettrie's "machine" raised to the level of electronics. Might we not fear under such conditions that our actions will be aimed only at earthly "projects" and will no longer be carried by this élan Blondelian dialectics saw in them?

These are the questions we are asking in this survey. It opens with the "Superman"—or rather the "Super-human"—whose advent was promised by Nietzsche, and closes with the Ultra-human which the mysticism of Teilhard de Chardin sees rising in the midst of the noosphere and then condensing and winding around the Omega point. The hope that temporal history would turn toward the highest spiritual life is in no way novel. Already in the eighteenth century, the enlightened priests thought they could go a long way with the atheists and adhere to the myth of progress. We do not wish to deny the value or, to a certain extent, the effectiveness of these generous intentions. Nonetheless, we believe that the concept of

[3] Cf. our work, *Barrès educateur*, (Gap: Editions Ophrys, 1946).

evolution must be handled with great caution. If everything is drifting in this universe, if no ontological structure is supporting a time that is—like fire—intrinsically indifferent to what it creates and destroys, if it contains the two poles of an entropy in which everything becomes stationary and of a zone of spirituality in which everything becomes animated and perfected, how can we speak of consistency, how can we justify a wager? Faith enlightens reason and guides it; reason in turn supports faith and justifies it. They cannot be set end to end and faith cannot be expected to straighten out an orientation which is not in its direction.

We do not believe either in the absolute value of socialization; we fear, on the contrary, that social inequality will become more pronounced, that the requirements of a rational organization will finally call for a system of education—who knows, perhaps even for biological "preformations"[4]—excluding all personal life. These inequalities would become more accented under the rule of "managers"—these "superior men" Zarathustra so disliked.[5] It may be that our attempts at conquering space are the symbol and the sign of the soul's will to escape which Plato has transcribed in the beautiful myths of Phaedo and Timeus. But might they not only accentuate a divergence which Saint Augustine pointed out, an irreducible divergence between a will that inserts its actions in the divine plan and a will which claims to make God unnecessary and to free itself from him? Can this duality be overlooked to the point of setting mutually exclusive orientations on the same axis?[6]

---

[4] Aldous Huxley presents a caricature of the world of tomorrow in his *Brave New World*; but this world has a lot in common with our present surroundings.

[5] Cf. the fourth part of *Zarathustra*.

[6] Cf. our work, *Saint Augustin: temps et histoire*, (Paris: Editions Augustiniennes) and, *passim*, the chapter on Dostoevski.

Though we condemn all euphoria and an unlimited confidence in "perpetual motion," we do not wish to yield to a morbid pessimism. At the very most we wish to point out the reservations which we believe should be made, to appeal to the human as opposed to the superhuman, to promote the development of all our potentialities instead of the surrender to a futile will to power. Christian thought has always displayed two trends with a great deal of mutual misunderstanding and perilous antagonisms. Thus the Manichees and the Pelagians and later the Molinists and the Jansenists have confronted one another. One side believed—and still believes—that we must trust man to complete creation, to raise the universe to God; the others dread the increasing weight of evil and believe only invisible supernatural interventions can redress our constantly perverse will.

In fact, we must beware of all excesses. For myself, I believe that the very triumphs of science testify to the existence of a structure of the universe whose progressive transformations—though they appear on a level beyond our powers of understanding—determine the paths we can follow and the limits of an escape contained in the divine plan. We must submit to this plan and to the mathematical relations that form its structure: This is how we are able to set our satellites and missiles on their orbits. We must therefore beware of any excesses for which we might have to pay with increased suffering and distortions. We have only to think of the monsters which might result from a reckless and too hasty incursion into the realm of life. What stone labyrinth[7] might we build to imprison the soul, this unknown that would thereby be deprived, even more than by its corporeal prison, of all chance of escape. What dreadful conflicts may be the price for the prolongation of our life span if it is not accompanied by a

[7] Cf. the novel by Dino Buzzati, Il Grande rittrato.

decrease in the deliriums of envy and resentment which are now growing every day! The formidable development of our technological thinking conveys and emphasizes an ancient disequilibrium which led to the supremacy of the *homo faber* at the expense of the human aspects of intelligence and of its ascent to higher orders of spirituality. The image of man arising in our times is a mutilated image, like the *Victory of Samothrace*. It exalts, on the threshold of the new Tower we are building, the eternal ambition of the Titans; but, like their daring project, it will not be finished.

At this crossroad we have now reached, another direction lies open to our efforts. Antonio Rosmini, one of the greatest metaphysicians of all times, pointed it out over a century ago. Let man aim at anchoring himself more firmly in being by harmoniously developing his powers, let him offer himself to the complement of light—of spiritualizing grace—that will enrich him with new structures; then—without in any way renouncing the earthly tasks he is called upon to perform—he will become synchronously united with a universe whose multiple aspects will gradually unfold before him. There is no way out for us as long as we insist on following the movement by which the universe is dilating away from its Center, swallowing us up a little more in each one of our attempts in the indefinite extension of space and time. We soon become discouraged at having to roll the rock uphill against the pull of the steep slope. "Sisyphus will be happy" only if he abandons the rock to its own weight. The human adventure, as Jean Rostand will say, however long it may be, will never be more than a fleeting moment in the history of the universe to which some would restrict it; the miracle it represents then appears not as a goal but as a mere accident. It is only in the instant in which time is gathered that this adventure can find a way out and a sense. For it is even more difficult for us to master this other time, that extends apparently indefinitely before and behind us, than a space which was once believed to be stationary. What is the sense in extending to the limits of a galaxy the drift of the earthly field in which our life has unfolded to this day, following the peaceful rhythm of the seasons, if this galaxy is itself drifting in the midst of a larger field which is without limits for us and which will finally set us on one of its orbits and impose a wider rhythm on our futile efforts?

I am afraid that the increasing socialization others are invoking will only yield this perfect order, these careful regulations which the Grand Inquisitor opposes to the silent appeal of Christ. Ensor sensed this when he painted, in the midst of the euphoria of a hilarious and derisory carnival, the Savior making his entrance into an exultant city of the future. This Christ is announcing the indifference brought about by the comforts of a civilization centered on earthly values. Albert Camus, with even more cruelty, will imprison us in a city "in a state of siege" in which the destiny of each one of us is fixed ahead of time. We are far indeed from the illusory "noosphere" whose density would increase indefinitely with the mere expansion of human communities. Auguste Comte's "Great Milieu" announced a similar future! But we are headed in a completely different direction. Increasing specialization awaits us, with the enslavement to precise duties which will erase, together with our disquiet, any desire for a personal life and even the will to create. Consciousness, which had been our main claim to greatness, will gradually fade away. The Ultra-human, like the Superhuman, might therefore turn out to be a regression instead of the progress we were anticipating. We were aiming at peaks we had glimpsed for an instant, where we thought we would breathe a spiritualized atmosphere. And now they have vanished! In their stead, we are faced with Zarathustra's Gateway. The road that passes underneath it and that, because of the invisible deviation in its course, appeared to be rising, is in fact leading us toward our past. Everything is beginning anew before us: desire and servitude. We are filled with despair as we see that by allowing ourselves to be guided by the bent of our reason toward technology, we have merely been endowed with a superior instinct.

Contents

Introduction:
The Duality of the
Renaissance Man

*E*very period has formed its own image of man; sometimes this image, like the Platonic Idea, became a model for those who had molded it out of their hopes and fears. Sometimes the distance between the ideal image and real man—caught up in the difficulties of everyday life—became greater. Man would then be dissatisfied with himself; he hoped for reforms, called for revolutions capable of filling this gap. Then, when the reform that brought him back to his sources was completed, when the revolution got bogged down or miscarried with dreams of freedom and social justice, it became necessary once more to toil in the present with the avowed or hidden awareness of defeat. For the Jew of Israel, the ideal image is that of the prophet; the same is true of the Moslem philosophers, Al Farabi and Avicenna. The prophet, says the Second Master,[1] combines fourteen almost contradictory qualities: To

[1] Al Farabi was given this name, the First Master being, of course, Aristotle. And the book we are referring to, the key book on which all his successors will meditate, is *The Model City as Opposed to the Cities of Error and Sin.*

1

prudence he must add wisdom; to wisdom, an aptitude for contemplating the hypostases; to this serene contemplation, divination; but while concentrating on this shape-giving Intelligence, he is, thanks to the alacrity of his practical mind, the wisest of all legislators. Some men come fairly close to this exceptional success of the prophet, to this absolute ideal. But in them some faculty will be stronger which will destine them for the role of guide, for that of sage, or for that of legislator. The people follow them, caught in the rut of traditions they do not question. In Ibn Tufayl's philosophical novel—in which are weighed the respective merits of the man living in society and of the anchorite—the autodidact who, detaching himself from worldly goods through a progressive movement of his intellect, rises to the peaks of mysticism and devotes himself to the contemplation of the One is thus of a higher rank than the theologian and, even more so, than the leader who tries to reach justice by preserving traditions and customs. To each one of these levels of intellection there corresponds a different understanding of truth. Intellection and faith discover its bright or enigmatic aspects: It is the philosopher who will reach the highest summits where dwells the Eternal.

The Greeks, on the other hand, opposed light to darkness, Apollonian serenity to Dionysian delirium; they nonetheless resorted to this delirium when they wanted to come in contact with the sacred, to penetrate the mysteries of a being of whom consciousness intermittently lights up only the outside. Before the soothsayer Prometheus, who though chained to his rock can read the future, even Zeus is powerless. He therefore sends him messengers to try and wrest his secret from him. Has Prometheus not learned how "to classify for the use of the ephemeral the thousand forms of divinatory art"?[2] But Prometheus reveals what he knows only through enigmas. Even

[2] Aeschylus: *Prometheus.*

2

Socrates, the wisest of all Greeks, turns to his inner daemon when he has to make an important decision; he resorts to "incantations" when he has to face the frightening passage leading from life to the ultimate mystery: that of death. Finally, Sappho, in order to be reborn, will throw herself from the Leucadian rock; only on this condition will wings free her from the prison of her body.

Thus there has always been a duality in the idea man had of himself. He aspires to wisdom and invokes the revelations of madness. He abandons Minerva for the frenetic bacchanalia. Dance reveals to him secrets which remain hidden from his reason. The divination of the prophet, the delirium of the pythoness or of the witch, are they not a sort of prefiguration of this "prospective" through which we now seek to throw light on a perilous present? To know the future by means of an illumination which follows no laws, to lift for an instant the veil which conceals it, how powerful the man capable of this would be! Hence the popularity of the Sibyls, of the oracle of Delphi, of astrologers and of priests for whom these secrets sometimes become clear. Very soon, archetypes arise, with their origins in man's unconscious. He sees them as benevolent gods or demons. Prometheus, by stealing the fire, frees him from darkness and distress and endows him with the most essential of all techniques. With its help he will someday be able to dethrone the king of the universe. Minerva tells him not to be so foolishly ambitious and teaches him how to fit into an order which is above him, how to subject his reason to the divine Logos. And thus, divided between ambition and wisdom from the very beginning, man is destined to conquer the universe; a perfidious voice incites him to rebellion, to proclaim the death of the One who claims to impose his law on him. But at the same time, another voice encourages him to master himself; it would be very dangerous to yield to the irrational part of his being, no matter how generous his inclinations, how rich the sudden intuitions he owes to it. Destiny represents this shadow which no prudence can dismiss since it arises from lucidity itself. Is Oedipus not the victim of this human, all too human wisdom which wanted to ignore the threat? The prophecy dooming him to the infernal deities will be fulfilled. But Athena takes him under her protection and guides him to this Attica where the rhythm of the laws has fixed the boundaries separating the just from the unjust. The chaos then subsides: the Erinyes become the Eumenides. Let us listen to the last warning he gives to King Theseus:

"How many cities, no matter how well they are governed, let themselves be driven to excesses! The gods know well how to find, even a long time afterward, those who, in defiance of their order, have turned toward madness. Be sure, O son of Aegeus, never to do this!"

The long wait for the millenium seemed to fix man in the attitude of a kneeling or recumbent effigy, or of a stylite. Why bother to look at this world if it is nothing but a temporary dwelling in which we go through a period of trial? The great hope for a near and triumphant resurrection, as shining as a Byzantine mosaic, the awaited apparition of the Judge above the turmoil of suddenly unleashed storms suspended all earthly ambitions and immobilized the pilgrim in meditation and prayer. We then find these "men possessed by God,"[3] these new prophets of a transfigured universe where the soul dissolves in the torrents of the flame of divine love. Then begin the long quests on the roads to distant holy places, the flights to the desert where nothing will distract the soul from its waiting, where it will see the signs, imperceptible to others, of the hoped-for arrival: "The monk in the state of complete

[3] Cf. J. Lacarrière, Les Hommes ivres de Dieu (Editions Arthaud), and J. Decarreaux, Les Moines et la civilisation (Grenoble, Paris: Editions Arthaud).

4

dispassion," wrote John Climacus, who retired to the Sinai in the seventh century, "is he who strives to confine his incorporeal being within his bodily house, paradoxical as this is. The cat keeps hold of her mouse, and the thought of the solitary holds his spiritual mouse. Do not call this example rubbish; if you do, then you do not yet know what solitude means."

The dispassionate man is aiming at the summits of asceticism; to reach them, he must oppose "the silence of his lips to the turmoil in his heart." The road to renunciation of the world and of oneself is a long one: Jerome Bosch, at the end of the fifteenth century, will depict it on one of the leaves of a diptych in the Palace of the Doges in Venice as an endless tunnel in complete darkness. The soul that sets out in it feels it will never reach the end, so weak is the light announcing the exit. For this image of the elder or of the monk—whose features are so similar in spite of the differences in perspective between the Oriental rite and Catholic orthodoxy—did not vanish with the advent of the year 1000. The slightest omen will bring it back to life. It arises again with the prophecies of Joachim of Fiore, the announcement of the reign of the Holy Ghost, the last stage before the apparition of the heavenly Jerusalem in the transfigured skies; it inspires artists: Dürer, whose mind will be haunted by the turmoil of the Apocalypse; Breughel, who will be obsessed by the Triumph of Death. The ruthless wars, the farmers' revolutions sweeping over the Low Countries, Flanders, and Western Germany remind men of their incapacity to free themselves without the help of a new supernatural intervention. Insanity is unleashed everywhere, the seven capital sins leave their mark on faces that have become nothing but masks. Embarked on the wandering ship, on the "ship of fools," or carried on the merry-go-round, men indulge in vice and in childish distractions. One must therefore listen to those who, like van Ruysbroek, oppose a pacified

5

picture to this caricature of man. Let this deceitful universe generated by vain lusts disappear, and let the spiritual world appear in which the soul can rise, appeased and purified! Such a call has crossed the centuries: It reappears in our times, so similar to the fifteenth century in their contradictory aspirations, proposing to us the life of the anchorites and of the saints, of the Elder Zosima or of Charles de Foucauld.

But in the Middle Ages, at the side of the praying man, we find the man of action. Is it not a remainder of lust for power, of impatient ambition, which prompts the vocations of the knights and leads them to adventure on the roads to the Holy Land? The turmoil of battle is less of a distraction from prayer when one is fighting the Infidel; and fighting alone is not sufficient for victory, but must be accompanied by the ardor of a faith willing to make the greatest sacrifices. In this commitment that was to lead Cervantes to Lepanto and let Don Quixote arise from his disillusionment, which weighed most: the share of applied religion, that of selfless heroism, or even that of interest? Louis IX may have been completely disinterested when he set out from Aigues-Mortes, but this was certainly not the case for those Crusaders who were lead to Constantinople by their ambition and the perfidious schemes of the Republic of Venice. The profane and the sacred are tightly interwoven in their soul, as they will be in those navigators who would soon cross the oceans. They will conquer empires and will think that they can impose their religion, as though by martyring the body one could bend the reticent soul; they will then go to sleep without fear under their slabs of stone, satisfied that they have risen above themselves and have freed themselves by offering to Christ these lands they saved from error and impiety. Thus we find again this same duality—however different in form—which we already met in antiquity and Islam; side by side, the anchorite and the conquerer go through these long centuries during which modern man is being shaped.

6

But this duality will become more pronounced during the Renaissance. The antagonism then becomes sharper, the conflict breaks out between wisdom, which obeys the law governing the universe, careful of the rhythm inscribed in it by a divine "Analogy," and the will to power, which becomes impatient and wishes to subject the universe to its own law. The Renaissance, therefore, with all the acuteness of its contrasts,[4] lies between the Greek world, which it recreates in an original form, and our modern world, which it announces.

We will dwell at some length on the huge fresco Gobineau painted of these centuries when everything was questioned anew; for no period is closer to ours than these fourteenth and fifteenth centuries in which man, pulling away from the past while trying to rediscover it, is wondering about his future. Even in Savonarola an anxious and ardent faith was intermingled in undistinguishable proportions with the will to power; it was the desire to dominate bodies and coerce souls which animated, unknown to himself, this great preacher who, for several years, seemed capable of making time flow back. He terrified his contemporaries by his apocalyptic prophecies; he demanded that even the beauty in the world be discarded. Was he giving in to feelings aroused by the awareness of his ugliness? Was he venting an obscure need for vengeance? Or was he really aiming at absolute renunciation? Only Dostoevski could have found his way in this dark underworld. Answering his call, however, adolescents and children will satisfy their aggressive instincts and give free rein to the resentment which already poisons their soul by destroying works of art, by mutilating statues. This lack of humility, combined with a very sound feeling for politics, is what characterizes this gigantic figure set, like those effigies in the Easter Islands, between two worlds. His pride makes him rise up against the Pope and set

---

[4] Benedetto Croce shows this very well in his book: *Vite di avventure, di Fede e di passione* (Bari: Le Terza).

himself up as a judge. The delirious crowds that follow him demand the miracle of the fire, from which he will finally shrink back. The idol then falls from its pedestal, but artists— such as the gentle and tender Botticelli—will remain deeply marked by his influence. And art will hesitate a long time between the nostalgia for the divine mysteries and the exaltation of man to whom the universe has been promised.

It is during these golden centuries of the Renaissance that we first encounter this faith in the ephemeral being who has been endowed by a half-god with powers which were very small at first but which are in fact unlimited. In this "prospective" the future already appears as the essential dimension of time. What is more, it takes on the same duality of aspects that it has today; Camus will realize this and ask when we too will see the dawn of a new renaissance. It is the statues of Praxiteles and of Phidias, it is the perfection of the Greek temple inserted in a scenery whose lines converge towards it that incite philosophers to see in man the microcosm of the universe: He measures the bodies with compasses and discovers those intricate proportions whose exact knowledge almost infallibly makes it possible to open the mind to the sense of beauty. Evil recoils and vanishes in the depths of the grotto where Leonardo's Virgin now expresses only the joys of motherhood; or, when its obscure menace still weighs over the world, as in certain paintings by Albrecht Dürer, it remains contained within the intricate combinations of the "golden number": Heroism triumphs over the hallucinations generated by the "slumber of reason." Already, in the Palazzo Medici-Riccardi in Florence, it was a dream both of majestic greatness and of innocent purity which guided the brush of Benozzo Gozzoli: In the back of the chapel, the procession of the Medici is coming down from the holy mountain, while behind the altar, children are playing in a garden that resembles that in which Meaulnes met Yvonne de Galais. Aspiration after another world slowly vanishes: It would seem that with a little perseverance man could transform the one in which he is living and restore the splendor and grace which embellished even the smallest creature in the first Eden. Anguish however does not vanish; Michelangelo's sonnets reveal the flight of a faith that remains unsatisfied; this prisoner each one of us remains, will he free himself from the marble or will he go further back into the dark stone, turning in vain to the sky his face that still bears marks of coarse animality?

But while some of these great artists, of these prodigious geniuses, are still hesitating between the past and the future, others turn confidently to this future and try to anticipate its appearance; da Vinci, for instance, who inscribes the persistent ambiguity of man in the faces of his models, is more aware than anyone else of the frightening mystery of the human mind and delights in its clair-obscure; but then, all of a sudden, he is imagining the conquests of the *homo faber*, without in any way neglecting stage effects. At his command amazing sceneries arise, fountains spurt up; wings will grow on the back of the conquerer of space he already anticipates, he already draws. And these navigators described by Jakob Burckhardt, setting out without the most elementary instruments to conquer unknown lands, did they not share in this desire and also want to knock down the walls of their prison by other means than prayer? The seas will be crossed in spite of the terrified crews; the Mediterranean Sea will no longer be the center of the world. The circle will cross through the New World and the fabulous Indies and will bring these daring explorers back to their starting point. Who will describe the complex mixture of feelings by which these navigators are crusaders, apostles of Christianity, and inhuman supermen all in one? Did not these first "colonizers" devaluate and discredit from the very beginning any attempt at colonization? Their fanaticism was mistaken on the very essence of the truth they

9

claimed to witness. When they resorted to iron and fire to impose their faith, they demonstrated that they were guided more by a spirit of domination than by that of sacrifice and that they had betrayed the message of Christ. And this mistake—has our greedy and cruel Western civilization ever stopped making it? And is it not because it has betrayed the ideals it teaches that it has lost all respect among other nations? One cannot forget in this connection the diagnosis and warnings of Doctor Schweitzer and of so many Christian missionaries.

Alas! this is not the only way in which the Renaissance prefigures our present times of uncertainty and crisis, this desert of nihilism we will have to cross before we can see the horizon pale at the coming of a new dawn. Their Machiavellianism seems to be revived today and to impose on us its most disgraceful maxims; we install ourselves in lies and think we can build peace on intrigues. We are witnessing a competition as to who will be most dishonest, who will cheat best. And we are discrediting Machiavelli when we claim to be following him. He at least could justify by the depravation of his country some of the advice he gave to his Prince; the failure of Savonarola had left him confused and hurt. Another leaf of the diptych he had painted opened onto antiquity and praised heroism and virtue; he found examples of these in the Greek cities and the Roman Republic. He had come to despair of mankind, and, seeing that wars unavoidably arise from famine or political intrigues, he could find no other way to master his centaur than constraint by a strong state or the ruse of political power.

Behind the screen of democracy do we not conceal a similar disregard for man? And do we not hide, behind clever artifacts, behind learned ideologies, a dialectic of master and slave which is far more ferocious than ever before? Berdyaev proved this irrevocably by showing the mechanism of the objectivi-

10

zation process which depersonalizes and alienates us. The Machiavellianism of old is but child's play to us: We have become masters in the techniques for violating the conscience; we know how to build the pyramid of actions on the simplest reflexes. Man is merely a somewhat more complex animal than Pavlov's dog. He too can salivate at the signal; obsessed by the recurrence of the same slogans, influenced by the violence of pictures or by the clever suggestion of symbols, he looses all control over himself; he abdicates his freedom for the sake of a false safety. Is not the greatest merit of a Simone Weil, of an Alexis Carrel, of a Teilhard de Chardin, to have tried to restore the self-confidence of this debased and perverted man, to have opened for him horizons filled with a future in which he could reconquer the sense of his dignity and of his value? In any case, this is why they are so popular. Thanks to them we are not tempted to yield to dizziness and hurl ourselves toward a destiny which some claim to be unavoidable.

There is perhaps a part of utopia and dream in this ideal. But who can tell where lie the imperceptible boundaries separating ideal from utopia? If we do not agree, without certain reservations, with Miguel de Unamuno's apologia of Don Quixote, let us at least listen to the measured words of Eliot. Like Berdyaev, he knows and tells us that we have to go through new Middle Ages—Middle Ages which will be brightened only intermittently by faith, where saints are rarely headed, where even the poets hear and transmit cries of despair rather than calls full of confident hope. He nonetheless claims that ideals which now seem incompatible will be reconciled someday. Man, thanks to a better knowledge of himself, will rise to the highest spirituality; he will no longer be this "unbalanced" being who might make bad use of his increased powers—this technician imagined by Renan, capable of ruling over minds by means of perfected tortures.

11

All writers and philosophers agree that a new humanism is necessary, and they all try to discern the features of the man, or superman, capable of building his future. But their previsions still diverge. The purpose of our investigation is to reach a conclusion which is as satisfactory as possible.

1

From Faustian Man to Superman

> *Set your mind at rest; I have not been happy; if one were to add up all the happy moments of my life, I was happy for at most one month. I always had to roll a stone which always had to be rolled up anew.*
>
> Goethe

*T*he Italian philosopher and historian Benedetto Croce cautioned us on several occasions against certain simplifying concepts. The division of history into "periods" is one of them. Sometimes we go even further: We make periods coincide with centuries, as if the birth of a new century brought about a radical transformation, capable of influencing ideas and habit. In fact, the nineteenth century extends through those first few years of the twentieth which we call "la Belle Epoque." The storms and crises which would soon divide Europe and cause its rapid decline went by unnoticed by those who witnessed, happy or sad, confident or anguished, the first hours of the twentieth century. Were they even happier than we are? They went through those violent social explosions which Emile Zola describes in *Germinal*, and, more important still, their life, like ours, unfolded at the level of the joys and sorrows of their family environment. As for historians, they foresee what they already know; it is by means of a recent past

13

that they explain a more distant one. It is afterward that they determine the course of events which occurred undetermined. The tocsin did not ring on the eve of the year 1900 to warn against events which could have been avoided with a little more wisdom and understanding.

As for the history of ideas, it is like those rivers which suddenly seem to waste away; their waters vanish from sight; they will reappear, miles further, purified and renovated, as from a spring. Nothing ever really begins or ends; trends, currents which seemed to have disappeared forever spring up again, as fashions recur which were for a long time considered outdated and obsolete. What is more, and because we are inclined to think of evolution as a continuous progress, we often consider as occurring one after the other events which in fact take place at different levels: just like these trompe-l'oeil sceneries which fit into one another and appear in succession only because this is required by the action on stage. One could never sufficiently emphasize the risks generated by this concept of a progress which is everywhere equal, without pause or regression. To peoples which are still surrounded by rough superstitions, rooted in their tribal traditions and customs, we offer, under the poor pretext of emancipating them, ways of life and institutions which cannot but dissociate and pervert them. History, says Karl Jaspers, has reached the axial age. But the axis carries along in its motion the scoriae and the refuse of unchanged cultures.

One cannot be too conscious of the interaction of time and space at the core of history, as they combine to form the frame of the universe: The age of boomerangs and poisoned arrows extends into a century where supersonic jets and missiles soar through the skies. And, even among the "civilized" people, life unfolds at the very different pace of the farmer and the manager: One lingers in a stable past and remains imprisoned by the seasons, deriving his equilibrium from their alternation;[1] the other reaches out for the future with such eagerness that he destroys his present. And while technology progresses with giant steps, man remains the unknown, enslaved by irresistible instincts of which Alexis Carrel spoke.[2] Intermittently lucid, he nonetheless continues to submit to this irrational substratum of his being wherein are superimposed the layers of ancestral attainments and violence, as the earth was formed bit by bit by its own convulsions. It is his shadow, says Pirandello,[3] which he casts on the rock of Mt. Caucasus to which he sees himself chained, and he stands appalled at the sight of this shadow. Contradiction and confusion, such is the man who calls himself "rational." His reason helps him only to wrap himself in the veil of reassuring explanations and false justifications. His dialectic hides, under the intricacy of motives and reasons, what merely arises from the antagonism of passions. Miguel de Unamuno will say of this conscious sleepwalker, who has emerged with great difficulty from the night of instincts, that he is a "diseased" animal. How could he be anything else, compelled as he is by his precocious knowledge to confront, unarmed, the certitude of death?

It is also said that he is "sociable." But this can be understood in so many ways! There are two very different forms of "sociability." The first raises us to the most intimate dialogue beyond the fecundating dialogue of "I" and "Thou," ranging

[1] "All this ageless countryside, with its objects at rest, its hidden horizons and its roads full of memories is altogether a mystery as full of our origins as History itself!" And Roupnel adds: "All the ancient sites are there; the layout has not changed; the fields are the same; the pastures have always been; and the forest fringe is still that where the leaves rustled during the first ploughings." Cf. Gaston Roupnel, *Histoire de la campagne française* (Club des libraires de France).

[2] Alexis Carrel, *Man the Unknown* (New York: Harper, 1935).

[3] L. Pirandello, *L'Umorismo*. Cf. our work *Luigi Pirandello*, 2nd ed. (Paris: Editions Universitaires, 1963), in which this text is translated into French and analyzed.

15

from friendship which is an emulation of virtue and enriches each one of the friends by urging him, to quote Jacques Rivière, to develop his own difference,[4] to the gift of oneself, which raised Saint Monica and Saint Augustine, Saint Clare and Saint Francis of Assisi to the summits of transnatural life. As for the other form of "sociability," it subjects us, without any possible communion, to the automatism of habit and custom and reduces us to gregariousness. Now the unlimited development of technology and the ensuing division of labor create anew the specialization and the inequality which our "democracies" claim to have abolished. We have then two often confused forms of the process of "socialization"; between them, how many degenerate forms and compromises! Vierkandt distinguishes between "society," "community," and Band.[5] The bonds of affection get stronger from one to the other, while the social fabric woven by interest becomes weaker. But is there really progress in this case? We have seen where the "communion" in the midst of the Band led the Third Reich! The greatness of man is rooted in his contrasts: Being both social and antisocial, he must escape "conformity" in order to become a creator. Will he still be one tomorrow? Who will discern whether we are going toward that which makes life meaningful or toward that which, by subjecting it to the cycle of recurrence, marks it as meaningless.

Always in quest of permanent and distinctive features, it has finally been said that man is essentially a "religious" animal. This brings us back to the definition proposed as early as 1720 by Giovanni Battista Vico, that genial precursor.[6] The

[4] Cf. our book De Renan à Jacques Rivière (Paris: Bloud et Gay, 1930).

[5] The chapters devoted to Tonnoies and Vierkandt in the excellent little book by R. Aron, La Sociologie allemande (Paris: Presses Universitaires de France).

[6] Cf. our books: La Formation de la pensée de J.-B. Vico, Vie de J.-B. Vico, Morceaux choisis de J.-B. Vico (Paris: Presses Universitaires de France, 1943–1946).

author of the *Scienza Nuova* discovered in man, no matter the times and the latitudes, three characteristics which distinguish him from the animals: 1. He cannot do without religion; absolute atheism would destroy any society. Thus God, after the dispersion of the sons of Noah, permitted idolatry, failing the true religion, to bring him back to towns and countries. 2. He contracts "solemn marriages," thus breaking away from the instincts and desires he shares with the animals; even rape then takes on a new import and weaves ties that cannot be broken. 3. Finally, he buries his dead, thus showing the respect he has for them; *inhumare* and *humanistas* have the same root. But here again, what diversity is covered by these customs, which are indeed constant; and how often do we find gold and dross intermingled within! It is true that even in fetishism and the most childish animism, there are signs, however faint, that the revelations which were made to man are not completely forgotten. But, down a slope which he could not climb up again by his own means, was man not led to human sacrifice? For what else could he project into these cruel deities but his own passions and aberrations? Even today, it is with difficulty that he defends himself from fanaticism and a false conception of truth. Even in the noblest rites we still find traces of these haunting memories, this substratum of primitive mentality which it is difficult to fight. On terraces where the moonlight brings shadows to life, we still see these masqued dances which claim to cast the dead out of the world of the living. The border between the sacred and the profane must be carefully set and maintained.

Must we conclude that man is a still an "unfinished" being, a being which must be "passed," or rather "surpassed"? This was, in the opinion of all—and even of Teilhard de Chardin—Nietzsche's great discovery. It is indeed this attempt to "surpass," this effort to always go beyond himself, which characterizes man. This perpetual unsatisfiedness, this dissatisfaction which draws him away from his work as soon as he has

17

created it is indeed what drives humanity onward; it is this
worry, this desire for novelty, this demand for enrichment
which drive the caravan toward the mirage of the oases, toward the ever-receding horizon of its destiny. Saint-Exupéry
shows this well in his delightful apologue of *The Little Prince*:
Why did he not stay on his tiny planet, with his volcanoes and
his rose? Like him, we dream of adventure, and we wish to
enlarge our prison indefinitely. Thus, always pushed forward,
driven by his own desire from his shelters and places of refuge, hurled toward his future, man would be the being which
can never realize itself, the existing compelled to invent its
"essence," according to the formula proposed by Jean-Paul
Sartre, who bases his humanism on this absolute primacy of
existence.[7] To be himself he would have to create new structures for himself and emerge into the superhuman:

"Man is a rope stretched between the animal and the Superman—a rope over an abyss.

"A dangerous crossing, a dangerous wayfaring, a dangerous
looking-back, a dangerous trembling and halting.

"What is great in man is that he is a bridge and not a goal:
what is lovable in man is that he is an *over-going* and a *down-
going*.

"I love those that know not how to live except as down-
goers, for they are the over-goers.

"I love the great despisers, because they are the great adorers
and arrows of longing for the other shore.

"I love those who do not first seek a reason beyond the stars
for going down and being sacrifices, but sacrifice themselves
to the earth, that the earth of the Superman may hereafrer
arrive. . . .

"Lo, I am a herald of the lightning, and a heavy drop out

[7] Jean-Paul Sartre, *L'Existentialisme est un humanisme*. Cf. *passim*.

of the cloud: the lightning, however, is the *Superman*."[8]

To rise higher than himself, man needs to set himself "models," "representative" men—as Emerson calls them—who have lived, toiled, and suffered, or characters drawn from fiction who still live a life of their own and are more real, says Pirandello,[9] than real people, since they have imposed their unique destiny on their creator and since they continue to propose it to others.[10] These models have changed for Nietzsche from *The Birth of Tragedy* to the *Ecce Homo*, where he will merely describe himself. In *Schopenhauer as Educator*,[11] he considers three possible ideals:

"There are three Images of Man fashioned by our modern time, which for a long while yet will urge mortal men to transfigure their own lives; they are the men of Rousseau, Goethe, and Schopenhauer." And Nietzsche feels that the first has "the greatest fire"; it still excites and still leads to revolutions:

"For in all socialistic upheavals it is ever Rousseau's man who is the Typhoeus under the Etna." He rebels against the classes and casts which oppress him. And when he cries: "Nature alone is good, the natural man alone is human," it is because he despises himself and aspires beyond himself. "The noble and the rare" in his soul then arise "from their utter depths."

The second image—that of Goethe—is only for the few, for "the contemplative natures 'in the grand style'"; and such a

[8] Friedrich Nietzsche, *Thus Spake Zarathustra*, Prologue, in Oscar Levy, ed., *The Complete Works of Friedrich Nietzsche*, Vol. 11 (New York: Russell & Russell, 1964), pp. 9–11.

[9] Cf. the prologue to *Six Characters in Search of an Author*, and the unfolding of the play.

[10] Cf. the book by Armando F. Zubizzaretta, *Unamuno en su nivola* (Madrid: Editions Taurus, 1960), especially Chapter 3, "La Persona y el Personaje," pp. 148–151.

[11] The quotations below are from *Schopenhauer as Educator* in *The Complete Works of Friedrich Nietzsche*, Vol. 5, pp. 139–141.

man is even, to some extent, "a corrective," a sedative to the dangerous excitation which carries away the "revolutionary." With great perspicacity, Nietzsche shows that Goethe first appears as a "revolutionary" similar to Rousseau's man. He curses Nature who made him full of desires and left him powerless, craving for the absolute but hemmed in by nothingness. But little by little his face changes:

"And here begins the new Image of man—the man according to Goethe. One might have thought that Faust would have lived a continual life of suffering, as a revolutionary and a deliverer, as the negative force that proceeds from goodness, as the genius of ruin, alike religious and daemoniac, in opposition to his utterly undaemoniac companion; though of course he could not be free of this companion, and had at once to use and despise his evil and destructive scepticism—which is the tragic destiny of all revolutionary deliverers."

But suddenly Faust calms down; Goethe too greatly loathed violence and action itself, which cannot be accomplished without violence, to give him for long the appearance of a rebel. Very soon "the universal deliverer becomes merely the universal traveller," the older brother of Wilhelm Meister. He will assimilate all the culture, and, connecting the future and the most distant past, he will make his own the history of humanity: "All the riches of life and nature, all antiquity—arts, mythologies and sciences—pass before his eager eyes, his deepest desires are aroused and satisfied." It seems that nothing can hold him back, not even the classicism of Greece or the beauty of Helen. Thus Mephistopheles is watching for that moment when weariness sets in, when his pinions will drop. But there is a divine power in the Faustian man, and against this power, the scepticism of the destructive spirit cannot prevail.[12]

[12] Unamuno will make a similar interpretation. For him, Mephistopheles is reason which negates and thus annihilates all values, as opposed to the generous impulse, the fundamental feeling. Faith is driving

Before going on to Schopenhauer's man, let us dwell a little longer on this remarkable portrait, for Goethe's Faust, just like the Don Quixote of Cervantes, still lives among us. Goethe's personality is in fact so complex—and, in the image of this personality, so is the portrait of the man he depicted—that Nietzsche, at the very moment he claims to break away from him, is actually inspired by him more than he thinks. What he rejects in this idealized picture is that which is already a sign of decadence: Goethe's classicism no longer has the vigor of that of ancient Greece, filled with contrasts and tensions which are surmounted only with great difficulty. In Goethe, as half a century later in Victor Hugo, we find a taste of the petit bourgeois mentality, marked more by common sense than true wisdom. Indeed, do we not see the author of a promptly repudiated *Werther* reduce, in *Poetry and Truth*, all that gives joy to life to the regular recurrence of natural phenomena. To simplify one's existence to the extreme and adapt it to the rhythm of the days and the alternation of the seasons, which brings back flowers and fruit to the branches made bare by winter, this is the ideal he sometimes sets for himself and for us—as if time, instead of hurling itself toward its term, flowed like a peaceful stream between enchanted banks.

We find in him a constant application to the task at hand. To come to grips with the obstacles; to succeed, after an extenuating effort, in making the initial conception of a carefully planned work coincide with its final realization; to reach in every detail, at the cost of endless corrections, the desired perfection, this is the secret of an art which, like that of Paul Valéry, relies only very cautiously on inspiration. There is no great human accomplishment which did not require a long

Faust in his search for himself through successive adventures and realizations. And this faith will survive all failures. This is why he will be saved in the end.

21

and laborious maturation. Thought which claims to fly over the earth, as would a bird of prey, has been involved for many years in a patient exploration. Nietzsche sometimes claims the opposite. We must however be wary of what he says about inspiration.[13] Zarathustra, this shadow which grew in the steps of the Wanderer, was not conceived in a day—no more than Faust, no more than Don Quixote. The face of the prophet changes from one dialogue to the next. The only thing which the young Faust who yields to the mirage of love has in common with the Faust who sacrifices the hut of Philemon and Baucis to his vision of the world is the "will to power"; Wilhelm Meister's long apprenticeship is necessary in order that he can start on a journey that will allow him to explore the human heart in which all things are mirrored. For all of them genius was acquired only at the cost of a great deal of perseverance. A writer, whether he be Nietzsche, Goethe, or Valéry, forges his style as Siegfried his sword.

It is indeed a strange paradox which opposes the traditionalist and conservative Goethe to the nonconformist and revolutionary Rousseau. One would expect that the first would be resolutely optimistic whereas the second would have great difficulty in overcoming his basic pessimism. However this is not at all the case.[14] Goethe finds it hard to overcome his con-

---

[13] Cf. the well-known passage on "inspiration" in *Ecce Homo* (Vol. 17 of the *Complete Works*), pp. 101–102: "If one has the smallest vestige of superstition left in one, it would hardly be possible completely to set aside the idea that one is the mere incarnation, mouthpiece, or medium of an almighty power. . . . One hears—one does not seek; one takes—one does not ask who gives: a thought suddenly flashes up like lightning, it comes with necessity, without faltering—I have never had any choice in the matter." Cf. our *Nietzsche* (Paris: Editions Universitaires, 1963).

[14] Goethe was tolerant, said one of the contemporaries of the author of *Faust*, but he adds: "tolerant without kindness." It is true that Rousseau sees in the history of mankind the endless conflicts between un-

tempt for man; Rousseau, naively, has illusions about him. If civilization had not perverted him, he would have remained good, subject to the God who reveals himself to him in the grandiose spectacle of nature. "The instinct of his conscience is reliable when the starry skies are shining above him." Then, says Kant, so close to him in so many ways, he is illuminated by moral law which, "even more than the starry skies, gives him a sense of the sublime."

But where can we find a more optimistic view of these long centuries of history which are marked by crimes and atrocities? Is it not naive to think that the alienation of man can be conquered outside of a deep reform of behavior, a complete transfiguration of our perverted nature?[15] A revolution, as Camus points out to Jeanson and Sartre,[16] merely changes the beneficiaries of the injustice; it does not in any way put an end to it. At the end of his life, Plato felt the very same way. The example of Dion proved to him that no "philosopher," no "sage" could govern the city without becoming perverted, or without handing himself over to his assassins—a tragic dilemma which led him, like Goethe, to withdraw with horror from the political scene.

healthy passions and declining civilizations. But he does not claim that the source from which these conflicts arise is an irrationality inherent in the very nature of man. On the contrary, he thinks that these conflicts will be overcome if institutions are reformed and if basic education follows the teachings of nature. It is therefore important not to shield Emile from experiences which, more than abstract lessons, will warn and guide him. Goethe, on the contrary, will say of the history of mankind: "It is an endless seesaw; some will suffer while others will enjoy well-being; selfishness and jealousy, the maleficent devils, will forever lead the game; factions will always quarrel."

[15] See our *Donoso Cortès* (Paris: Editions Archives de Philosophie, Beauchesne, and "Antihistorisme et théologie de l'histoire chez saint Augustin" in *Recherches Augustiniennes*, I.

[16] Cf. *passim*, especially Chapter 6.

Rousseau saw in democracy the best form of government but one that was suitable only for a people of gods. He therefore proposed democratic institutions only to nations which, like Poland, carried the respect of the person to extremes—and at what risk!—or to peoples which were protected by their geographic situation, such as the blessed island governed by the wise Sancho Panza—or Corsica. Who could blame him for not trusting large empires, whose unbounded ambition and tyranny cast a shadow on any culture, of which they smother the "golden flower"? As with Stendhal later, it is in a small principality that he would have liked to live; only there, he felt, would it be possible to make useful political experiments at the level of man. Goethe, believing that all institutions are much the same, advocated concern for man alone and felt that one should strive to know his most intimate structures. Education is of use only if man is finally enlightened as to his misery, his unreliability, his instinctive servility, and this jealousy which makes him incapable of tolerating any superiority.[17] "The true study man should undertake is that of man."

This man, whom he pities in his good days, one must try to make him happy in spite of himself, to transform into a springboard that fate which endlessly "knocks at the door,"[18] and to teach him never to get discouraged. Is this not how Faust triumphs over death, which can in fact interrupt nothing, how he models himself on his creation and wins immortality?

---

[17] This is indeed, according to Saint Augustine, the first cause of man's fall and of his progressive decline. The sin of Judas is a repetition of that of Cain, who killed his brother Abel because he was concerned only with the City of God. Cf. *Confessions, The City of God,* and our work *Saint Augustin, temps et histoire,* published in the Editions Augustiniennes.

[18] Beethoven frequently uses this expression.

Are we really far here from the Superman ideal? It is true that Goethe advocates a moral hygiene, an ethics which tries to restore equilibrium between violently antagonistic forces, and excludes this dangerous game in which Nietzsche will delight; but he nevertheless does not condemn all excessiveness. We even find him admitting that there can be no genius without some excess and some imprudence. Does he not say about Byron, who was being criticized in his presence, and probably to please him: "We must not always try to find the elements of our culture in that which is, beyond dispute, pure and moral. All that is great enriches us if we are able to discern it."

He nonetheless took it upon himself (and who could do otherwise?) to wear a mask and kept without publishing it, in a carefully wrapped parcel, that which might have caused scandal by revealing his innermost thoughts.

The problem which preoccupies Goethe and which Faust will have to solve by fighting against the main enemy of man —the spirit of doubt personified by Mephistopheles—is the very one which has continuously been discussed throughout the twofold Christian tradition, Protestant and Catholic: Is the human heart condemned to incurable perversity? Can it be saved only through the free gift of grace? Or does there linger in its darkness enough light, enough pure dispositions, that it can escape the powers of evil by its own efforts? Goethe, following both Luther and Erasmus, solved the problem in the spirit of Pelagianism. Or rather, to a naive optimism and a destructive pessimism he opposed a constructive optimism.[19] If the deed is always the most important, faith is necessary to found and support it. Man should be seen for what he is, but one should trust him because: "Who e'er aspiring, struggles on, / For him there is salvation."

---

[19] It is the Faustian man we will find again in Teilhard de Chardin.

After his long journey around the world—and his descent into the spirals of hell—Faust, thanks to his deeds, will escape damnation. He has understood that, to obey divine law, man must also become a creator, that he creates himself only by performing great tasks. True, it is not without regret that he destroys the hut where live, immortal in their own way, Philemon and Baucis. Such a paradise is no longer suitable for us: It has become a shelter and a refuge—the symbol of an introversion, of a refusal to live which Goethe condemns. Such a narrow setting cannot contain the ideal of the Faustian man. He must, while remaining faithful to moderation and fitting his actions into the Order which contains them, dry up swamps, push back the sea, transform that Zuider Zee which claimed so many ships and where so many dikes were carried away by a furious sea. A supreme temptation, this pleasant and easy life offered by Mephistopheles. Faust's ambition is henceforth quite different. Let us consider the final dialogue which explains everything:

> MEPHISTOPHELES: Then, swelling with self-conscious pride I'd raise
> A pleasure-castle in a pleasant place.
> Hill, level, meadow, field, and forest glade
> Into a splendid garden I'd have made. . . .
> And then I'd build, for loveliest women meet,
> Sung villas, each an intimate retreat.
> I'd pass there endless time in joyous mood,
> Blessed by the dearest social solitude.
> "Women," I say, for here, as everywhere,
> I think in plurals of the ladies fair.
> FAUST: Sardanapalus! Vile and new, I swear!
> MEPHISTOPHELES [the sceptical mind who does not understand Faust's aspiration]:
> Who could devine toward what you aspire?
> It must have been sublimely bold, in truth,

Toward the moon you'd soar and ever nigher;
Did your mad quest allure you *there* forsooth?
FAUST [*with self-confidence*]:
By no means! For this earthly sphere
Affords a place for great deeds ever.
Astounding things shall happen here,
I feel the strength for bold endeavour.
MEPHISTOPHELES [*still jeering and sceptical*]:
So you'd earn glory? One can see
You've been in heroines' company.
FAUST: Lordship, possession, are my aim and thought!
The deed is everything, the glory naught.[20]

Goethe dreams of removing all barriers; beyond national misunderstandings, he invites all men to concord and union. It is by this feature perhaps that the portrait of the man he offers differs from that of the Superman. One could become oneself only by passing through others, by becoming a "universal" man. This is the goal Goethe proposes to Germany; thus it would have found its true greatness.

"Instead of keeping to himself, of shutting himself behind his frontiers, the German must receive the world in order to influence it."

Thus Goethe foresaw the "giants" which would mold the future. He invites Europe to unite to build a canal from the Danube to the Rhine, which would be a source of prosperity for all, and then to connect two inland seas by another canal, the one which Lesseps was to realize: the Suez canal. Turning toward America, he traced the Panama canal. Such was the ideal of an extrovert who saw beyond the quarrels of his time —and of ours!

[20] *Faust* in *Great Books of the Western World*, Vol. 47, *Goethe* (Chicago: Encyclopaedia Britannica, 1952), pp. 247–248. See all the sequel: "Your bitter, sharp, and hostile mood,/How does it know what men count good?"

In Schopenhauer, Goethe saw one of his emulators. When he met him in a salon in Weimar, he went up to him congratulating him for writing the On the Fourfold Root of the Principle of Sufficient Reason, the conclusions of which would later be developed in his great work on The World as Will and Representation. Fifty years later, Nietzsche would buy this book in a bookstore in Leipzig. It was to be a revelation for him, and under its spell his first encounter with Wagner took place: "I belong to those readers of Schopenhauer who know perfectly well, after they have turned the first page, that they will read all the others, and listen to every word that he has spoken."[21]

What Nietzsche admires in Schopenhauer is not only a style which no other can approach[22]—where indeed can we find a writer who can say that which is deep with simplicity, that which is touching without unnecessary rhetoric, that which is strictly scientific without the slightest pedantry?—but it is also, and mostly, a certain ideal of life, different from that of Goethe and Rousseau though perhaps of greater educational value. Honesty, joy, aspiration after holiness,[23] which he himself says he might have attained had he been touched by grace, these are the qualities which Nietzsche will see in Schopenhauer. His contemporaries did not understand him and he

---

[21] Schopenhauer as Educator, p. 114.

[22] "I only know a single author that I rank with Schopenhauer, or even above him, in the matter of honesty [for Nietzsche this is the only true virtue, the only one which wears no masks]; and that is Montaigne. The joy of living on this earth is increased by the existence of such a man." In Montaigne, as in Schopenhauer, Nietzsche claims to find another quality which is as valuable as honesty: "a joy that really makes others joyful. 'Aliis laetus, sibi sapiens.' " Schopenhauer as Educator, p. 116.

[23] "He [Schopenhauer] turned away with a sad look from the picture of Rancé, the founder of the Trappists, with the words: 'That is a matter of grace.' " Ibid., pp. 127–128.

had to face the greatest of all perils: isolation. His lucidity perceived the precursory signs of decadence and he faced them without fear; he understood that humanity had to cross this desert, without making fresh provisions of heroism and detachment. The philosopher he presents to us cannot but fear a destruction and a total degeneracy of culture, the unmistakable symptom of which is the acceleration of the decline; this sudden haste which takes hold of all men makes them unsuited for contemplative life and makes all simplicity impossible!

"The waters of religion are ebbing, and leaving swamps or stagnant pools: the nations are drawing away in enmity again, and long to tear each other to pieces. The sciences, blindly driving along, on a *laisser faire* system, without a common standard, are splitting up, and losing hold of every firm principle. The educated classes are being swept along in the contemptible struggle for wealth."[24]

Unperturbed, Schopenhauer's man crosses the desert of souls. He stoically accepts this unfurling of idle activity, this delusion of false culture. He knows that these are but deceitful appearances, that behind the veil of Maya is hidden the unity where this multiplicity, though more and more fragmented and incoherent, has its source—the universal Will. Thus he prepares "the complete transformation of his being, which it is the inner meaning of life to realize."

Schopenhauer does even more: He reveals to us the tragic, the terrible condition of man. Does it not seem, when we consider this obviously unfinished being, that "after yearning for man so long and at last reaching him by her labour, Nature should now recoil from him and wish to return to a state of unconscious instinct."[25] Terrible uncertainty, perilous retreat,

[24] *Ibid.*, pp. 135–136.
[25] We will also find this theme in Miguel de Unamuno, Pirandello, and mostly in Kafka.

29

which leaves mankind on the brink of life, abandoned and without other resources than the heroism to which it finds itself, in a sense, condemned.[26] Nature should have decided to go all the way in the line of knowledge, and now it recoils as if it were afraid of the consequences.[27]

"It is something to be able to raise our heads but for a moment and see the stream in which we are sunk so deep. We cannot gain even this transitory moment of awakening by our own strength; we must be lifted up—and who are they that will uplift us?

"The sincere men who have cast out the beast, the philosophers, artists and saints. Nature—*quae nunquam facit saltum* —has made her one leap in creating them; a leap of joy, as she feels herself for the first time at her goal, where she begins to see that she must learn not to have goals above her."[28]

A presentiment unfolds for Nietzsche horizons which will be his and not those of Schopenhauer, who, like Wagner, will be intoxicated by a tardy fame. At least, Schopenhauer will remain a misogynist, skillful at avoiding Ariane's snares. Did he not one day make his servants carry down, to some overly enthusiastic young girls who hoped to be introduced to him, his full-length portrait, which he saved for just such occasions. Already, though unknown to himself, Nietzsche speaks for himself. His own future becomes clearer:

"To rise as high as any thinker yet into the pure icy air of the mountain, where there are no mists and veils, and the inner constitution of things is shown in a stark and piercing clarity"![29]

---

[26] The example Nietzsche gives most readily at that time is Beethoven.

[27] Nietzsche already stigmatizes attitudes of retreat and flight: "The hurry is universal, because everyone is fleeing from himself."

[28] *Schopenhauer as Educator*, p. 152.

[29] *Ibid.*, pp. 152–153.

There, far above the abysses, the pine tree takes its roots and presents a proud brow to the storms, the pine tree—symbol of a culture which, while extending into the most distant past, assumes the future and accepts risk. For the past must be used but should not lie heavy and hinder the impetus which cannot unfold without some leeway. Thus Schopenhauer's man is replaced by another who does not wish to renounce but wants to create himself, to be his own sculptor.

It is true that the change is imperceptible, for Nietzsche does not yet dare to speak for himself; there is merely a new emphasis which changes the meaning of words. This hero, this saint[30] which Schopenhauer presented to us, is he really in a permanent state of war with men and institutions? Does he not rather seem anxious to pull away from the state before the curtain falls on the last act of the drama? Did he really advocate a "heroic life" because "a happy life is impossible"? If suffering is the result of an accidental individuation of the will to live which causes everyone to try to perservere in his own existence, of what use is heroism which obstinately pursues its futile conflicts? To renounce is to be wise: to cast off the temptation to hold back a fleeting life, to pull out even its roots and, after facing fate and the ingratitude of men, accept "being absorbed into the nirvana," this is the teaching of the Hindu philosophy adopted by Schopenhauer. This is how he becomes an educator, how he teaches the best of us, those who can understand this austere metaphysics.

To the others, however, who remain in the grips of the tenacious illusions of individual existence, he proposes two powerful antidotes: art, thanks to which we delight in the

[30] "Finally, Nature needs the saint. In him the ego has melted away [into that of the others], and the suffering of his life is, practically, no longer felt as individual, but as the spring of the deepest sympathy and intimacy with all living creatures." (*Schopenhauer as Educator*, p. 154.) The saint is the man who mortifies his will.

multicolored weave of the phenomena woven by the will to live and perfect in ourselves, if we are capable of it, the game of deceptive representations by the artifices of our own genius; compassion, which allows us to dilute our suffering in the universal suffering until, finally, the desire which prompts us to live for and by ourselves subsides in us.

Soon, Nietzsche will no longer approve of this transformation of the original will into nonwill. We will join the ranks of the dancers and the bacchants following Dionysus, the god who never ceases to recreate the world from its own fragments, who creates by destroying and destroys by creating, like fire, the symbol of both life and death. It is vitality he will praise, and it is from vitality that he will obtain the joy which will lead him to the ultimate sacrifice. He will then understand that in Schopenhauer's man he had seen the lonely man whom no failure can discourage, who, like Dürer's knight, goes his way without wavering, through the darkness that is filled with devilish apparitions. Stoic and hard, unmoved by pity, never deluded by appearances nor succumbing to the temptation of a peaceful life in the midst of the flock, the hero tries to reach his extreme limit. If he renounces his individual existence, it is not to lose himself in the peace of nirvana but to wage war everywhere so that through him will be born the one before whom Nature has retreated: the Superman. Far from rejecting it, he will let himself be carried along by life and its passions; he will climb to the peaks where soar the birds of prey; he will submit to the acceleration of a time which will cast him as a holocaust to a future he will not know. He will scarcely see the crimson fringe of the first of the triumphant dawns which will be witnessed by a mankind redeemed by his sacrifice.

2
The Search for the Superman

> And Zarathustra spake thus onto the people: "I teach you the Superman. Man is something that is to be surpassed. What have ye done to surpass man?
>
> "All beings hitherto have created something beyond themselves; and ye want to be the ebb of that great tide, and would rather go back to the beast than surpass man?"
>
> Thus Spake Zarathustra[1]

*M*oderation and equilibrium allowing man to fit into an order he must mirror in himself if he is to try and subject it to his will; protest and rebellion against social injustice, or against an absurd destiny; renunciation of the illusion of individual life, the source of all suffering, and return to the blessed nirvana: such are the three ideals which Nietzsche assigns to Goethe, Rousseau, and Schopenhauer. They will always exist, as will this refined amateur of pleasure, this subtle egotist —Don Juan or Guiscard—whom Mephistopheles offers to Faust's ever-renewed desire. To this animal whose consciousness emerges intermittently just enough to let him witness his own downfall,[2] to this "monster" from which Nature recoils

---

[1] Prologue, in Oscar Levy, ed., *The Complete Works of Friedrich Nietzsche*, Vol. 11 (New York, Russell & Russell, 1964), p. 6.

[2] Though Nietzsche is very reticent in his judgment of Baudelaire (he probably could not forgive him his panegyric on Wagnerian art), their ideals are identical: "To be a hero and a saint for oneself." Baudelaire, *Carnets intimes*.

after accidentally letting him arise from the long line of instincts, Nietzsche will propose another ideal. Since Nature, his mother, did not complete her task, it is up to him to go ahead heroically and create by his conscious efforts this being which did not see the light—the real man, the Superman. This will be a new genesis, a *pathetic* birth if ever there was one, since it is his destiny man must now assume in order to transform it into freedom. Is it not clear that the example, the irreplaceable model of this inhuman tension of an unyielding will is no other one than Beethoven?

"Is true man the slave of his surroundings or is he free? Does he not save his best Self from all the storms and, what is more, from all the pleasures of this life? The world is within his bosom: is it part of the elemental mass? And that which often stirs and ferments within this mass, can it influence that world? Can you be crushed, O Man?

"However, there are times!—Yes, there certainly are! But thank God they are only fleeting moments, when man, overwhelmed by a more powerful nature, believes that his highest self is but the toy of the waves. At such times, the deity is showing us the distance separating it from us; it punishes the criminal rashness of man in his desire to set himself on equal footing with it and throws him back into nothingness. At such times, the sage is swallowed up by dust—is he not the son of dust!—however, he soon rises again, purified; he escapes from the hands of fatality and proclaims thus his almighty power before the divine will. You too will rise again! . . . What can I do?—Be more than your destiny?"[3]

Beethoven, whom nothing could subdue and who transformed the rumblings, the crackings, the uproar filling his mind into sometimes demonic, sometimes divine harmonies

---

[3] This is a quotation from Z. Werner's *Söhne des Thals*, copied down by Beethoven in his *Notebook*; he also copied fragments of the *Iliad*.

and who, struck down by suffering and treason, rose again to create, renewing himself and renovating music till the last, was the first bond between Nietzsche and Wagner, who even wrote a book about the celebrated composer. These were the delightful days in Tribschen.[4] The row of poplar trees, scarcely stirred by the breeze, formed a screen between the old house and the lake; it did not completely conceal it however, and the melody reflects the glistening of the water. At that blessed time, alone but appeased, Wagner had imposed his choice and created his own happiness. He was composing the *Siegfried Idyll*; once more the hero was escaping from the spell of the forest. The Superman was replacing the gods. No barrier of fire could keep Brunehilde from him; no law could set back his almighty will. The superior man creates his own laws, and "the iron claws of Destiny," which tear only the flanks of the weak, have no hold on him. He lives in an atmosphere beyond what ordinary men call "good and evil." In the blessed moment of creation, even "harrassing" time lets go. He can really say of himself: "You are your own Destiny." "You are the image of the Eternal." Nietzsche will never forget those happy hours when genius appeared to him: a marvelous revelation, but also the greatest of all perils, for is it not necessary to break all ties in order to be oneself and realize oneself according to one's own laws? And the Superman to whom the future will belong, is he not even beyond that? Beyond what cannot but be a halt followed by an unavoidable regress. One must generate something real and not what might still be only a pretense. A born comedian offering himself in Bayreuth to the adoration of the crowds, a genius gone astray who allowed himself to become "someone," that is what Wagner turns out to be, and what a disappointment![5]

[4] Cf. our book: *Pour connaître le pensée de F. Nietzsche* (Paris: Bordas, 1964).
[5] Cf. Pirandello's play: *When Someone Is Somebody*.

Thus Nietzsche realizes more and more that we cannot turn to the past for models! At the very most, on condition one goes back as far as ancient Greece, as did Beethoven, von Kleist, and the too tender Hölderlin, one can hope to find motives for exaltation. One must create the man of the future, invent the culture which will be suited to him, wrest him from all-destructive time, install him in an eternity which is not static but dynamic. But if there is nothing beyond time, if it contains no dimension which opens up onto Being, how can it be surmounted if not by itself and by its own coiling around? The serpent is the symbol of Eternal Recurrence, this hypothesis Nietzsche could not dismiss, though it filled him with a terror he once confessed to Lou Salomé. How then can one conquer a Destiny inscribed in the very heart of events, avoid the shipwreck of the drift of time? Endlessly, the cycles begin again, in which we must consent to be no more than a never abolished instant; each one of us is a "fatality." To fulfill his role, ever the same one, to try and transform into joy what is accompanied by an indescribable anguish, this is finally the only goal which the Hero can set himself, he who must work at a statue which has already been sculpted so often and so often destroyed!

But let us leave for a moment this Gate through which passes the road to a future which is merely our past, let us forget Eternal Recurrence and try to describe the Superman. This is no mean task. It might be easiest to compare him with his direct opposite: the last man, the gregarious animal who seeks shelter in the warmth of the flock, Panurge's sheep! Nietzsche saw that if mankind is left to itself and allowed to follow its own course, it will slide down the incline of instincts until it reaches the elementary reflexes; everything combines to bring it back to the ant nest, to make it yearn for the chain and the yoke. Man flees from the consciousness which awakens in him; he fears nothing more than solitude and silence.

This is what Edgar Allan Poe is saying in what is perhaps his most beautiful poem in prose, though it is not very well known.

Having unsuccessfully tried to conquer man by leading him into a dismal country where there is no rest or silence, the Devil fixes all things in a motionless rest.

"Then I grew angry and cursed, with the curse of *silence*, the river, and the lilies, and the wind, and the forest, and the heaven, and the thunder and the sighs of the water-lilies. And they became accursed, and *were still*. . . .

"And mine eyes fell upon the countenance of the man, and his countenance was wan with terror. And, hurriedly, he raised his head from his hand, and stood forth upon the rock and listened. But there was no voice throughout the vast illimitable desert, and the characters upon the rock were SILENCE. And the man shuddered, and turned his face away, and fled afar off, in haste, so that I beheld him no more."[6]

Catherine von Gunderode, Bettina von Brentano's friend,[7] had a similar vision and described it in her *Apocalyptic Fragment*. She could not bear the tragic certitude of Eternal Recurrence; disappointed in love as well as in her ideal of greatness, she committed suicide:

"I then saw a vast ocean in front of me, with no shores either to the north or to the south, to the east or to the west. Not the slightest breeze to disturb the water, and yet this huge sea was stirred in its depths, as by an inner fermentation."[8]

[6] E. Poe, "Silence, A Fable" in *Complete Stories and Poems of Edgar Allan Poe*, (Garden City, N.Y.: Doubleday, 1966), p. 605.

[7] Though Nietzsche never speaks about Catherine von Gunderode, he mentions several times her great friend Bettina, a fervent admirer of Goethe, who was to marry the writer von Arnim.

[8] *Les Romantiques allemands* (Bibliothèque Européenne), pp. 606–607.

We would not be so afraid of death if we were sure, as soon as we crossed the threshold, of finding a guide or an intercessor in the unknown no-man's-land we will have to cross. Little by little the last swirls of the current that carried us have died away; the hand which held ours is no longer there to reassure us. If only we were not alone when facing this ultimate trial! Catherine von Gunderode lies alone, shrouded in her long hair, on the banks of the Rhine where the genius of Wagner will resurrect her. But Heinrich von Kleist, whose torment Nietzsche would often evoke, would not return to the paradise lost without the heroic woman his destiny allowed him to meet after so many fruitless leads.[9]

When facing such perils, one seeks for the reassuring presence of another, if only through commonplace words. The presence of the flock around us can be so appeasing! Kafka himself tells us in his Diary of his happiness when, one Sunday, he went for a picnic in the country with his neighbors. He forgot everything, the coarseness of the conversation, the banality of the place where they stopped, the stupidity of his companions, in order to enjoy the bliss of being able to avoid the tête-à-tête with himself and his sense of guilt. His "hunter Gracchus" will never find the road leading to the other world; henceforth, in his coffin, he will wander from one shore to another, welcomed here, cast out there: a new and even more pitiful image of the Flying Dutchman whom no love will redeem. Nietzsche, the eternal wanderer, had only the company of his shadow. And when from this shadow arose the very best of himself, the prophet Zarathustra, this incarnation of an Idea left him unsatisfied. What he needed was a physical presence.[10]

[9] Cf. Les Romantiques allemands, and our Nietzsche (Paris: Editions Universitaires, 1963) Chapter 1.

[10] "The friend of the anchorite is always the third one: the third one is the cork which preventeth the conversation of the two sinking

However, greatness is the reward for absolute renunciation. The old friends have fled, horrified by the audacity of the prophet; the new ones will not reach the peak where is inscribed, in letters of fire, the new table of values. Those who listen to Zarathustra do not sense his persiflage, eager as they are to avoid all responsibility and to get lost in the satisfied crowd. Popular dictatorship, this is clearly the fate of humanity at the end of a decadence which began with the decline of the Greece of Aeschylus, Sophocles, and Heraclites.

"Lo! I show you the last man.

" 'What is love? What is creation? What is longing? What is a star?'—so asketh the last man and blinketh.

"The earth hath then become small, and on it there hoppeth the last man who maketh everything small. . . .

" 'We have discovered happiness'—say the last men, and blink thereby.

"They have left the regions where it is hard to live; for they need warmth. One still loveth one's neighbour and rubbeth against him; for one needeth warmth. . . .

"No shepherd, and one herd! Every one wanteth the same; every one is equal: he who hath other sentiments goeth voluntarily into the madhouse."[11]

Stage by stage, mankind returns to the animality from which it emerged with such difficulty. Would this decadence be leading to a new barbarism—that of the mind—which would be intensified with the development of technology? To what excesses will the inventions of the biologists lead us if there are no ideals to restrain them? The "brave new world," of which Aldous Huxley describes the prefabricated hierar-

into the depth." "Ah! there are too many depths for all anchorites. Therefore do they long so much for a friend, and for his elevation." *Thus Spake Zarathustra*, in *The Complete Works of Friedrich Nietzsche*, Vol. 11, p. 63.

[11] *Ibid.*, pp. 12–13.

chies, would be the end result. Nietzsche would have recognized the city of the last men. Huxley also foresees that in order to avoid the economic and social confusion which will result from excessively increased power, one will have to resort to state dictatorship. Castes will reappear in a new form, and no one will be able to get out of that caste in which he has been imprisoned even before he was born.

A really "efficient" totalitarian state would be that in which the almighty Executive Committee of the political leaders and their army of directors would rule over a population of slaves which would not need to be constrained since they would love their servitude.[12]

Who would even think of rebelling? Propaganda will have so many ways of training the human animal and prompting him to accept the halter, and everyone will be satisfied when he sees that his condition is identical to that of his neighbor. A society based on imposed or, better still, suggested obedience, where the strings of jealousy and resentment are pulled at will, this is what mankind is condemned to if there do not arise from it these "dominators" who will be the announcers of the Superman. For Zarathustra is patient; he knows that there are many obstacles on the road at the end of which the Superman, the "Dominator," will finally appear.

"He who gives, he who creates, he who teaches—these are the precursors of the Dominator."

First, there will have to be models, who are still not perfect but lie halfway between man and Superman; their influence, if they succeed in having any, will prevent mankind from sliding down the fatal incline. Will they succeed? The temptation to seek a refuge, to take on alibis, to enjoy one's well-being is very strong indeed. Everything possible will be done in order to do without these models, so great is man's hatred for any-

[12] Cf. Aldous Huxley, *Brave New World* (New York: Harper, 1946), p. xvi.

40

thing superior! Zarathustra's task will be accomplished if
humanity starts off again, if the equilibrist progressing along
the rope taut toward the future is no longer the toy of ancestral
mistakes:

"Zarathustra is happy that the struggle between castes is
ended and that it is now at last the time of the hierarchy of
individuals. Hatred for the democratic leveling system is only
on the surface; in fact, we should be happy we have come this
far."

For it is now that the Prophet, the Announcer of the future,
must set to work. He must mold these mediators between the
past and the future, this new race of strong and resolute men
which stands on the dividing line of "Midday." Those who
will replace God will come later, those in which new structures will be set which will make them capable of conquering
the world. Beneath them, "the eudaemonic and social ideal"
—which brings mankind backwards—will have generated "the
ideal slave of the future, this indispensable lower caste."[13]

Let us proceed by stages, taking on Zarathustra's great
patience. Let us examine these "mediators," these models who
open for mankind the road to the Superman. Let us make a
portrait which does not appear as an intaglio, by contrast with
its antagonist—the last man—but one which stands out,
carved out as in a medal. Antiquity and the Renaissance have
yielded many examples of such heroes; and Nietzsche liked
to evoke their rugged features, in Basel with his colleague
Jakob Burckhardt.[14] Navigators, artists, humanists, even patri-

---

[13] All these revealing texts are taken from the *Posthumous Works;*
they are "fragments" in which Nietzsche's intentions are clearly
described.

[14] Cf. Jakob Burckhardt, *The Civilization of the Renaissance in Italy,*
which first appeared in 1860. Nietzsche was inspired mostly by Part II
(The Development of the Individual) and by Part IV (The Discovery
of the World of Man); as for the *History of the Renaissance in Italy,*
it would appear in 1867. Nietzsche came to Basel in 1869.

41

cians who, in Genoa, piled up treasures in houses built to their image, each one unique as they were themselves, these are indeed those who really give—for they give themselves up completely to dreams and utopia—those who create by creating themselves, those who teach not by abstract lessons, as would professional teachers, but by their works and their life, educators who mold the body and carry away the mind; without being in any way compelling, they invite and stimulate. Among them, and foremost, we find Christopher Columbus:

> "Dearest," said Columbus, "never
> Trust a Genoese again.
> At the blue he gazes ever,
> Distance doth his soul enchain.
>
> Strangeness is to me too dear—
> Genoa has sunk and passed—
> Heart, be cool! Hand, firmly steer!
> Sea before me: land—at last?
>
> Firmly let us plant our feet,
> Ne'er can we give up this game—
> From the distance what doth greet?
> One death, one happiness, one fame."[15]

The "Model" is therefore the man—whether he be artist, hero, explorer, or even saint (in the sense of Baudelaire and Nietzsche)—who stands out from the crowd by asserting himself in his singularity, the "noble man" as opposed to the "good" man. The "noble man" is not so much the man who belongs to a family that can boast of its ancestors, as the "strong man" whose "will to power" cannot be fettered by any threat, any scruple, and whose personality unfolded without

[15] "The New Columbus," in The Complete Works of Friedrich Nietzsche, Vol. 17, p. 162. Cf. our Nietzsche (Editions Universitaires), p. 64.

any restrictions. Thus we see a new type of man appearing in fifteenth-century Italy: "Man became a spiritual *individual* and recognized himself as such. In the same way the Greek had once distinguished himself from the barbarian. . . ." Another example of this emancipation is the humanist: Politian, Leon Battista Alberti, Leonardo da Vinci especially, who "was to Alberti as the finisher is to the beginner, as the master to the *dilettante*." Did they not both dare to claim: "Men can do all things if they will." This individual man is also the "universal" man whose culture takes in all places and times, such as Pico della Mirandola, who exalted man in his famous speech: man, the masterpiece, the end and the spire of creation!

"God made man at the close of the Creation, to know the laws of the universe, to love its beauty, to admire its greatness. He bound him to no fixed place, to no prescribed form of work, and by no iron necessity, but gave him freedom to will and to move. 'I have set thee,' says the Creator to Adam, 'in the midst of the world, that thou mayst the more easily behold and see all that is therein. I created thee a being neither heavenly nor earthly, neither mortal nor immortal only, that thou mightest be free to shape and to overcome thyself. Thou mayst sink into a beast, and be born anew to the divine likeness. The brutes bring from their mother's body what they carry with them as long as they live; the higher spirits are from the beginning, or soon after, what they will be for ever. To thee alone is given a growth and a development depending on thine own free will. Thou bearest in thee the germs of a universal life.' "[16]

The past, however, only gives us a sketch of the Superman. The prisoner has not yet succeeded in freeing himself of his gangue. A man alone cannot give birth to the Superman. And

[16] Jakob Burckhardt, *The Civilization of the Renaissance in Italy*, Part IV, The Discovery of the World and of Man, (New York: Harper, 1958), pp. 279–352.

moreover, how many so-called superior men offer themselves
as models to the admiration of the mediocre. Each great man
has his jester to imitate him. To draw up the list of these imitators who fool so many people, Nietzsche added a fourth
song, more grimacing than harmonious, his *Zarathustra* poem.
He knew what skillful simulation can accomplish; he had seen
clever producers prepare the background for their easy triumphs; he himself was an expert in the art of disguise, of hiding behind a mask. There is the leader who claims to be a
"guide" while merely flattering the passions of the rabble, the
false saint who feigns to be virtuous, the braggart who plays
the hero, and the false artist who uses only shams. In *The
Case of Wagner*, he does not hesitate to exaggerate, not without an injust cruelty of which he was not completely unaware;
will he not come back all upset from Monte Carlo after hearing the prelude to this Christian *Parsifal* he so loathed.

It is true that in Michelangelo, Leonardo, Christopher
Columbus, Dürer, Beethoven, Goethe, and Hölderlin—the
poet of misery—man had reached his highest form; but they
are still only "representative" men, as Emerson would call
them. The artist has molded the clay and outlined what he
wanted to create; he has covered with gold, like Ghiberti the
bas-reliefs on the bronze doors of the baptistry in Florence; he
has changed the rhythm of words to make them express feelings that are violent, like Kleist, or full of tenderness, like
Hölderlin. But this is not at all the main point; the obstacle
which fetters the progress of the species must be removed.
Just as mankind had to create for itself other structures than
those it inherited from the animals, so Supermankind must
take the leap which will emancipate it from human servitude;
a threshold must be crossed beyond which a new being will
be born.

This is where we have not understood Nietzsche. Had he
known Gustave Moreau, he would have recognized in this

great artist the lucid mind capable of solving the enigma. Myth finds its full and rich expression in Nietzsche; it emerges from the northern fogs where it had been kept prisoner by the confused genius of Wagner. A lot has been said about the determining influence of Darwin, whose works Nietzsche apparently read between 1874 and 1878 during what Andler calls his "positivistic" period; but the "selection" described and advocated by Nietzsche is very different from Darwin's mechanical selection which eliminates the less adapted. Nietzsche knows that man is the most unstable, the least adapted of all animals: Weak and deprived of everything, as Lucretius said, he has to invent everything. But it is because he is so deprived that he has the audacity to undertake everything; he risks his life to save it; he has to discover a way out, to find an opening, to break through the static equilibriums; in an agonizing childbirth he taxes his strength to the utmost; and the bud bursts open and lets the blossom unfold in the first effluvia of spring. But the bridge which must be crossed at all cost is man himself; darkness hovers over the abyss and it is we and not God who must make shine the light that will dissipate it. There is no other creator than the man who climbs on the stake in order to be born greater.

It has been said that Nietzsche, like his master Schopenhauer, reduced intelligence to a practical role to give a higher place to the will, which it too often paralyzes; he therefore condemns it under the name of Socrates. It is true that this opposition of Will and Intellect can be found in his works; what we call "truth," he says, is nothing but the vital lie that misleads us, while the tight weave of motives hides from us the spurt of mobiles which govern our actions. Thus intelligence plays at the surface of our being; it delights, like a child, in the colorful bubbles which form and dissolve in the light air. But if intelligence forgets the illusions it delights in, if it stops to unfold the veil of appearances, if it refuses to be at the

45

service of our ephemeral individuality, if, by turning back into itself, it follows the movement of the vital flux which carries us along only to abandon us, which generates us only to destroy us, then latent potentialities will develop in it; it will become, beyond the deceiving distinction between Good and Evil, the servant of that Will to Power which creates its own values.

The same is true of these functions: memory and imagination, which intelligence maintains within the limits of its cool calculations. Of the first it only asks, by revealing to it the part of the past which is most useful to its own purposes, that it give a basis for its wise previsions; as for the second, it tempers its flame, demanding from it a methodical exploration of the future which removes risk, dismisses adventure. But the excess of culture in which decadent civilizations took pride[17] is only a hindrance. Of what use is a "too full head"? asked Montaigne, that judicious master. Life does not bother with calculations; to reach its goals, which are always improvised, it must forget its earlier failures; it opens up, as it needs them, unexpected roads upon which it then sets out. Who does not see that "lived" history demands that one take no notice of the lessons of "written" history? Action is effective only by pulling itself out of the ruts it has made; it grows only through a shaded zone; it progresses against a background of irrationality which alone authorizes, legitimates, its daring deeds. Rousseau has left deep imprints in Nietzsche's mind. The "innovator," father of the Superman, is not the sage, the "moderate man" who is generally only a "mediocre man" frightened by respon-

---

[17] In an earlier book, *Pour connaître la pensée de Nietzsche*, we emphasized the importance of the second "Intempestive" (on the dangers of history), the theme of which will recur in France in the works of Paul Valéry and in Italy in those of A. Tilgher, while the dangers of excessive culture will be exposed by Thomas Mann.

sibilities,[18] it is the "revolutionary man" whose exalted imagination is afraid of nothing. He has grown wings[19] and, like a bird of prey, he soars above the peaks, far above the abyss; fearless of heights and lightning, imagination prospects the triumphant future.[20] On this condition only will it invent, though it will be accused of carelessness and even of madness by the "wise men"; it is obeying this fundamental Will which pushes it forward, like the daring pilot who risks in the storm the lives of his crew and the terrified passengers.

Let us carry the extrapolation further: We then see the profile of a more encompassing, more mobile culture, which will be that of the future. No one understood better than Nietzsche how man, initially tied to his "condition," masters it through a progressive broadening of perspectives. This is the meaning of a very beautiful poem describing the fir tree growing more and more deeply into the rock, which might give way under it at any moment, in order to raise its branches as high as possible.

> —But thou, Zarathustra,
> Still lovest the abysses,
> Lovest them as doth the fir tree!
>
> The fir flings its roots
> Where the rock itself gazes
> Shuddering at the depths,—
> The fir pauses before the abysses
> Where all around
> Would fain descend:
> Amid the impatience
> Of wild, rolling, leaping torrents

[18] Nietzsche carries out anew the analyses of the great French moralists he admired: La Rochefoucauld, Vauvenargues, and Chamfort.

[19] Nietzsche was well acquainted with the Pythagorean views.

[20] For Nietzsche imagination will always be what it was for all romanticists: "The queen of all faculties."

> It waits so patient, stern and silent,
> Lonely. . . .[21]

It is true that this double exploration, into the depths of the past and into the future beyond all possible previsions, exposes the fir tree to a double danger. It may slide into the abyss or lightning may strike it:

> O'er man and beast I grew so high,
> And speak—but none will give reply.
>
> Too lone and tall my crest did soar:
> I wait: what am I waiting for?
>
> The clouds are grown too nigh of late,
> 'Tis the first lightning I await.[22]

Nietzsche boasts of speaking in "enigmas," like the sphinx, and each enigma has several meanings. The fir tree symbolizes the growth of man whose consciousness, at first restricted to the immediate present and prisoner of a particular place, expands little by little to enclose, for the best men, the totality of space and time. Our starting point, for all of us, is the spot where we were born—that pine tree burnt by the sun near which Pirandello found himself projected into his native Sicily[23]—and the universe is reduced for us to the limits of our field of vision. Time is even more restricting, for beyond it how many fruitful meetings could have taken place!—Chateaubriand will be too old when he meets the woman he could have loved. But now this horizon is widening a little, for some of us at least. But how many will go back into their family, their house, their village and refuse to be chased out of them!

[21] "Between Birds of Prey," in *The Complete Works*, Vol. 17, p. 178.

[22] "Pine Tree and Lightning," *ibid.*, p. 161.

[23] Cf. our *Luigi Pirandello*, 2nd ed. (Paris: Editions Universitaires, 1963).

Some will say they are wise, others that they are afraid of taking risks. But the future yields only to the adventurers, to the Christopher Columbuses who are afraid of nothing, to the Argonauts in quest of the eternal Golden Fleece.

Now begin the idle questions, and Archetypes arise in a consciousness that has become unbounded.[24] Beyond the place in which I am fixed, I sense that there are others; beyond my village there are towns, full of noise perhaps but also full of all I desire, and harbors where one can embark for the happy isles; I wonder about the time that went by before I was born and I try to find a meaning for it. Suddenly I feel dizzy in the face of the infinite unfolding of time-spaces. For time and space join and blend together in such a way that it is impossible for me to separate them, and this endless surf which has brought and taken so many lives before me, which after me will leave them on the shore, headed for identical shipwrecks, how can I not loose my foothold when listening to its endless murmur? To avoid these unanswerable questions, we must stop clinging onto that "individuality" which every day eludes us, to see in it only the manifestation of a Will, a Vitality which has no other aim than to create in order to destroy. To consent to be only a transition, or rather to use this impetus and make it cross the threshold which opens the way to higher realizations, to offer oneself as a holocaust so that the Superman may come, this is the mission Zarathustra sets forth to man.

We can only give an outline of this Supermankind which will arise from an "ascending" selection through the deliberate sacrifice of the best men. Each Superman will have chiseled himself to the point of displaying the hard crystal of his transparency; he will no longer have any use for masks, since he will have found the Oneness of a completely self-

[24] Cf. the painting by Gauguin which bears the exergue: "D'où venons-nous? Qui sommes-nous? Où allons-nous?"

sufficient person; in a quasi-timeless intuition he will have brought together not only his own past and his own future but the past and the future of a universe with which his consciousness will coincide, while his Will will be identified with the will to power which creates all forms of a multiform existence. He alone will be fully autonomous, for autonomy can not consist of obeying some categorical order valid for all but of inventing one's own laws. Emancipated from gravity so that nothing can hinder the flight of his mind, dexterous and joyous as a dancer, he will have found, beyond the insurrection of the lion, the full freedom, the airy lightness of a child at play:

"But tell me, my brethren, what the child can do, which even the lion could not do? Why hath the preying lion still to become a child?

"Innocence is the child, and forgetfulness, a new beginning, a game, a self-rolling wheel, a first movement, a holy Yea.

"Aye, for the game of creating, my brethren, there is needed a holy Yea unto life: *its own* will, willeth now the spirit; *his own* world winneth the world's outcast."[25]

How will the Superman generate a community of Supermen? And on what feelings will this community be based? It is true that the Superman looks for "fellow-creators," "fellow-reapers," strong men whom no task can frighten and who "know how to whet their sickles." But what ties will unite these Supermen, apart from their common task, since each one will have no other law than his own law, since they will not know pity and will turn away scornfully from those who cannot follow them? What will become of this lower humanity they have abandoned behind them, that vile herd of which they will not even condescend to be the herdsmen? Finally, will they triumph over time or will they be carried away by it, since there is no world-beyond where this higher being they

---

[25] *Thus Spake Zarathustra*, p. 27.

will have mastered, this Super-ego they will have formed, can blossom forth and fix itself in the plenitude of Action.

Once more Nietzsche feels the dizziness he thought he had mastered. The idea of Eternal Recurrence had been haunting him for a long time. Suddenly it becomes clear to him under the double appearance of the Gate and the Serpent. To accept the Eternal Recurrence of all things, is this not the only way to gather together all the past, to take on all the future, both coinciding underneath the Gate. But can the fusion of being and time occur only at such a cost? Must the best men be destroyed, annihilated in order that everything may come back again? How can this terrifying revelation be transformed into joy? And must one not renounce intelligence itself to admit that "Everything has returned: Sirius, and the spider, and thy thoughts at this moment, and this last thought of thine that all these things will return,"[26] to understand that "the timeless and time can be compatible," indeed that they can coincide? Only an instant separates the completed conscious life from the first glimpse of the new life, but if creatures could count they would measure this gap in millions of years. As soon as we dismiss and destroy the Christian God, the moral God, there remains but one hypothesis which, through endless repetition, transforms temporal becoming into eternity.

Such are the terrifying thoughts which fill Nietzsche's mind and which he dares mention to neither Lou Salomé,[27] nor Overbeck,[28] nor Peter Gast.[29] He defends himself as best he can against this climactic conflict; and one winter's evening in 1889 he will succumb to this tension: Is it madness or an ultimate mask behind which he conceals his misery to himself?

[26] *The Eternal Recurrence* in *The Complete Works*, Vol. 16, p. 248.
[27] Lou Andréa Salomé, *F. Nietzsche* (Paris: Grasset, 1932).
[28] He will advise Madame Overbeck to remain faithful to her religious beliefs.
[29] Cf. the letter to Peter Gast dated August 14, 1881.

For there is always a share of simulation in madness. At the end of this pathetic effort to create his own destiny, the man who is almost a Superman finds himself caught—oh, irony!—in a cyclic process in which he is but an instant, caught in the Karmic wheel which has determined his place forever and fixed his role *ne varietur*. And the person is reduced to the level of a mere character!

The same obsession will torment Pirandello; his six characters will impose on the author and the producer a role they are not free to change. More bitter than Nietzsche, he will draw for us in his last, unfinished play—*The Mountain Giants*—the caricature of the pseudo-Superman. Gone are the days of poetry and charm, destroyed by the excesses of criticism and the progress of technology! Mankind has detected the falseness of the spectacle. It rejects the actors by whose acting it had been deceived. It is only within the confines of another world in which the magician Cotrone is trying to keep them that the enchantments the public delighted in for a long time can remain valid. Henceforth, in the depths of subterranean forges, at the top of mountains which have not been explored in ages, these "Mountain Giants" who have abdicated all humanity will go on toiling. Hard-working but ruthless, they create a world from which all charm and all spirituality have been excluded. Can man survive and remain himself when all mirages have vanished, when the myths on which rest the authority and even the prestige of laws have disappeared, when the legends woven by imagination, by the "spontaneous wisdom"[30] of nations have been dispelled as mist by the wind?

The Promethean theme, however, was haunting other minds and inspiring other masterpieces. Nietzsche was familiar with Lipiner's *Prometheus;* he did not hide his admiration

---

[30] Vico will often use this expression.

52

for Carl Spitteler's *Prometheus und Epimetheus.*[31] It is a sublime and not sufficiently appreciated poem, which begins in the same tone as *Zarathustra.*

"This was the time of his youth. He was full of health and vitality and stronger every day.

"Prometheus, overflowing with pride, said to Epimetheus, his friend and his brother:

"Arise! Come! Let us no longer be like the crowd, like those who swarm in common time!

"For if we make our behavior conform with the common example, we will soon be of common value, and we will never again know noble joys or those sufferings which enrich the soul."[32]

The distinction Carl Spitteler makes between "myth" and "epic" is very similar, indeed almost identical, to that which Nietzsche makes between Dionysian art—participation in the suffering of the world, in the mystery of uninterrupted creations and destructions—and Apollonian art, which imposes a plastic form full of luminous serenity on this painful creation. We find the same fierce individualism in both works,[33] in which the symbolic animals are very similar: the Lion and

[31] "As regards aesthetics, he is the finest of all writers," said Nietzsche. One might ask whether Spitteler's mythical epic work, which appeared in 1880–1881, did not somewhat influence Nietzsche's *Zarathustra*: a very limited influence of course, if it is true, as we believe, that Zarathustra first appeared to Nietzsche as early as 1876, in one of the "happy isles," Ischia. After his *Prometheus und Epimetheus*, Carl Spitteler wrote *Olympischer Frühling* (*Olympian Spring*), full of memories of ancient Greece; he would once more take up the theme of Prometheus in a work of a completely different inspiration, *Prometheus der dulder* (*The Patient Prometheus*).

[32] Carl Spittelter, *Prometheus und Epimetheus.*

[33] Spitteler will say about Nietzsche in an article which appeared November 8, 1888, in the *Bund*, in Berne, concerning *The Case of Wagner*: "Nietzsche is a giant." Nietzsche will send him a copy of his *Zarathustra* (an honor only Overbeck was to share).

the Dog in *Prometheus*, the Eagle and the Serpent in *Zara-thustra*. At the beginning of Spitteler's poem, Prometheus appears as a giant full of indignation over deceit and injustice; though he is the "strong man" whom no concern with caution can lead to compromise or resignation, he nonetheless has respect for the gods and is mindful of their laws:

"We have seen," says Romain Rolland," what Spitteler has in common with Nietzsche; but this generous, overflowing, healthy nature was not made to remain in this state of para-doxical, total, and mad tension to which Nietzsche con-strained himself up to the final break. Spitteler is not a tense and striken genius. If he lived the Nietzschean drama in his own way, it was to transcend it and to solve it."[34]

A common admiration for the virtues of ancient Greece, for the heroic effort which makes it possible to throw an Apol-lonian light on the darkness of evil, an identical rebellion against hypocrisy and injustice which relate them both to Rousseau, this is what brings Nietzsche and Spitteler together. But very soon their paths diverge. At first there is nothing to moderate the violence of Prometheus; he is the unsatisfied wanderer who rejects the false peace of home; the god is wor-ried by his obstinate intransigence and prefers the dutiful and obedient Epimetheus. Prometheus is also the inspiration which overflows all of a sudden, the fiery torrent which clears a way for itself without thinking of anything but its own im-pulse. He is willing to submit to the god's order but only on condition that he ratify this order. This ardent soul, carried forth by prophetic instinct, will have to go a long way before it can become understanding and conciliating without ceasing to be true to itself. The hero will evolve like his Creator, whose voice will be heard one day in defense of freedom and preaching peace to a mankind divided by resentment and ambition.

[34] Romain Rolland, *Compagnons de route* (Le Sablier, 1936).

Contrasting with Prometheus, we find his brother, Epimetheus, whose docility is reassuring. Epimetheus is the conformist conscience, law-abiding and respectful of the established order; in the end he will accept another law, no longer divine but human, which will be dictated to him by a crowd that is hostile to anything beyond itself which it does not understand. His weakness will make it possible for a jealous people to kill the divine children entrusted to his care; the worst of all sins will be committed which will lead mankind to perdition. Like Faust, Epimetheus has sold his soul, but nothing can save it. For Faust remained faithful to the inspiration which animated him; the same thirst for the absolute drives him and against it the negating spirit is powerless. This thirst misled him once, but oriented toward noble deeds, it will allow him to mold the universe; thus he escapes from the snares of the Devil. It is for an earthly kingdom, for a conscience at the level of societies and states, that Epimetheus has sold his soul. Now, conformist minds, as soon as they are faced with a crucial problem, as soon as the "sacred" is in question, are lost and helpless; they turn out to be incapable of solving a situation which, since it is beyond the familiar scope, requires innovation, calls for an original solution.

It is true that the Prometheus-Epimetheus conflict is that of the individualistic and singular mind with the conscience that is nothing but a reflexion of society, "the others in us" Pirandello will say.[35] The Creator stands up against tradition and opposes personal law, whose origin is divine, to juridical legalism.[36] But it is also something else, which prefigures Bergson: the opposition between "closed" morality—which imprisons itself in rigorous obligations to which it wishes to subject genius itself, where the future is nothing but the repetition

[35] Cf. L. Pirandello, *Right You Are.*

[36] The problem had already been set in these same terms in the "philosophical novel" *Hayy ibn Yaqzān,* by Ibn Tufayl.

of a past restricted within the limits of the city or the state—and "open" morality, in which are shown more generous norms[37] that are valid for a mankind which is pacified at last. Spitteler is thinking of this mankind and, first of all, of a Europe in which all families would have a place in the love of a common fatherland.

"A European poet," he says, "that is the right word. I never was a Swiss poet, or a German poet, but a European poet, international and timeless. It is by mere accident [that of birth] that I used the German language."

Nietzsche will sometimes echo this statement: "I see over and beyond all these national wars, new 'empires,' and whatever else lies in the foreground. What I am concerned with—for I see it preparing itself slowly and hesitatingly—is the United Europe. It was the only real work, the one impulse in the souls, of all the broad-minded and deep-thinking men of this century—this preparation of a new synthesis, and the tentative effort to anticipate the future of "the European."[38]

Nietzsche was thinking of the European and of the "leveling" he implies, and it is perhaps to the level of the Superman that he wanted him to rise. He would then have justified this short definition, probably the best one he ever gave of the man of the future: "He who gives, he who creates, he who teaches." But he saw standing out against him the shadow of

---

[37] "And on that accursed day," admits Epimetheus, "I handed over my divine soul for a fabricated Conscience which, by dint of words like 'tion' and 'ism,' did a marvelous job of leading me along the path of virtue to complete ignominy.

"And now I am frustrated and deprived of all my being, and all that is left of me fills me with hatred and contempt." *Prometheus und Epimetheus.*

[38] *The Genealogy of Morals* in *The Complete Works*, Vol. 13, p. 224.

mediocrity and fear, and this disease, the worst of all, which undermines and destroys our civilization: our sense of guilt to the point of humiliation.[39]

[39] Nietzsche stresses the extreme frailty of civilizations: "Civilization is but a thin film above a fiery chaos."
I am sorry that I can no more than mention a great European, Guy de Pourtalès, the author of one of this century's greatest novels, *La Pêche miraculeuse*, and of that unfairly neglected book: *Les Saints de France*.

3

An Almost Unknown Gobineau: The Calenders, Sons of Kings

The moral world is in every respect like the deep round bowl of the sky whose starlit splendour we can see. My gaze only wants to uncover and search out and see those radiant beings with scintillating crowns who have grouped themselves intelligently in infinite space, attracted and joined by the laws of some mysterious and undeniable affinity.

Gobineau[1]

*I*n Gobineau, even more than in Dostoevski whose religious anxiety he would not have tolerated, Nietzsche saw a fellow-mind. They have the same horror for the imminent mediocrity, for leveling from below. "In the dwarfing and leveling of the European man lurks our greatest peril. . . . We see today nothing which wishes to be greater, we surmise that the process is always still backwards," says Nietzsche.[2] "Nations, or rather 'human herds,' will henceforth wallow in the torpitude of their nullity, like ruminant buffaloes in the stagnant waters of the Pontine marshes," will be Gobineau's bitter conclusion.[3] It is true that Nietzsche, who had read in Basel the

---

[1] *The Sons of Kings* (*Les Pléiades*), trans. by Douglas Parmée (London: Oxford University Press, 1966), pp. 18–19.

[2] Nietzsche, *The Genealogy of Morals*.

[3] Gobineau, Correspondence with Count Prokesch, quoted by J.-E. Spenlé, *Nietzsche et le problème européen* (Paris: A. Colin, 1943), p. 113.

Essay on the Inequality of Human Races—Gobineau, alas!
even today is known only by this work—will regret that the
Wagners had got their hooks onto this masterful mind and
had "turned him away from him";[4] he nonetheless praised
him for his excellent portrait of the "noble man," for showing
how "all higher civilization arose on this earth."

These two men have so much in common! Nietzsche, the
son and grandson of Lutheran ministers, invents a Polish ancestor—Count Nietzky; Gobineau, heir to the fortune of a
wealthy, traditionally Catholic family from Bordeau, discovers
an Aryan ancestor, the Viking Ottar Jarl. Gobineau, who lived
in Athens for a long time, considered Greece his true fatherland; it was in this beloved country that he became a sculptor
and a writer. For Nietzsche, who knew it only in his dreams,
Greece was the educator par excellence. They both greatly
admired the Renaissance: this blessed period during which
Greek classicism seemed to bloom again in all its vigor, thanks
to a few outstanding minds. Their eyes delighted in the sight
of the same patrician city before closing six years apart. It was
in Turin that Gobineau died, in a coach on his way to the sta-
tion; it is in Turin that Nietzsche wandered while madness
was invading his brain. Beyond these two different deaths, the
same derisory fate will reunite them. Because of a disciple of
limited intelligence, Houston Chamberlain, Gobineau was to
become the inspirer of what he would have hated most: German national socialism, which came to power by flattering the
basest wishes of the crowds. Nietzsche was to have a similar
fate, he who had condemned Germany and its "political"
decadence.

In order to really get to know Gobineau as a man—great
not by his family ties but by his own genius; full of intelligence but also of passion; fond of tradition but, by another

[4] Correspondence with Overbeck, quoted by Spenlé, *ibid.*, p. 109.

contradiction, leaving at the end of his life the family he had loved above all in favor of a tardy affair;[5] a tireless traveler, carried by his eager and searching mind; fascinated by man, though he claimed to despise him; above all craving for light and beauty—one must read his lengthy correspondence with another humanist, Count von Prokesch.[6] He was still very young when he first developed his veneration for the Renaissance, together with his plan to try and describe it:[7]

"I who am always engrossed by the sixteenth century, who compare everything with those artists, who see only them, who live among them, high up, when I climb back down to this century it is to see talented men, no doubt, but without love for what they are doing, without respect for beauty and form."

As years go by, though the project becomes clearer, the perspective changes. When he finally gets to work on his masterpiece, thirty years later in Stockholm where he has been sent as ambassador, the initial idea—"in reaching maturity"—has considerably changed. It is no longer a novel or a history book extolling men "of faith and passion,"[8] but a huge fresco: Gobineau will depict in it the contradictory and conflicting aspects of the Renaissance in which he had been living for so long. Almost at the same time Renan set himself an identical goal in his *Drames philosophiques*, but he will not be able to

[5] He will go to live in Rome with a very intelligent young woman, the Marquise de la Tour.

[6] *Correspondance de Gobineau et du comte Prokesch* (Paris: Plon, 1933).

[7] As early as May 24, 1841, he announced to his father his intention of writing a history of the condottieri, and he added: "In the biography of each of these condottieri, I would fit all my views on this marvelous period."

[8] *Vite di avventure, di fede e di passione*, is the title of a book by B. Croce which was similarly intended to extol "vitality."

substantiate his ideas in this work.[9] In Gobineau's successive tableaux, on the contrary—and though they are too vast and too confused for stage performance—we see a crowd carried along by the enthusiasms and passions of the leaders of the hour; unstable and quick to yield to all emotions, it can change instantly from love to hatred, from passive resignation to anger, from veneration to resentment. Though we witness the rise of the "condottieri," the atrocious betrayal at Sinigaglia which Machiavelli considered the political act par excellence, though Machiavelli himself, the leader of this skillful and daring game, is very much in the limelight, Gobineau nevertheless most willingly dwells on the artists. In his view, as in that of Nietzsche, the ability to create—much more than virtue or a discerning mind—is what characterizes the Superman, the "calender," the king's son.

It is therefore important to read very carefully the three following works, so different from one another though they were written almost simultaneously: the *Nouvelles* (Asiatic and Greek), the *Sons of Kings* (*Les Pléiades*), and this Renaissance he was to call *The Golden Flower*. Among the short stories, there is one whose perfume still lingers: *Akrivie Phrangopoulo*; it was inspired by Gobineau's tender friendship for a young Greek woman, Zoé Dragoumis. Some of the descriptions recall Ulysses' encounter with Nausicaa. Jean Mistler is right in rating these delightful tales higher than those of Mérimée: "his irony is not dry and arid, it is brightened by a ray of poetry"; as in Alain-Fournier's *Miracles*, everything is transfigured by beauty, that fragile flower which blooms, alas! only for a moment, on a stem that might break at any time.

But let us not dwell any longer on what was for Gobineau but a pleasant pastime and a homage to that country where the "golden number" is inscribed in the proportions of the

---

[9] Cf. our *Ernest Renan* (Lyon-Paris: Vitte, 1956).

temples. And let us examine his real purpose in painting the Renaissance. For it was not the man of a certain period he wanted to draw, however great that period, but the "universal" man; "I am, in short, trying something new, to write a book I can only compare to a large fresco which will explain, or at least which should explain its meaning, not in what is particular to it and in a sense archaic, but in what it contains that is generally and constantly human."[10]

The intuition guiding our author is that certain periods are more suitable than others to display the constant aspects of human nature; truly "representative" men meet during these periods, confronting their views and their lives. Now what period more than the Renaissance—apart from Greece in the days of Pericles—revealed to us man both in his basest instincts and in his loftiest aspirations? It was followed by what Gobineau disdainfully calls "the swamp of the seventeenth century." His nature was instinctively too generous for him to subscribe, without reservations, to the views of Machiavelli, who in his bad days saw nothing in human nature but "envy, hatred, fear, pride, unrestrained lust for conquest and possessions, vain ignorance, uncontrollable desire for vengeance, restlessness due to unlimited ambitions and desires, suspicious and mistrusting minds, instinctive malignity, and a constant inclination toward desiring the misfortune of others,"[11] in short a "vipers' tangle" which must be cut by strength or handled with cunning. Gobineau also could be quite cynical, but the harshness of his judgments was due to his constant dis-

[10] "I am engrossed in the sixteenth century in Italy." Letter to Prokesch, April 25, 1873.

[11] Regarding Machiavelli, read F. Meinecke, *L'idea della ragione di stato nella storia moderna*, Italian translation (Firenze: Sansoni); B. Croce, *Storia come Pensiero e come Azione*, Chapter "Meinecke," (Bari: La Terza); E. Garin, *L'Umanesimo italiano*, (Bari: Le Terza, 1938).

appointment. He could therefore discern the same suffering in the Secretary of Florence. Machiavelli also had believed in the efficacy of moral ideals, and, willing to become the disciple of Fra Savonarola, he had listened to his vibrant sermons; then he saw this great and noble personality submerged by popular storms, in a frenzy of hatred. He then asked himself the agonizing question par excellence: Might not the highest aspirations lead to the same results as vice? Does not the slightest deviation of the sense of religion lead almost inevitably to fanaticism and intolerance?

But Gobineau had a more optimistic outlook. He felt that history, like life, is constantly being fashioned by the action of two principles: the first passive and receptive,[12] the other active and fecundating, and that it presents the alternation of two periods: one of slow and almost static maturation, the other of sudden movement and crisis. He even thought of writing a book on the migrations of peoples which preceded the decline of antiquity.[13] But he soon realized this would be too great a task, and thus to verify, so to speak, what would have been his hypothesis, he chose this privileged moment of history, the Renaissance.

Let us open the Introduction at the first scenes of the drama: They are set in Florence—that amazing city which, in the sixteenth century, had inherited the genius of ancient

[12] He wanted to express this symbol in the two statues he sculpted in Athens: *Love* and *Night*. He had borrowed it from Apollodorus, who wrote: "The active principle and the passive principle create the world: gods and men." Letter to Prokesch, June 8, 1868.

[13] He borrowed the following distinction from Machiavelli (it can also be found in Renan's works). Machiavelli made a distinction between three types of wars: political wars with limited objectives; ideological wars, which are much more dangerous and cruel, and the wars caused by large migrations of peoples or of tribes driven by famine or poverty, those which ravaged Europe as the Roman Empire was weakening.

Greece. Like the land and the enveloping ocean, the moral world, says Gobineau, reveals only its most superficial aspects. Above "the accumulated waves of time" there stand "a certain number of epochs that may be compared to continents."

"The portions that are high, disclosed and clearly seen, illuminated by the sun, and considered of all ages especially worthy of interest, are few in number; they occupy but scant space in the expanse of the ages. To enumerate them is a quickly finished task. There is the epoch in which Pericles ruled; there is the opulent period of the Selucidae and of the Ptolemies. Then appears the Roman splendor under Augustus; this ends with the Antonines, and a great gulf separates it from the period in which Christian theology, inspiring the feudal hierarchy, produced the genius of the twelfth and thirteenth centuries of our era. At this point the ascent halts anew; like a smoking lamp, history gradually dims its light and is enveloped in shadows; it seems to flicker out, and it finds no new life until the second half of the fifteenth century.

"During the periods that lie between these luminous moments, the days, the stream of days, the stream of facts, flow on, troubled and indistinct; this is the sterile sea, the Homeric bard would say again. But no! It is the fecund sea, stirring in its depths, bearing on its surface the germs of future things, leaving to float humbly upon the face of its waters that interlaced vegetation, devoid of brilliance but ever constant, that upholds amid tufted leaves, plated upon the sombre cloth, the golden flowers, great marvels of human vitality. For they are golden flowers, those splendid times in which men built the Parthenon, the Capitol, the cathedrals of Beauvais and of Amiens, and when all Italy was ablaze with life, with myriad colors, with wit, intelligence, with genius and with beauty."[14]

---

[14] Cf. Arthur, Count Gobineau, *The Golden Flower*, trans. B. R. Redman (New York: Putnam, 1924), pp. 5–6.

A constant movement, a surging life always ready to be reborn through constant metamorphoses appears thus in the moral as well as in the material world. And perhaps this world in which some rare personalities blossom forth above the universal mediocrity of the nameless masses, which sway like trees in the stormy wind, is only the cosmos itself carried to its highest expression. On the ruins of what time has destroyed we see new civilizations arising, following a rhythm that evokes the very breathing of the sea; or rather, when a great era comes to an end, the crumbled materials it leaves in its wake are ready to be used in new combinations. It is true that nothing that has happened will ever happen again. It is therefore not without melancholy that the sage examines that "which will never be seen twice," but one should have faith in the powers for renewal which lie in the heart of nature. Let a masculine principle arise and from "the Greek detritus, held suspended in the depths of men's minds and touched by Roman intelligence, emerges the Age of Augustus." "Nothing is destroyed; all the means save one—a capital element, it is true—exist for the production of new creations. Along with the value, the savor, the perfume, the particular stamp of the extinct period, with the structure that was peculiar to it and the special soul that animated it, has disappeared forever what one may call the masculine germ that is contained, and which conferred upon it the individuality of its being; this germ is dissolved, it counts no more in the total of the world's wealth, it will never appear again. But behind it remains the floating mass of what may be called feminine elements endowed with a receptivity calculated to result in new creations when a new plastic cause, furnished by a new race, shall have reawakened the paralysed fecundity."[15]

There is a secret affinity between the calenders in *Sons of*

[15] *Ibid.*, p. 9.

Kings, Conrad Lanze, Louis de Laudon, Wilfrid Nore, and their leader, Prince John-Theodore, and the artists whose genius blossomed like a golden flower during the blessed days of the Renaissance. The same dream of beauty brings them together, the same effort to fix their ideals in themselves or in the marble. They have converged from everywhere, like these stars which suddenly combine to form a harmonious constellation, called toward one another by a mysterious affinity, and here they are together, on the terraces of Isola Bella, facing a lake of unequaled splendor, or in the gardens of the Medici, in a city beyond compare which also deserves the name of beauty. The strong bond uniting them is love, love aroused by the perfection of forms; alas! this love too is passing, fleeting, and so quickly carried away by all-destructive time. Thus Prokesch was mistaken when he reproached Gobineau for departing from his original plan. He would have liked the young prince to be more greedy for power, that he lead the "rabble" to "the flogging"; thus exceptional beings would have asserted their primacy and satisfied their ambition. But Aurora charms the prince away from any such thoughts, or rather, in his young cousin he finds the true purpose of his existence, as did Raphael when he met the Fornarina. Who could forget the charm of Aurora, so marvelous that it is impossible to think that it might wear off with time! "I have mentioned Aurora Pamina's name, but I haven't yet talked about her. She was tall and slight and slender, with a ravishing figure, graceful and delicate. Her hair was the loveliest you could imagine, her blue eyes were infinitely gentle and deep, questioning and charming as well. . . . Seeming interested in everything, graceful in everything she said and did, and with a character which was a blend of sparkling wit, reasonableness, and sensitivity."

Gobineau had tried to fix this beauty in the stone, this beauty that causes the artist to rebel at the thought that it might vanish. He had admired it in his eldest daughter, Diana

—though she was prouder than Aurora—and in the young, graceful, and lively Greek woman he immortalized as Akrivie. Nature seems to curve around these delightful figures, like the sky around the sparkling constellations. But how can one hold on to this rare moment when beauty reaches its apex? Odette Swann's umbrella protected her only against the rays of the sun; soon her beauty will be only that of an artificial flower. How can nature be forgiven for being so careless as to abandon its masterpieces to the whims of time? This rebellion, which is probably the main cause of Proust's incredulity, how acutely did Gobineau not sense it also!

History however will provide the author of the *Pléiades* with some figureheads that appear as though sculpted outside time: soldiers, politicians, princes, a pope, marvelous figures of women so unjustly calumniated and so unhappy in their greatness, such as Lucrezia Borgia, but most of all artists: Aretino, Botticelli, Raphael, Titian, and finally Michelangelo. Between the scenes where these giants appear, a breath of pity brushes humble faces, the faces of those who do not make history but must endure it: poor devils, farmers, common people, women carried away by the storm, their dead child in their arms, unable to understand what hit them. Their eyes, dried up by tears, are filled with a stupor nothing will ever be able to erase. The dialogue alternates with these apparitions of a chorus which is no longer satisfied with commenting on the sufferings of the great but relates its own misery. War, in its most cruel aspects, irrupts onto the stage itself. Gobineau adopted a partitioning similar to that of Michelangelo in the Sistine Chapel, of Raphael in his *Stanze*. Each part of the fresco is the complement or the commentary of another, while, in a daring innovation which we will not find again until present-day drama and novels,[16] events which are separated

[16] Cf. in particular the novels of Jean-Paul Sartre and the plays by Anouilh.

only in appearance by space and time are represented as contemporary. By suddenly turning the set, changing the lighting
and showing in succession events that occurred in different
places—Florence and Milan, Venice and Ferrara, the battle-
field of Fornovo, and the camp of the mercenaries at Sinigaglia, then Rome where the fate of Savonarola is being settled—
Gobineau wanted to show how the threads of human intentions and of destiny are intermingled; we see them intertwine
before us, get into knots, then unravel, creating an illusion
of respite, until intermingling anew they sever a human life.
Thus in the *Iliad* and the *Odyssey*, the designs of the gods
themselves are powerless against the Ananke: the wise Ulysses will wander on the seas while the death of Patroclus will
hasten the disastrous fate of Troy. Gobineau's mind is saturated with these themes he encountered in Asia as well as in
Greece: in his works, Love and Night express the permanent
opposition between Good and Evil.

But fate has no hold over some exceptional beings who
know how to impose the decisions of their will or of their
genius. Through all the scenes, whether they be atrocious or
burlesque, pathetic or laughable, inspired by Dante's Inferno[17]
or by Jerome Bosch's paintings, there transpires a light, there
flows a song filled with hope, thanks to two or three exceptional people. We first see Lucrezia Borgia, terrified and full
of indignation at the horror of the murder of her husband by
her own brother Cesare. The arguments used by Alexander VI
to encourage her to be resigned may surprise and shock us;
and yet, do they not belong to the arsenal of reasons of state

[17] Some of them seem to have been borrowed from Dante or Vasari;
the latter, indeed, mentions a young girl "*ora innamoratissima d'un bel
giovane, il quale pareva che poco di lei si curasse.*" We will find her in
The Renaissance, where she dies, her mind aglow with love and unable
to repent.

in which we continue, in this century of progress, to find arguments and justifications?

"Know henceforward that for the kind of persons whom fate summons to dominate others, the ordinary rules of life are reversed, and duty becomes quite different. Good and evil are lifted to another, to a higher region, to a different plane. The virtues that may be applauded in an ordinary woman would in you become vices, merely because they would only be sources of error and ruin. Now the great law of the world is not to do this or that, to avoid one thing and run after another; it is to live, to enlarge and develop our most active and lofty qualities, in such a way that from any sphere we can always hew ourselves out a way to one that is wider, more airy, more elevated."[18]

Where can we find a more accurate statement of the maxims that will inspire the now-conscious beast of prey and justify the crimes of the "great"? Never was the primacy of might so cynically asserted, together with its aptitude to create a new law.

Is this creed then the message of the *Renaissance?* In that case the morality of Gobineau would be remarkably close to that attributed to Nietzsche. I do not think this is the case. First of all, Lucrezia does not follow these precepts. We will soon find her protecting the arts and delighting in the verses she reads to Bembo: "There is nothing great in this world save the love of art, the love of the things in the intellect, the love of those whom one loves, and moreover, when life in its course has raised you to one of those table-lands where the flowers become scarcer and the horizons more stern, perhaps you will still find pleasure in wise reflection on certain eternal matters

[18] Arthur, Count Gobineau, *The Renaissance*, Oscar Levy, ed. (London: Heinemann, 1913) p. 67.

69

about which we trouble less in our first youth. . . ."[19]

Some years go by and the diorama brings us back to Madame Lucrezia's study. But what a change! We no longer see the young girl with flaming hair portrayed by Pinturicchio and whom we met in the "Savonarola" episode—sorrowful and naive, indifferent to politics in spite of her father's pleas—nor the young woman of the following tableau conversing with Bembo and dividing her life between politics and the arts, but a grave and calm woman with greying hair appearing from under her simple velvet coif. She is writing to her old friend Bembo, now Cardinal, and her letter is tainted with anxiety rather than hope:

"The love of literature, that once had such power to delight my leisure hours, has lost its spell; religion alone keeps me up; it offers many threats as well as promises."[20]

Is this then the course of all lives, at first carefree and serene, full of games and laughter, later turned toward love, then strained by ambition and relaxing, when not at work, with learned conversations and the arts, until other perspectives and more exacting calls appear to the soul?

Another actor however is holding some of the threads of the plot unfolding before us. A perspicacious observer of events over which he admits that man has very little influence, he will not turn to religion for comfort. In his youth he was one of those who believed in the reforms of Savonarola and in the primacy of morality over politics. He was happy to see how people filled the churches and deserted the taverns. But he witnessed the inconstancy and the ingratitude of the crowd, anxious to miss none of the tortures inflicted upon the prophet it had but yesterday hailed as a saint. He will not forget this scene, and understanding that all men—or almost all—are

[19] Ibid., p. 229.
[20] Ibid., pp. 283–284.

governed by interest and passion, he will be attracted by very different virtues: that of the strong man who knows how to use in turn violence and ruse in order to satisfy his will to power and dominate these beings he scorns and over which he has full control. But however skillfully Cesare Borgia directs his intrigues, however great the absence of scruples which allows him to realize his schemes and the tenacity with which he carries them out, a single little mistake will suffice to ruin it all and hand him over, helpless, to those who had feigned to accept his cooperation only so that he would be more at their mercy. Would there be other threads in the weave of history than those spun by human hands? And does Providence make use of the passions and interests of man to reach goals which are beyond us? Would the true face of events, which is hidden from us, reveal a plane in which morality is avenged? Gobineau considered this hypothesis; Machiavelli, mindful of the teaching of Tacitus, will not retain it. History appears to him, as it did to Voltaire, as a series of unrelated tableaux; folly and insanity transform it into a series of atrocious scenes in which the wretched actors think only of plundering and stealing.[21] A superior man sometimes arises, only to be swallowed up in the night, leaving behind him nothing but those ashes one calls glory.

Those who, like Charles V, think they are the masters of the world are in fact nothing but the toy of a terrible fate; their palace echoes the footsteps and the cries of their victims, and the religion they profess sinks into the horrors of the Inquisition. Thus man, mistaken as to his real feelings, satisfies his thirst for blood under the cover of false virtue.

"When Fra Girolamo Savonarola came to preach his doctrines, I was a young man; I loved my fellow-creatures; I loved my country; I loved Italy; I believed in the possibility of rea-

---

[21] Cf. *ibid.*, the abdication of Charles V and his dialogue with Philip II, pp. 334–337.

son and virtue. I exhausted all my strength so as to build them
a house. What has been the result of my hopes? Let us not
speak of it. As, however, I had still a little of credulity left, I
fancied that an able man like the Duke of Valentinois could
create a noble kingdom, endow it with wise laws and good
ordinances, send the foreigners back to their homes—in short,
that there was still something to be desired. The Duke of
Valentinois failed. To-day, it is the fashion to regard him as
the most frightful of monsters, although, so far as individual
or general cruelties are concerned, he never dreamed of a tithe
of the useless brutalities carried out by Charles V, among
others the sack of Rome and the re-establishment of the Inquisition. But the minds of men are so constituted that they
need a number of scapegoats to bear the burden of the crimes
of a period; naturally, they do not choose the wolves, who are
doing most harm. They take those who can defend themselves
least, those whom the dogs have already rent or throttled,
because above all, they are cowards themselves."[22]

Are these Gobineau's conclusions? One might think so, if
one only considered his more bitter remarks. His famous
mot: "We're not descended from monkeys, but descending to
them" is hardly modified in Machiavelli's statement: "I am
dying, and the Italian world will live, but utterly discredited.
You are all great men, I mean you and your friends; but when
you have disappeared, as you soon will, there will remain
only your imitators, who will imitate you badly; and then will
come the apes, who will transform your heavenward flights into
ludicrous gambols; then it will be all over with your work."[23]

We are reminded of Renan's disillusioned comment: "We
are now living on the shadow of a shadow. On what will
people live after us?" But this disillusionment, this bitterness

[22] *Ibid.*, pp. 318–319.
[23] *Ibid.*, p. 319.

can be explained, if one recalls that Renan wrote his philosophical dramas and Gobineau his *Renaissance* just after a bitter defeat and an atrocious insurrection. We can then appreciate better the pathetic undertones of the dialogue between Machiavelli and Michelangelo. How much disappointed love, how many frustrated hopes are concealed in Machiavelli's cry: "I am a wretched official of the most wretched of States, and I loathe that State, I loathe Florence. . . ." Upset in his most tenacious illusions, driven to despair by Savonarola's failure, convinced that the fatherland is nothing but a delusion and Florence an unnatural mother, that man is a madman or a wretch, Machiavelli has decided to retire from the world and to sit back and enjoy the sight of the universal madness: "It is far wiser to contemplate men as a passive spectator than to mingle in their affairs. I am not in the least surprised at the strong taste that many have for conspiracies, seditions and revolts. Of all games of chance, this is incontestably the one that sets the greatest number of faculties in motion. Every moment an unforeseen event! Men breathe a boundless hope of indefinable things; they talk, they shout, they bustle, they think of nothing, and they drink, drink, drink without ceasing in a cup of emotions whose savour is constantly changing!"[24]

"Man is a strange animal indeed!" exclaimed Montaigne, who had also stopped acting and delighted in watching the spectacle with an amused indifference. La Rochefoucauld was to do the same thing after the defeat of the Fronde. But Pascal refused to let man be so humiliated as to forget his greatness. And neither does Michelangelo: "For my part, I confess to you that, with or without hope, I will serve my country; I will use all my knowledge to defend it, and if it succumb, I shall at least have fulfilled a duty, or what seems to

[24] *Ibid.*, pp. 317, 313.

me one."[25] But it would be a mistake to see in this trait the whole of Michelangelo's character, a complex character indeed, and at times full of lassitude and discouragement, and ready to give up. We soon see that he is sustained by hope and that in him too the voices of heaven and earth are intermingled:

"Whether a man works only upon himself, or applies his activity to inert matter and breathes into it movement and life, the achievement is in both cases the same: he sets up models for his fellow-men. We can say with truth, when we reflect on the similarity of the results, that the most virtuous men are those like Polygnotus, Zeuxis, Polycletus, Phidias, these most accomplished artists being as great missionaries as are the philosophers and the saints."[26]

This is indeed the perspective in which a great artist works; and this same ideal will animate the almost nameless sculptor to whom Violaine will sacrifice her beauty, as an humble token of love, while the never-satisfied ambition of the conquerer is ironed out, like a pleat.[27] To have painted Creation on the ceiling of the Sistine Chapel, is that not to have understood the mystery of life and death? The belief in his vocation, the mastery he had to acquire have already prepared Michelangelo to rise above scepticism and resignation; for him there is a meaning in what seems to the sceptical mind merely absurd or amusing. He has entered into a world in which were revealed to him the true joy and comforting certainty; these are the share of the creator who, like the God of the Genesis, rested only after completing his work. Let us listen to him, in his studio, chiseling his ideas into the marble:

"It is pouring with rain. One can hear the shower smiting the roofs and falling on the flagstones of the courtyard like a

---

[25] *Ibid.*, p. 320.
[26] *Ibid.*, p. 345.
[27] Paul Claudel, *La Jeune Fille Violaine* and *Tête d'or.*

great river. It has been a fearful storm. Lightnings furrow the shimmering blackness of the windowpane. But behind all this stern uproar, what calm! The distant rumblings of the thunder and its majestic roarings, but no human voice, no false, lying, peevish, imperious or stupidly arrogant voice is raised to vex me! I can *create* . . . my spirit is free . . . I am happy! . . . I am wholly in the power of all that is worth my entire devotion, and the hard bosom of the marble opens . . . the living head begins to appear. . . . White, white, it palpitates beneath the chisel that sets free its features one by one. . . . Out of the material they spring . . . they speak."[28]

Thus the sceptical mind bows to this will that triumphs over ugliness and evil. In the heat of the creating effort, doubt vanishes, the anguished questions find an answer:

"I am, admits Machiavelli, only a huckster of ideas, and events prove that I have been but a dreamer. There is a great distance between seeing and creating the truth. From ugliness itself you make immortal beauty . . . your world may perish, you remain a god and live. But I?"

Art fixes the ephemeral in the timeless. But behind what is still but a universe of figures bereft of the most precious of all gifts—the fugitive expression given by life—another world is apparent, in which the rough work will be completed. Michelangelo knows that this curtain must be raised before everything can become meaningful at last and the nightmare vanishes:

"You are weary of life?"

"On the contrary, I am greedy of life. I wish to shake off from the limbs of my true being these fetters of flesh that bind them. I am athirst for complete freedom of spirit. What I can divine, I am eager to seize; what I can comprehend, I yearn to behold. If, in my sojourn here below, I have grasped some-

[28] *The Renaissance*, p. 275 .

thing and can express a portion of the truths I feel, what shall I not succeed in accomplishing when once the walls of barren rocks that surround me have fallen for ever into the abyss of the past? No, no! it is not death that I feel coming, but life, life whose shadow alone we can perceive down here, and which I shall soon possess in its entirety!"[29]

Recreated by Christian faith, endowed by it with a more solid substance, the Platonic myths appear, forming the background of the Renaissance. Behind Michelangelo, all these artists, these writers, these poets—Marsilio Ficino, Pico della Mirandola, Luca Paccioli, Politian, Bembo—rush toward us, fleeing from the cavern in which they were deceived by shadows. Blinded and stumbling at first, they perceive forms of which they measure the exact proportions and fix them in their works. The original mind, says Pascal, finds diversity where the average man sees only a dull uniformity. How many talents, how many different geniuses appear to him who, in spite of everything, set his trust in man! Instead of only one type of Superman, how many deep and original minds! The human drama is made up of these great voices answering one another through the centuries, expressing the universal man in their rich individuality. Ideas clash, incarnated by people who fill the stage but for an instant, sliding imperceptibly, as Calderon shows us, from the crib to the tomb. What an infinite range of attitudes for the enjoyment of the moralist who aims at complete detachment! But this moralist does not know or does not wish to know that it is not just a question of contrasts, a show in a puppet theater that one can watch with amusement. Each time, a destiny is at stake, not merely a brief existence. This is what Michelangelo is saying, he whose stature is even greater than is shown in the fresco, in which he will be the last to speak:

[29] *Ibid.*, pp. 319, 343–344.

"We are dying badly, unhappily. What matters? There have been beautiful spirits, glorious spirits in Italy, she that is henceforth enslaved and prostrate. I do not regret having lived."

"A soul like yours" he will exclaim to Dona Vittoria, whose loving care brightens the artist's old age:

"A soul like yours is at the summit of greatness, and that summit is virtue."[30]

We are far from a defense of reasons of state and from a special morality for the Superman. An anecdote will reveal how close Gobineau's sensitiveness is to that of Unamuno. It was during one of his last conversations with Richard Wagner, in Venice, in the palazzo Vendramin. Wagner is finishing the last act of *Parsifal*; his mind is already looking for other, lighter, more ethereal topics. He has read *Undine* by La Motte-Fouqué and this legend delights him. He is thinking of giving it the density of a myth. But the visitor and his host happen to discuss Cervantes and his immortal hero Don Quixote, this Don Quixote of whom Gobineau was always so fond. He exclaims: "It was criminal of Cervantes to do such a thing!" How Nietzsche would have seized this new chance to condemn the obtuse German mind! For Wagner does not understand and is indignant. Gobineau then stresses the heroism of the Knight of the Rueful Countenance. How could one forgive Cervantes? He had no right "to make lowly minds laugh at this king's son."

Don Quixote, a "calender," exalted to the level of the young aristocrats of *Sons of Kings*, is this not a revealing trait? Gobineau's cynicism has the same origin as La Rochefoucauld's bitterness. Rejected by some, deceived by others, swept away in the adventure of the Fronde, the victim of a heartless woman he loved passionately, the author of the *Maxims* no

[30] *Ibid.*, pp. 348, 342.

longer believes in virtue. He sees it as nothing but one of the many faces of selfishness. Having once sought refuge in a dream of beauty that was destroyed by the ruthlessness of time, Gobineau takes the view that man is degenerate, incapable of emancipating himself from his animality. However this is but the reverse side of an aspiration for the absolute, a refusal to compromise with the ideal. He too rides through the forests, above the abysses, unperturbed and haunted by an inaccessible ideal.

4
Demonism and Angelism: Gogol, Dostoevski, Pasternak

> Dim light scarcely touches my bedstead.
> It gives me such comfort to drift
> And feel that my life and my lot are
> Thy priceless and wonderful gift.
>
> While dying in fading surroundings
> I feel how thy hands are ablaze,
> The hands that have made me and hold me
> And hide like a ring in a case.
> Boris Pasternak[1]

*T*he question frequently arises of what criteria determine a work of lasting value. This question is especially important these days when artificial limelights can confer immortality upon essays that are outdated before they are ever written. The present is demanding, it reduces to ephemeral dimensions what should lie outside time, what should not be influenced by its acceleration. It is true that every book remains inserted in the period in which it was conceived and is therefore vulnerable to this aging process, this progressive obliteration which threatens even the most incontestable masterpieces. Baudelaire saw two elements in beauty: an "unchanging and indestructible" element fixed in the essence, and a "transient and fleeting" element in which is reflected a culture which will itself vanish. In fact, there is even a third element

[1] From "In Hospital" in *Pasternak Fifty Poems*, chosen and trans. by Lydia Pasternak Slater (London: George Allen & Unwin, New York: Barnes & Noble, 1963–1964), pp. 80–81.

79

originating from an even more fleeting factor, fashion.

The only works which will not suffer from the flight of time are those in which, through the man of a given period, we see the eternal man facing the hopes and failures of his "condition." This is the everlasting drama we witness in the tragedies of Aeschylus, Sophocles, or Racine, in Shakespeare's *Hamlet* or *King Lear*, in Goethe's *Faust*, in the *Don Quixote* of Cervantes. The tragedy is sometimes inspired by recent events: I was thinking of Julien Gracq's *Le Rivage des Syrtes*. What raises this novel to the level of an authentic masterpiece is that through the decline of Orsenna, reflected in the now stagnant waters of the lagoon, and through the helpless despair accelerating it, we not only see the recent history of France but inscribed in filigree, as in two different keys, we see the ambition of an anguish which makes us hope for death even though we fear it[2] and the fate of all civilizations, destined to decadence as soon as they are born. The painful cries of Tristan, the invocations of Zarathustra are echoed in this work, expressed in a language whose sumptuous richness surprises and delights the reader.[3] As for the crafty novelist who dwells merely on nuances or delights in painting morbid states, though his contemporaries may recognize themselves in traits that flatter or scandalize them, he will enjoy only a fame he must hurry to make the best of.[4]

In works with an audience that is all the more lasting for being belated, we find conflicts which concern us all because they are tied up with the "condition of man." In the play or in the novel, or even in the essay—according to the perspectives peculiar to each one of these genres—are set these "eternal problems" of which Renan once said that we cannot help

---

[2] We will mention only one example: a story by Marcel Proust, "La mort de Baldassare Sylvande," in *Les Plaisirs et les jours*.

[3] We are sorry we are unable to devote more time to this novel and to Julien Gracq's other works, especially *Au Château d'Argol*.

[4] Also by Julien Gracq: *La Littérature à l'estomac*.

setting them though we know we are unable to solve them. Sometimes art conceals their acuteness, as in Proust's *Remembrance of Things Past*, but nevertheless we wonder with the author if Bergotte will survive only through his books; we would like to be able to follow him beyond the yellow wall he desperately fixes.

No novels deal with these problems as extensively as those of the Russian writers who, like Gogol, Dostoevski, and Boris Pasternak, have gone through hell and have tried to escape.

It is quite obvious that the theme of evil and of the Apocalypse has obsessed the Russian mind[5] to the extent that it forms the background common to all Russia's novelists and philosophers, that it is like the second leaf of a diptych in which the other leaf is the awaiting of a transfiguration of heaven and earth. Do we not find the two panels of this diptych even in the works of Russian musicians, who are also so deeply attached to their native land—in Rimsky-Korsakov's *Easter*, in the harrowing andante of Rachmaninoff's concerto, in the vigor of Stravinsky's *Firebird?* We are aware of our injustice in retaining only the names of Gogol, Dostoevski and Pasternak; they are the closest to Nietzsche, the most involved, like him, in the search for the Superman. In all three, however, the Superman contains a demonic element, as though the "sense of the earth"—instead of meaning, as for Nietzsche, the vanishing of the world beyond, the reevaluation of the temporal universe in which we must desperately toil, or, as for Teilhard, the unfolding of the mind in the midst of opaque matter—implied the refusal of all divine assistance and the proud insurrection of the man-god.[6] In fact, an impassable

[5] Cf. in the *Cahiers de la nouvelle journée*, the collective work devoted to the "Russian soul."

[6] Love for the earth is shared, however, by Ivan Karamazov, in whom the demonic postulation will triumph, and the "angelic" Zosima and Alyosha.

81

frontier separates good and evil.[7] Left to his own devices man can create only a technological civilization, in which the soul will fade away and disappear. Proud of his power over matter, he will invent robots and monsters which he soon increasingly resembles—as though a dual mimicry were inscribed in nature, that which makes us similar to angels and that which gives us the odious and grotesque features of the Devil. Thus, always inscribed in the history of the Russian nation was the failure of the liberal-minded, of the optimists, of the pseudo-revolutionaries who had faith in man and thought they could secure him happiness by emancipating him:

"They [the liberal-minded] do not realize," Dostoevski once said, "that the end of all their progress and other nonsense is at hand. They do not realize that the Antichrist is already born and is coming. The Antichrist is coming, and the end of the world is near, nearer than we think."[8]

Gogol—that amazing genius—announces the perils inherent to our technological civilization, and he depicts characters in which we can already sense Pirandello's *Mountain Giants* and the heroes of Bernanos, fighting against dizziness. The "Sun of Satan" shines on mankind, while we watch the final decomposition of this living corpse, Monsieur Ouine.[9]

We first note a phrase that foreshadows the direction that will be followed by many present-day painters and artists who are haunted, unknown to themselves, by the dread of this break, this dislocation threatening a mankind that is searching in vain for a principle of unity and of symmetry: "The Devil broke the world up into a multitude of little pieces and

---

[7] Cf. the terrible tale by Edgar Poe, "William Wilson," whose theme will occur again in Oscar Wilde's *The Picture of Dorian Gray*.

[8] Cf. in particular *The Origin of Russian Communism*, by Nikolai Berdyaev.

[9] Bernanos, of all French writers, is closest to the Russian novelists, in particular by the important role of "illogic" in his works.

82

then mixed them up higgledy-piggledy." Since *Les Jeunes Filles d'Avignon* was Picasso not obsessed by this lack of harmony and of meaning which, in his view, reached its climax at Guernica? Gogol had already searched in vain for the human face, for its celestial beauty; instead, he saw only fragments: a nose, holes instead of eyes, torsos without heads, automatons whose faces are snouts; Jerome Bosch's universe was very similar, with Saint Anthony riding monstrous animals through a sky full of flames and smoke. Gogol, like Bosch, sees human reality, or what remains of it, from inside: Between paradise and man, submerged in the horror of sin, there lies a long, endless tunnel.

Let us take a look at Chichikov in *Dead Souls*. This is no ordinary woman hunter, like Montherlant's Guiscard—or, like his Don Juan, a ridiculous old fogey. He covets much more than the refined pleasures of food and lust; he announces this "nocturnal" atheism Berdyaev will distinguish from the "diurnal" atheism of the age of enlightenment; or rather, he first combines their features, and then, with a diabolical smirk, denounces the noxiousness of the mixture. He too formulates with relentless clarity the vision of the last men—happiness in prosperity, a higher standard of living for all, the purpose of life limited to procreation. The human race will build statues only to itself; the anonymous immortality of the species rather than that of individuals, this is, he says, "the immovable axis of modern civilization," the pillar replacing the religious chimera of the end of the world. He will be a burlesque victor, this man of "future times," with his face painfully contorted in a self-satisfied sneer: "The present generation laughs and, full of self-sufficiency, begins anew." It is carried by just such a hilarious crowd that Ensor's Christ will make his entry into Brussels.

But another image now strikes the Russian writer: that of the oyster . . . without pearl. On all continents, man is yawning. And there arises a technological world providing means but no ends. Gogol compares these "dead souls" we will meet again in Bernanos' novels with computers capable of solving a multitude of problems but unable to set a single new one: "The struggle for survival and concern for their descendants monopolize all the energy of the human race and distract it from the knowledge of the purpose of man."

But such an absence of being, such a complete "nihilization," this mechanization transformed into a cult cannot but doom man to a slow death; the world is nothing but a cave in which larvae are creeping. The Revizor casts his shadow on this cave, prefiguring Kafka's messenger of the Emperor of China. It is very far away, this Supreme Government to which one must go immediately, delegated by a power which is also indifferent and merciless.

Let us not be fooled; it is the trumpets of the *Dies Irae* which are going to sound on a world devoid of all spirituality. The Revizor, the terrible Messenger, is indeed the announcer of the Antichrist.

"Soon, very soon, the Tempter, the Antichrist, will come to the world."[10]

How could it be otherwise? Does not the coming world justify the words of Isaiah: "We have harbored in lies and sheltered in illusions."

Extremely lucid, Gogol knows both what art can depict or suggest and where lie its limitations: "A lot has been said about me; several of my characteristics have been analyzed, but no one ever found the essential one, except for Pushkin. He used tell me that no other writer had this gift (that was mine) of revealing so crudely the triviality of life, of describing so powerfully the weakness of man—so sly by nature—in such a way that the unnoticed vulgarity bursts forth and im-

[10] Gogol, *The Portrait*. This prediction appears in the first version of the story.

84

poses itself to the view of all. This is indeed the quality which I seem to possess and which seems to be lacking in all other writers."

We will have to wait for Milosz and the *Amoureuse Initiation* before we again meet the burlesque of the tragic farce;[11] however, in the great Lithuanian poet, light reaches even the very deepest corners of the caves; little by little the larvae resume their human appearance; an obscure aspiration wells up, transfiguring even the most atrocious vulgarity, wresting from his excrements the unfortunate who wallows in them. In the coarsest gestures, in the most carnal libido, in the sensual pleasure sought for in the arms of the dreadful courtesan, there is a regret, an obsession: the inflaming of the soul by another Love. Gogol already senses this modern art in which Milosz will be such a master; he sets it over against the luminous art of yesterday:

"Formerly things would be questioning in their confident expectation, and the artist would answer by making them live anew under his creating eyes, by restoring their virginal innocence, by leading them back to their first ingenuousness. The modern artist, before looking at the world, questions his soul and applies his disintegrating vision to things: he projects himself into a universe he has previously dislocated."

But, by no longer reflecting the universe in its naive primitiveness, art fails in its mission. It loses its unity and its purpose. Who will show us once more the "green paradise of children's love," the garden where Benozzo Gozzoli's adolescents converse, and this rustle of wings flying through Michelangelo's sky? Sin has changed and destroyed everything, and art can now see only through the screen of a distorting "I." A

---

[11] Milosz realized the dangers threatening the man who wants to become a god and goes astray in his search for the Superman. This work, one of the most important of our time, deserves a longer discussion than I can give it here.

transfiguration would be necessary to restore the initial harmony of this monstrous universe. But, led astray by its craving for pleasure, fooled by leaders who build their power on this deviation, how could the crowd enjoy true art in this increasing triviality in which the very reflection of the world beyond disappears? Gogol senses the syncopated and dissonant rhythm of jazz, a faithful expression of these conflicts. What has become, he wonders, of this art "that reconciles us with life"? This art that introduces order and harmony into the soul? Art is reduced to a "fleeting passion" if the artist "does not perform the miracle of transmuting into love and forgiveness" the soul of his audience.

It is true that this mistake has no grip on eternity, but it corrodes time and breaks it up into unrelated and meaningless moments, into *drops of nothingness*.[12] In what we call good, there remain only infinitesimal atoms of good: "For the most tragic substitutions disfigure Good to such a point that, *behind the mask*, empty eyes are looking at us." Once more we think of Ensor's masks drifting, hilarious or tragic, through this carnival which life has become through their own fault,[13] or of those specters returned from the no-man's-land in which they cannot find their way, to beg a little heat from a derisory stove.[14]

What Gogol wants to show us is that art is not self-sufficient; aestheticism will be really meaningful only if it is oriented toward asceticism, but the religious principle must then be introduced: "The desire for Good and the desire for Beauty coexist without being in any way related, or rather, what is even worse, they diverge. Only the religious principle can reconcile aesthetics and ethics and make them converge freely

[12] Kierkegaard uses this expression.
[13] Cf. *L'Intrigue* and *La Vieille aux masques* (or also *Les Masques et la mort* in the Museum of Liège).
[14] *Squelettes voulant se chauffer*, private collection, United States.

86

toward unity."[15] Atheism, by eliminating God, makes this ailment inscribed in the very essence of human nature even more virulent and incurable.

Gogol, and also Pushkin, these are Dostoevski's sources, this writer whom Nietzsche—how wrongly!—considered merely a psychologist. Dostoevski himself protested against this appellation: "They say I am a psychologist, but this is not true; I am a realist in the highest sense of the word, since I show the depths of the human soul." He leads us indeed through the innermost recesses of this "maze"; he unveils the hidden and perverse man, this "underground" man he is himself and whom we all are: "I am very fond of realism, which most people consider fantastic and strange. These very words express the essence of reality."

If Gogol reminds us of Ensor and Picasso, Dostoevski recalls R. Breslin and Odilon Redon: They too saw hallucinating shadows arise in the midst of everyday realities. These shadows haunt the mind of Raskolnikov, of Dmitri and Ivan Karamazov, and even more their father Feodor Pavlovich, whose cynicism will horrify the Elder Zosima. From crime to crime—like these spiteful Erinyes generated by remorse—they will lead the wretched Stavrogin to suicide.

Thus good and evil are waging a merciless war in man's soul. The Superman, or the man who thinks he is a Superman, is the man in whom, usually after a fierce struggle, evil has the upper hand. The demonic element triumphs in him; but it seems that there is a secret agreement between events, nature, and the demonic man, so that the fate that is carrying him along is but the outward appearance of this agreement. Unknown to ourselves, we are driven by some gravity from fall to fall down to the bottom of the abyss where our face is no

[15] Nikolai Berdyaev will take up this theme again.

longer recognizable, as in the portrait of Dorian Gray:[16] grace alone (a grace understood in a perspective which is not that of Catholicism) could protect us against this fate. Sonya, Alyosha, Prince Myshkin are creatures of light; but public opinion rates them as "visionaries," "misfits," "fools," "idiots." How else could their idealistic vision of the world be explained, their naiveté and even their unexpected replies? Anyone who isn't "down to earth" is an "idiot"; Prince Myshkin and Don Quixote have a lot in common; such men will always be fooled, but for them the world is diaphanous and transparent; the earth itself takes on a supernatural glow. They can read minds and penetrate the most secret feelings; sometimes they can even read the future: witness the Patriarch Tikhon, or the Elder Zosima.[17]

Nietzsche was thus mistaken when he saw a spiritual relationship between Dostoevski and himself—or rather he discerned in the Russian novelist only the psychologist capable of removing all masks, of penetrating into the inner recesses of the mind. And this is not very surprising since he never read Dostoevski's major works. He had only read *The House of the Dead* and *Notes from Underground*—perhaps *Raw Youth* and *Insulted and Injured*, which Peter Gast had sent him. Had he known *The Brothers Karamazov*, *The Idiot*, *Crime and Punishment*, or *The Possessed*, he would have rejected this sombre metaphysics dominated by the sense of guilt and the mirage of a world beyond. He would have seen in Dostoevski another victim of Christianity. As genial as Pascal but haunted by identical ghosts, this is how he would

[16] And also the god Glaucus, whom Plato described, imprisoned at the bottom of the sea, where he has been covered and disfigured by incrustations and shells.

[17] For the first, see his conversation with Stavrogin (in the *Notes*); for the second, the dialogue with Dmitri Karamazov, who, sensing he has been exposed, runs away in terror.

have described this writer whose flashing intuitions he had too readily admired; in his characters he would have seen victims of this resentment which allows the "weak" to paralyze and rule over the "strong" by suggesting vain scruples to them. But the humility of Dostoevski's best heroes is quite different, as they call for light and forgiveness from the bottom of their agony.

In fact, Dostoevski is right to refuse the name of "psychologist"; in the abysses in which his analysis descends, he discovers something quite different from feelings related to one another by causes whose links follow the intricate logical pattern of motives. Like Gogol he is moving in a cave or in the underworld; he wrestles there with pure illogic, with the absurd, with nothingness. No one realized better than he did the disparity of conscience, with its two alternating slopes, of which Jung proposed the logical explanation: The balance is suddenly upset, and all that was hidden comes to light. Driven beyond all possible harmonization, the discord, the antinomy in the heart of all men gives rise to the "double"; however this "double" is not the genius which sleeps in some beings— Zarathustra, the prophet hidden by the Shadow—but the maleficent and evil being that lives and stirs within all of us. *The Double* is of course but a clumsy beginner's work; it is far from the poignant intensity of Edgar Poe's "William Wilson," for whom the devil triumphs over the angel, or this *Dorian Gray*, who will retain his youth and his apparent purity as long as the stigmas of his vices continue to be inscribed on his portrait. However, *The Double* yields the first outline of Dostoevski's basic theme. In all his heroes, apart from those in whom the angelic nature has won and who are covered by the cloak of God, the duality is apparent. In Dmitri Karamazov, who suffers from his fieriness and violence, he has harbored demons who could be exorcised by the saintly Bishop Zosima, if only he would let him. How many generous impulses, how many noble feelings are stifled in his brother Ivan by the terrible Karamazov heredity of which he is aware without being able to get rid of it! And then there is another double in the person of Smerdyakov, their half brother, in whom the image of the crime each one of them planned will take shape.

Kirilov would be heading for saintliness if he did not wallow in doubt and negation to the point of letting himself be tempted by an absurd wager—the very opposite of Pascal's—since the only way out for him is suicide. He is a strange god indeed, this man who could prove his divinity only by committing suicide! When he is not tormented by his insane hatred, when he is not obsessed by the atrocious crime of which Bishop Tikhon has forebodings, Stavrogin has the stature of an archangel. For the fall is all the more irreparable as it affects beings created to unfold in beauty. The anonymous sculptor of the church in Niederrotweil[18] understood this well, as witness his portrayal of Lucifer's progressive downfall: at the top of the fresco we see a sublime figure, full of grace and purity; then, at each stage of the fall, the snigger becomes more pronounced and the features more sagging, and a monstrous being is finally swallowed up in the abyss.

Not a psychologist but a metaphysician, such is Dostoevski in his masterpieces; the characters in his novels unveil the passionate, alogical substratum of their being, which they do not succeed in mastering; they are fighting not against ghosts, like Hamlet, but against these "realities"[19] called hunger, crime, vice, or death. The salvation of their soul is constantly at stake; they endlessly take sides for or against a God whose existence is proved by their emphatic negation; they constantly gamble their salvation, pledging an original freedom of which they

[18] *The Transformation from Angel into Devil*, altar in the church of Niederrotweil (Baden). We only know the initials, H.L., of the author of this masterpiece.

[19] This is the meaning of the word "realist."

cannot rid themselves and haunted by the memory of a sin from which only a public confession can free them.[20]

After Nietzsche's Superman, here is his caricature! Here also Dostoevski is a master; what diversity! He does not offer a type on which barely sketched personalities like the "higher men" encountered by Zarathustra[21] would model themselves, but real men living under our very eyes, facing their destiny: the old Karamazov, dissolute and cynical, imprisoned in his violence; Ivan, with his occasional dreams of saintliness; Kirilov or Raskolnikov, who, after trying to justify his crime, frees himself from it by confessing it—a strange and very noble figure who will be saved by the compassion of a woman; next to him even Wagner's Flying Dutchman is amazingly conventional.[22]

We first see Golyadkin, the hero of *The Double*, this double who little by little chases his luminous brother from his "ontological environment"—for each one of us has his ontological environment in which he dwells, alas! only too rarely, his existential basis from which he derives the attributes of his authentic being: unity, identity, individual uniqueness. Hunted from this environment, Golyadkin subdivides, mul-

---

[20] During his imprisonment in Siberia, Dostoevski realized that the most cruel punishment imposed upon the convicts was not the blows they received, nor the cold, nor starvation or pain, but the constant presence within them of the crime that barred them from all human community; so that their "hell" was not so much the prison to which they had been exiled as the "frenzies" of envy, resentment, and hatred isolating them from one another. Had they been sympathetic to the misery of their fellow-prisoners, had they helped them to carry their cross, they would have found the narrow exit from the maze in which their soul was agonizing. The theme of *Crime and Punishment* arose thus from the atrocious scenes Dostoevski witnessed in Siberia.

[21] In the fourth part of *Zarathustra*.

[22] Senta, with her redeeming self-sacrifice, is more alive, more touching, though very similar to the gentle Sonya.

tiplies. He is now nothing but a ghost, a puppet; the impostor he has become has given rise to a swarm of doubles, or rather, he is nothing but masks; one would search in vain for his true face behind his various masks. Does he even still have a face? And is it not his punishment that he can no longer recognize and identify himself? *"Maschere nude"* Pirandello will say, though in a somewhat different context.

It is not easy to recognize oneself in this gallery of distorting mirrors in which we live. Things become blurred, confused, indistinct. Beauty itself, which by its very essence is related to holiness, becomes enigmatic; it takes on a dual aspect in this universe generated by an unhealthy, tormented consciousness which distorts everything. "Not only does it offer itself to save," Prince Myshkin will say, "but it also tempts with its charms and causes death."

The Prince will sense this menace even more acutely in the museum of Basel, in front of a painting by Holbein, this *Deposition from the Cross* Nietzsche had also contemplated. He is greatly perturbed by it: "If death is horrible, if the laws of nature are so powerful, how can we surmount them? How can we win when the very one whom nature obeyed when he was alive has been vanquished by it? When we look at this painting, nature appears as one of those modern machines which has stupidly grabbed and swallowed up the admirable being who was worth more than nature and all its laws put together, this very nature that was perhaps created only to produce him?"

This is the very intuition we will find developed by Nikos Kazantzakis and which Teilhard de Chardin will express in its highest form. In Dostoevski's view, the resurrection is the only testimony which gives a basis to the greatness of man, which makes creation meaningful. But all the earlier arrangements, all the inclinations inscribed in nature from the very beginning so that, reflected or rather carried in an exceptional soul to their full expression, they would be brought to their full completion by this soul, have been invalidated. Man has isolated himself, turned toward himself, cut himself away from creation;[23] he wanted to become God.[24] In doing this he became similar to the Devil of whom Saint John once said: "When the Devil tells a lie, he is acting according to his nature."

We now have the portrait of Orlov, the convict who prides in the condition that cuts him away from mankind, and is thus the prototype of all demoniacs:

"Never in my life did I meet a man whose will was more firm or inflexible. . . . Orlov was a *brilliant example of the triumph of spirit over matter*. He had complete command over himself. He despised punishment, and feared nothing in the world. . . . I was struck by his haughty air. . . . I don't believe anything had the least influence over him. . . . I tried to ask him about his adventures. . . . When he realized that I was endeavouring to see through him and discover in him some trace of repentance, he looked at me with a haughty and contemptuous air, as if I were a foolish little boy whom he honoured too lightly with his conversation. I detected in his countenance a sort of compassion for me. After a moment's pause he would laugh out loud, but without the least irony." (This is absolute laughter, the sardonic, demoniac laughter

---

[23] "What, then, will man become? Will he be equal to God or to the brutes? What a frightful difference! What, then, shall we be? Who does not see from all this that man has gone astray, that he has fallen from his place, that he anxiously seeks it, that he cannot find it again. . . ." Pascal, *Pensées* in *Great Books of the Western World*, Vol. 33 (Chicago: Encyclopaedia Britannica, 1952), p. 247.

[24] To tell the truth, it is no longer possible to distinguish the true from the false or good from evil in this prism in which everything is distorted and confused. The soul is destroyed by this lie in which it comfortably settles, reassured by alibis, led astray by misunderstandings.

that originates, says Baudelaire,[25] from a superiority complex carried to its paroxysm.) "But in reality he must have despised me, for I was a feeble being, in all respects contemptible, and guilty above all of resignation."

This is indeed the attitude of the Superman who sets himself above all laws and whose tremendous personality unfolds beyond good and evil, the arbitrary inventions of a morality by means of which the weak, the docile, the mediocre try to hinder the free and confident flight of the "noble man." Here evil is not due to weakness of character but to a will to dominate which nothing can stop; such is the somber grandeur of evil which also gives rise to a sense of the sublime but of a sublime which, even more than the convulsions of nature and the furor of the ocean, is terrifying and horrifying. Far from being due to a victory of the flesh, it is on the contrary the total victory of the spirit over the flesh; it is, so to speak, a reverse spirituality.

We are haunted by many other figures: Some are tormented by remorse and cannot maintain the mask of pride and arrogance they had put on. They will try in vain to reassure themselves with fallacious justifications: the perfection of a crime that cannot be solved; the lamentable and derisory nature of the victim, a horrid old pawnbroker; the use they can make of a fortune now going to waste in other hands.[26] A day

[25] Cf. Baudelaire, The Essence of Laughter, and our study in the Revue d'Esthétique, 1953.

[26] This search for justification is very well formulated by Dostoevski: "Having committed a reasonably useful crime, Raskolnikov planned to be, for the rest of his life, honest, firm, unshakable in the accomplishment of his duty toward the betterment of humanity." Cf. also this pertinent comment: "In my novel I also hold the view that the punishment set by law is much less frightening to the criminal than the legislators seem to think, partly because he himself morally demands it."

Damnation is not, as Tikhon will try to explain to Stavrogin, the direct consequence of the crime; it really depends on how the criminal

will come when this front will crumble. Raskolnikov, in *Crime and Punishment*, does not have the stature of Orlov in *The House of the Dead*. A sudden thawing will soon set in. By confessing his crime, for which he would not have been caught, he will reconcile himself with his fellowmen and gain inner peace. Thanks to confession, the order he destroyed by committing the crime will be restored.

Let us take a closer look at Stavrogin; here we go beyond the frontiers of horror. Stavrogin is one of the characters who gave Dostoevski most trouble. He had conceived him quite differently, redeemed by his beauty. But there is a demonic beauty, which, far from turning toward good, freezes in the contemplation of its cold perfection. Such is the beauty that obsessed Baudelaire:

> Man, I am lovely as a dream of stone,
> and my breast where each is bruised in turn
> is made to inspire the poet's love alone
> to last like matter and be as taciturn.[27]

Such is also Stavrogin's beauty ("repulsive" rather than "attractive" Dostoevski will say when he is not disfigured by his insane temptation or when he is not possessed by the irresistible need to scandalize or to torment. In his *Diary* the novelist admits that his hero finally escaped him and ended up by imposing his own destiny on the writer, according to a logic whose rules are disconcerting. He will not enter into his universe, as Dostoevski would have wished, as a Christian on

reacts to his crime: Either he says nothing, uses it, glorifies himself with it, and dooms himself; or he refuses to let it bind him, to let himself be caught up in it, and can be saved. This is the very contrast between the two thieves of Calvary.

[27] "La Beauté" in *One Hundred Poems from Les Fleurs du Mal*, trans. by C. F. MacIntyre (Berkeley and Los Angeles: University of California Press, 1947), p. 45.

his way to salvation but as a tragic mask condemned to damnation from all eternity. Dostoevski was the first to discover what
Unamuno and Pirandello will affirm later: A character has a
life of its own; he obeys in his development a law over which
no one but himself has any control. As though man, this im-
perfect creator, also had the power to project into the world,
in which luminous and tenebrous[28] heroes are dwelling, benefi-
cent or maleficent powers over which he loses all control as
soon as they have taken shape.

Nietzsche's "nihilism" is the decomposition of a culture:
It started sooner in the Occident, but—says Dostoevski in his
notes—it will have even more tragic results in the Orient because calculating reason will not oppose it. Its starting point
has been—as is proved by the examples of Kirilov, of the
brothers Karamazov, of Orlov, and of Stavrogin—the introduction of atheism. For there is but one question which must
be answered affirmatively or negatively, by hearty agreement
or by refusal: "Can one be civilized and still have faith?"—
that is, believe without reservations in the divinity of the son
of God, of Jesus Christ (for faith consists of this, and this
alone). In Stavrogin the proud refusal will cause his character
to be petrified; this prince is all of one piece; it would be even
better to say that there are no cracks or flaws in him; he forms
a whole: "The Prince is somber, passionate, demonic—a dis-
orderly character, out of all proportion, molded in his entirety
by the sublime question which leads to being or not being";
thus very similar to Byron's Manfred.

Thus Stavrogin—Dostoevski's most perfect creation (together with Ivan Karamazov, who is in fact more complex, so
that his salvation is still possible)—says he believes in the
Devil but not in God. He is the very realization of Lucifer,
who has assumed his features and seeks to impose on them an

---

[28] Cf. another novel by Julien Gracq: Le Beau Ténébreux.

apparent immobility; his actions are the counterpart and hideous caricature of those of the Savior. This "fine and strong" spirit, "this man whose beauty is but a mask," has divorced himself from the Creator, he has shut himself up in his "I," he has loved himself to the point of despising all others, of despising God, and his cynicism is the projection of his scorn. In doing this, he wanted to be a god himself, to usurp all divine power, to gain unbounded freedom. To the pole of God who became incarnate in order to take on the misery and suffering of man, there corresponds another pole, a demonic pole: that of the man-god. And all humanity gravitates about these two poles. Some, like Zosima and his disciple Alyosha, like Sonya in *Crime and Punishment*, are all purity, all humility, all grace. Prince Myshkin, the Idiot, has remained a child; he belongs to another aeon, original sin has no hold on him; he is an abstract being, miraculously preserved. He is the Truth which has burst into a world of lies, and this leads him to do things which most people would consider unreasonable and childish. Had he loved Natasha with an impure love, the only one possible on this earth, the young woman would have been saved. The very spirituality of his tenderness will be her ruination; she refuses this pity, this heavenly love, though she secretly yearns for it with all her might; for her, as for Kirilov, death is the only way out. Claudel's Violaine is also unreasonable, out of her right mind, when she kisses the leper Créon. Such is the choir of Archangels who prefer Christ to the truth, or rather who believe that the truth cannot be such that it makes faith impossible.

But on the other hand, as in a painting by Jerome Bosch, we see the demonic army: Dmitri Karamazov, his brother Ivan, Smerdyakov, and even more so the one who is leading the dance, their sinister jester of a father, and especially Stavrogin, who will declare one day:

"I know neither good nor evil, and not only have I lost all

97

sense of these things, but I know that there is neither good nor evil: it is all but prejudice."

But Stavrogin will not be able to keep up his cynical attitude to the end, for it hides a deep despair which will either save or damn him, as Bishop Tikhon understood so well. Before Bernanos, Dostoevski recognized and analyzed this dialectic of despair, this endless spiral staircase individuals and peoples will descend and then hurl themselves into the abyss, into nothingness. It is to this dizziness that nations are succumbing when, embarking in total war, without concern for their own survival, they accumulate destruction over destruction. Once the game is started it continues of its own accord; is this perhaps how mankind will perish? Here again the absolute is being pursued, but "the wrong way round."

"From me nothing has come but negation, with no greatness of soul, no force," exclaims Stavrogin, and then goes to hang himself.

Superman, supermankind, these are two similar affirmations of a will that wants to be almighty; they both imply a negation: that of being.[29] The world created by God is governed by a centripetal force, union in love;[30] to this force, the proud personality opposes a centrifugal force, power in isolation. From Raw Youth to the Brothers Karamazov, Dostoevski centers his universe around a dynamic image which symbolizes and measures the fight between two antagonistic forces: the aspiration to unity and the demonic splitting up. To love that unites he opposes not hatred but power, the unbounded appetite for power of which hatred as well as scorn are merely

[29] The three categories of being: unity, identity, uniqueness are the basis of ethics, for they condition a concrete, living Truth which is destroyed by the lie of temporal existence. Cf. the chapter on thought in our work Les Dimensions de l'être et du temps (Lyon-Paris: Vitte, 1943).

[30] These are almost the very words Teilhard de Chardin will use.

consequences. By its very nature power is demonic; it generates not a spiritual community but a materializing collectivity, not the kingdom of God but a communizing ant nest. Dostoevski has described the two forms it can assume: the brave new world—the crystal palace—or the state which exchanges happiness for freedom, as the Grand Inquisitor offers it. Everyone is familiar with those remarkable pages, but I do not think that the description of the "Crystal Palace" (in *Winter Notes on Summer Impressions*) is as well known. On first sight the picture painted by Dostoevski is rather similar to that drawn by Nietzsche, but closer inspection reveals different intentions:

"You sense the terrible force which has drawn these people without number from all the world into a single herd. . . . Baal triumphs everywhere, the ant nest is set up for good." The author outlines here his theory of the earthly kingdom of the Antichrist; his critique of the bourgeois order, along the same line as that of Herzen, suddenly assumes the form of an Apocalyptic vision. The capitalist regime is the kingdom of Baal, of the Devil to whom human sacrifices are immolated. He has assembled men in herds; he has built the giant ant nest.

"But if you saw how proud is the powerful spirit which created that colossal setting, and how proudly convinced that spirit is of its triumph and of its glory, you too would have trembled for its pride, its relentlessness, and its blindness, and for those over whom this spirit hovers and holds sway."[31]

An authentic community assembled around the Good Shepherd in an act of trust and love, or an anonymous herd in the service of the Superman, led astray by his will to power—this is not, alas! simply a dilemma but a permanent conflict between two antagonistic forces, two axes about which the whole universe can rotate. Prince Myshkin picks up a little

[31] *Winter Notes on Summer Impressions*, trans. by R. L. Renfield (New York: Criterion, 1955), pp. 91–92.

Russian earth in which is inscribed the mystery of creation. Alyosha sees in it all that gives roots to man and brings him back to his origins. It is Stephen Verhovensky who finally has the right outlook when he humbly professes his faith:

"My immortality is necessary if only because God will not be guilty of injustice and extinguish altogether the flame of love for Him once kindled in my heart. And what is more precious than love? Love is higher than existence, love is the crown of existence; and how is it possible that existence should not be under its dominance? If I have once loved Him and rejoiced in my love, is it possible that He should extinguish me and my joy and bring me to nothingness again? If there is a God, then I am immortal. Voilà ma profession de foi."[32]

This constant presence of the Russian earth which survives, unchanged, the superficial agitation of revolutions and under which flows the invisible stream of the nation, who has expressed it better than Boris Pasternak?[33] We will however speak less about Doctor Zhivago than about four less known short stories in which are assembled, in a few deliberately enigmatic lines, the essence of his message.

First "The Sign of Apelles." At first sight it is all very simple: an artist, passing through Florence, does not find at home the friend he had come to visit; he does not leave his name

[32] The Possessed (London: Dent, New York: Dutton, 1931), Vol. 2, p. 296. Note the ideal the Devil proposes to Ivan Karamazov, the description he gives of the mankind of the future when, together with God, traditional morality will have disappeared: "Men will then unite to extract from life all possible joys, but in the world only. The human spirit will rise with a gigantic pride and thus mankind will be deified."

The Superman will stand at the top of this pyramid, blindly followed by a herd of slaves.

[33] On Pasternak, see: Michel Aucouturier, Pasternak par lui-même (Editions du Seuil), and an outstanding work by Robert Payne, The Three Worlds of Boris Pasternak (New York: Coward-McCann, 1961).

but a simple line traced on a card with his blood. But did not
the painter Apelles make himself known by a similar line?
This artist who can be recognized by his style, does he not
show us in which direction human nature can and must be
fulfilled? One can go down to the very bottom of the underground without finding the authentic man; it is not in these
depths that the "Apelles line" is formed. Another zone of preconsciousness in which the creative work is prepared exists at
the point where aspiration to the Transcendental finds the
answer it was seeking. In the "shapeless" unconscious, man
wears masks behind which he hides and rejects his vocation.
One must rise to the level of perfect purity in art—where the
very excess of simplicity makes heroism possible[34]—before the
face will appear, casting off its finery: "You can consider these
things with a keen intelligence. You know the trait that is
unique."[35] This obligation we have, at the limit of a heroically
obtained wisdom, to reconcile the requirement of fully becoming the individual being we are, with that of becoming an
active and generous member of a community, is it not expressed in every page of the Bible and even more clearly in
the gospel? Where did Pasternak find this sense, which communism will not succeed in destroying, of the individuality of
each human destiny? It is true that the future in our world
of this seed entrusted to each one of us—our soul—seems to
him very precarious. But we must make it blossom at all cost
in the turmoil of revolutions and wars, in these centuries
where everything is questioned anew, where we must become
reconciled with insecurity.

"In our days, men are slowly adopting a new attitude toward life. I would like to make one thing clear: in the nineteenth century, bourgeoisie was the leading class; our literature

---

[34] We know that Proust, only a few hours before his death, used his
own experience of agony to correct his account of Bergotte's death.

[35] "The Sign of Apelles."

101

shows it very well. Mankind then sought security in money,
land, possessions. Now, it realizes that possessions do not imply security. And this is true not only of the Russians. In our
times of world wars, in this atomic age, values are changing."

And this is why we must set out on this bridge, on this narrow footbridge leading toward an uncertain future: grandiose
or filled with the clamor of pending cataclysms. This is why
we feel our aching and nostalgic heart panicking within us.
Here is the leader talking to the fascinated crowd:

> He was the face which spoke to them:
> [that of ineluctable facts]
> When he appealed to the facts,
> He knew that when he rinsed their mouths
> With the momentum of his voice,
> History was pouring through them.[36]

The Revolution, by chasing us from our refuges, by raising
us to greatness in spite of ourselves, has shown us the power
of the irrational, the power of this wave that drives us along;
history has carried us along and rolled us like pebbles. We
have discovered in it this Ungrund, this abyss described by
Jacob Boehme in which being and nothingness come together.
The bourgeois era let us chose between a shallow religious conformism and a "diurnal" atheism promoting the cult of reason. But now a great clamor has filled the earth, and disquiet
and hope rise side by side:

> The rain smiled at a birdcherry; drenched
> The lacquer of cabs, the tremor of trees.
> In moonlight, pop-eyed, the fiddlers filed
> To the theatre.—Citizens, close your ranks!

[36] Lenin, in "Sublime Malady." Translation is from Robert Payne,
The Three Worlds of Boris Pasternak, p. 136.

102

> Wind, pools of rain. As a throat choked
> With tears, the innermost heart of roses
> With jewels aflame! Rain, spout new joy
> On roses, brows, eyelashes, clouds![37]

If one had lived through these days filled with cries and calls, when injustice seemed to loose its foothold, when a richer community was forged on the anvil, how could one forget them and go back to the shameful stagnation of bourgeois comfort? But happiness has its exigencies: Like a fragile flower clinging to the rock and searching for a drop of dew to survive on this arid soil, it wants to find itself a shelter and live there its shared dream, the humble dream of love. This is the drama Pasternak confesses shyly, discreetly, in his poems, and in almost every page of *Doctor Zhivago*. The Ural mountains cast their protecting shadow over the novel; they still conceal an oasis where the storm does not reach. There the miraculously preserved soul of the poet can meditate, this soul that is to be the "tomb" of all those who "have died in the torment." The duty of the poet in times of despair is to preserve the "sacred trust" and to transmit it. He remains the confidant of all distresses:

> In this selfish age
> And whatever the cost,
> Be the urn in the crypt
> In which rest their remains![38]

How comforting when, lonely and dejected, we return to the desolate house, to discover in it the Apelles mark, the sign of a mysterious visitation which proves to us that someone

---

[37] From "Spring Rainstorm," in *My Sister Life*, 1917. English translation from Boris Pasternak, *Poems*, trans. by Eugene M. Kayden, 2nd ed. (Yellow Springs, Ohio: Antioch, 1964), p. 14.

[38] "When the Skies Clear," 1956, translator's translation.

thought of us, that heaven is not empty under the smoke of the fires, that we are not completely abandoned.

In another story—"Tula"—Pasternak sets more directly this problem of the role of the artist, of the purpose of the poet. And he then remembers perhaps the visit of the poet Rilke, when he was still only a child. What worries him most is to see human relationships become more and more tainted with lack of understanding, a lack of understanding that extends even into the family circle. The poet feels as though he were merely transient in an "inn"[39] in which all lights have been quenched; he finds himself surrounded by strangers, threatened by an obscure hostility. Who will make it possible for an almost dead consciousness, like the ashes in the hearth, to send up once more its "devouring" flame? It is sometimes in the humblest, the most despised people that the light remains. How beautiful is the description of the death of the old comedian, in whom the flame had continued to burn!

It is not surprising then that Pasternak, like Henri Bosco, "dreamt" his childhood—not an actual, endured childhood, which is so often so painful, but a happy childhood that occurred "out of time." And they are not mistaken: We dream of childhood as we dream of limpid water dropping from a clear vase, when time was still lingering. Jacques Rivière said it: Childhood is idle, happy play; there is no hurry. There are hawthorn hedges; there is meandering along the river where one would like to linger; there are countries unknown to grown-ups where it is lovely, infinitely lovely to wander. Genia, the little girl in Pasternak's "The Childhood of Luvers," knows like Meaulnes that the real world sometimes makes way for another world where nothing is impossible, where roses bloom in tears of crystal on the frosted windows. Grown-ups do not know these mysteries because their life is no longer anchored in being; time carries them

[39] This same feeling inspired one of Baudelaire's finest poems, "L'Horloge."

far away from these lands one should never leave. One night Genia wakes up in tears. Beyond the fence, there is the factory; leaving her garden full of life, she finds this monstrous "thing": a stone image in which souls are imprisoned,[40] the factory; the factory—that is, something which does not exist gratuitously, which does not exist in itself, free from all ties, but only because of the use that is made of it; a painful revelation that hovers over all relations between objects and men, between men themselves, caught up in the mesh of means and ends and inevitably devaluated by this reciprocal alienation.

At the end of the suffering road, as soon as one goes beyond the fence, there is hell; we find it in the fourth story, "Aerial Ways." We no longer see the gentle Genia lingering in her green paradise, but a retarded child with a nurse to take care of her. One day, the child disappears, and no one will be able to find her; there are many lost children and many stray dogs in our depoetized universe. Even the landscape undergoes strange deformations, as in some of Vlaminck's paintings: "The fields are swept by wind, darkness and fear, as by a gigantic three-pronged rake."

Doctor Zhivago will also wander in a universe that is disfigured by hatred and fear, offering only some fleeting moments of love, until he dies, anonymous and adrift, in a streetcar of the gray suburbs of Moscow. And yet, behind the grandiose decor of the Revolution, which was not the work of the multitude but of a handful of determined men[41] capable of altering the course of history, the eternal debate goes on:

> We were people. An epoch now . . . .
> When winds in the morning confound
> The thatch of the roofs, a debate
> In the congress of trees will resound,

[40] Cf. Dino Buzzati's *Il Grande rittrato*.
[41] The poem "The Caucasus" symbolically expresses this power held only by men without scruples, men with granite souls.

105

Astir with immortal speech
Where the shingled roofs do not reach.[42]

All this turmoil will come to an end; and, of this Revolution that had seemed to rock the foundations of the world, nothing will remain but the memory of the atrocious agony of innocent children:

But be forever unforgiven
The children's fear and pain!

This age will pass. A brighter day
Will dawn, a time of peace.
But the woes of children maimed in wars
Live across the centuries.[43]

"The sense of the earth," for Pasternak as well as for Nietzsche, is not the innocent reality of the obsession with the afterworld but what remains fixed as opposed to what is passing. While the passing guests disappear whom no one will remember, what time does not affect stays behind; it is in this setting that the human drama is played, the only one that matters:

The steaming foliage is translucent
Like figures in stained-window glass.

[42] From "We Are Few," in Pasternak, *Poems*, trans. by Eugene M. Kayden, p. 64.

[43] From "The Tragic Story," *ibid.*, p. 173. Though, like Kazantzakis, Pasternak has great admiration for Lenin (they both consider him the very type of the Superman), he held a very different opinion of Stalin, who was so harsh, so ruthless to intellectuals, denying them all freedom, even that of expression, and thus transforming them into terrorized servants of his dictatorship: "Now rises the obstinate old man, the old man with the iron will. And the terrified people, withdrawn within themselves, hardly dare to murmur."

Thus from the church's narrow windows
In glimmering crowns, on spreading wings
Gaze into time in sleepless vigil
Saints, hermits, prophets, angels, kings.[44]

We find here this "ontological environment" in which we remain, unknown to ourselves, while the scenes of our life on earth unfold from the gates of birth to those of death. For this is the role of art: to make us realize the fixation in the timeless of the characteristic gesture, the characteristic action; through it everything assumes an eternal value, alas! the crime as well as the impulse of trust and love.

One day Pasternak became more clearly aware of this power of art which he had already realized intuitively in Venice:[45] in the monastery of Ghalili, in Georgia, some remarkably well-preserved mosaics delight the viewer with their marvelous colors. There is a tomb, decorated with precious stones, which tradition claims to be that of King David. Now, on these mosaics generations are spread out in depth, like time itself according to the various spatial planes which compose it. That which is successive appears simultaneous to the artist.

No matter therefore the course of our earthly life and the sufferings we must endure. What is true is that which is fixed

[44] From "When It Clear Up," in *Pasternak Fifty Poems*, trans. by Lydia Pasternak Slater, p. 75.

[45] "Venice, a golden lake, overflowing with life, fed by countless springs, one of the initial abysses of creation." Pasternak sees its churches as "anchored vessels, the wind filling their sails, and Venice itself seemed altogether so youthful one might think it had just been born."

It is in Venice that Pasternak first met his favorite painter, Tintoretus, and it is perhaps in the San Rocco museum, contemplating the beautiful scenes of the Passion, that he felt the faith of his youth flow back and invade him. "Italy," he will later recall, "had incarnated and crystalized within me that to which we unconsciously aspire from our very earliest youth."

on the stained-glass window, these scenes that come to us through the centuries and in which we discover we were present, though not yet born. The Revelation is inscribed in the heart of all centuries, the attitudes of each one of us are set in the humble garden where Christ is agonizing. From our birth till our death, our existence is but an instant to which a single answer given in the very deepest of our being will bear witness.

> "I will suffer death and on the third day rise
> Again. Like rafts descending on a river,
> Like a caravan of sails, the centuries
> Out of the night will come to my judgment seat."[46]

How could he not have understood the message of Christ, this witness of cruel times who had endured until death the sufferings of the innocent?

> A change will come. The capital,
> Rebuilt, will live again.
> But be forever unforgiven
> The children's fear and pain!
>
> There's no forgiveness for that fear
> In faces seared and old. . . .

But once more, like the Passion scenes on the church window, events are superimposed which we wrongly take to be successive . . .

> The doers of the evil deeds
> Like Herod in Bethlehem.[47]

Thus little by little there emerge from the fog the episodes of drama which has divided history and given it its meaning.

[46] From "Garden of Gethsemane" in Pasternak, *Poems*, trans. by Eugene M. Kayden, p. 229.

[47] From "The Tragic Story," *ibid.*, p. 173.

For all that has occurred since and all that will occur is prefigured in these days of the Passion during which each one of us was redeemed and called. To Zhivago, who is reluctant to accept the resurrection of the flesh "in the coarse form in which it is formulated for the consolation of the weak," Vidniapin, his teacher, answers:

"Until now it was thought that what mattered most in the Gospel was the moral maxims and rules contained in the commandments. In my view, the essential is that which Christ expressed in parables taken from everyday life, illuminating truth with the light of everyday events. At the bottom of all this, there is the idea that the ties binding men are immortal, and that life is symbolic because it is meaningful."

Now if this is the case, it is not only the duty of the poet, of the artist, which takes on a new dimension, but the very meaning of history is altered. Revolutions are nothing but the scum on the waves roused by the storm, and the Superman is powerless as soon as one goes a little deeper. Here again we must listen to Vidniapin, who represents that which, for Pasternak, remains anchored in being, while Zhivago is only its earthly appearance wandering through the plains of Russia: "What is history?" asks Vidniapin. "It is the launching of the works destined to elucidate the mystery of death and to surmount it one day." The soul is indeed given to us like the seed that fell on barren ground. The task is more difficult in times of anguish, but the sheaf will be all the more beautiful when it is bound by the divine Harvester.[48]

---

[48] Cf. the admirable finale of the "Garden of Gethsemane": "I will suffer death and on the third day rise / again. Like rafts descending on a river, / like a caravan of sails, the centuries / out of the night will come to my judgment seat." Cf. also *Boris Pasternak*, choix de textes précédés d'une étude d'Y. Berger (Paris: Seghers, 1958).

5
The Tragic Sense of Life

So far as I am concerned, I will never willingly yield myself, nor entrust my confidence, to any popular leader who is not penetrated with the feeling that he who orders a people orders men, men of flesh and bone, men who are born, suffer, and although they do not wish to die, die; men who are ends in themselves, not merely as men; men who must be themselves and not others; men, in fine, who seek that which we call happiness. It is inhuman, for example, to sacrifice one generation of men to the generation which follows, without having any feeling for the destiny of those who are sacrificed.

Miguel de Unamuno

Without illusion, impudence, or fear. But this is not enough; take a further step: battle to give meaning to the confused struggles of man.

Nikos Kazantzakis[1]

It is hard to go on believing in man when we see the ever deeper chasm separating his thoughts and his actions, when this substratum of alogic and passion over which his reason has no control is getting more important, when it becomes obvious that he is unable to realize the ideal of truth and justice he so vehemently proclaims. Pascal had already noted this discordance in man. "We have," he said, "a need for truth impervious to all Pyrrhonism, and an inability to prove impervious to all dogmatism." But for him this dilemma was solved by grace, and God, letting our heart feel his presence, made sensible to us the only truth necessary for our salvation. But now that God is left to the discretion of man and the gap between the light of reason and faith has grown beyond measure, we witness these frenzies of resentment and hatred which

[1] Miguel de Unamuno, *Tragic Sense of Life* (New York: Dover, 1954), p. 16; Nikos Kazantzakis, *The Saviors of God* (New York: Simon and Schuster, 1960), p. 78.

110

torment the "underworld" man. But can we hope, we who can discover the mathematical structure of matter and follow the slow progress of life from the cell to the animal, can we hope someday to be able to control these sudden eruptions, this unleashing of violence which, washing away our hesitant inclinations, appears as the manifestation of a negative aspect of the sacred? Is there no remedy for the conflict between Dionysius—with his train of drunken bacchants—and Apollo, whose serene art endeavors to unfold the curtain of comforting but deceiving appearances? And is this struggle inscribed in the very nature of man, condemned as he is, facing nothingness, to confront his useless destiny? Would Penthesilea, the proud Amazon who, in the paroxysm of her desire, mangled her conquerer Achilles, be the symbol of a life doomed to unsolvable conflicts?[2]

At this stage, there are two possibilities.

Realizing his situation in the world and most of all the contradictions in his nature, man can stiffen in a "pathetic" attitude, become fully conscious of the unavoidably "tragic" nature of life, of the unsurmountable opposition between the exigencies of the *élan vital* and the conclusions of his reasoning, and not only accept this divorce but see in it the very reason why one should persevere in a heroic and useless endeavor; he can also find in this contrast, which, the more he thinks of it, makes him appear perfectly ridiculous, his revenge against an oppressing destiny and a bitter satisfaction. However contrasting in appearance, these two poles of the "pathetic" and of the "ridiculous"—between which oscillates the *aesthetics of décadisme* reinserted in the existential flow—are closely interwoven and sometimes even merged in contemporary novels and plays: We are thinking of Montherlant's King Ferrante and of his Malatesta, of Jean Anouilh's poor Bitos and of his

[2] In the play by Heinrich von Kleist.

Lieutenant de Saint-Pé, of Camus' monstrous Caligula; the pathetic here still conceals the ridiculous, which will come to the fore—sometimes burlesque, sometimes cruel—in the works of Pirandello, Ionesco, and Kafka.

Though he is ever more haunted by the absurdity of a life that unfolds against the background of failure, man can also assume his destiny, accept himself as "ephemeral," endeavor to base on the density of an "instant," during which lucid consciousness is at its keenest, a humanism which will be inscribed in time alone. This is the attitude of some great writers who, while remaining faithful to the Nietzschean message, will dismiss as a mere mirage the hope for the Superman and will reject eternal recurrence as a perilous temptation. What will this instant be? Opinions differ on this point. For some it is the elating minute of creation during which man feels himself equal to God, this God in which he no longer believes; Faust will ask Mephisto to give him only the power to invent words, to develop an inimitable style that would express the very movement of life in its endless ebb and flow. In this success, promised not to inspiration but to the alchemy of a methodical mind, resides the only superiority at which we might aim: The ultimate problem is therefore to forge "a style that will embrace all the modulations of the soul and every leap of the mind, a style that, like the mind itself, can at times return to what it expresses, just to feel that it is the thing expressing it, asserting itself as the will to express, the living body of the speaker, the sudden awakening of thought, startled that it could have identified itself for a time with an object, even though that identification is its essence and its function."[3]

For others—André Gide and, sometimes, Montherlant and

---

[3] Paul Valéry, *Luste or the Crystal Girl,* in *The Collected Works of Paul Valéry,* Vol. 3 (New York: Pantheon, 1960), p. 33.

also Camus—this unique instant to which all the rest can be sacrificed is that in which desire is at its most intense, the moment of surrender on a sun-drenched beach when the body yields to the warm sand, that in which one finds at last the well that will quench one's thirst, that of the hunt as the coveted prey gets within reach, that of drunkenness carried to its paroxysm by a monstrous satiation. Paul Valéry's Faust will merely caress the gentle Luste with an immediately checked amorous caprice.

But should we not reject these morbid temptations which are the delight of a decadent "existentialism" that has reached the extreme limit of its contradictions? Pleasure, whether of the mind or of the flesh, will soon vanish and the anguish reflecting the conflicts of a disintegrating society will reappear even stronger. We must give man other goals, transform these economic structures which are at the source of harrowing alienations; we must exalt everyday life instead of gathering it under the sign of death; we must restore the true value of work, or rather consider work as the unique source of all "values." Karl Marx's message should not be underestimated, nor the greatness of the humanism he wanted to found. We can all see, however, that communistic societies are now plagued with those very contradictions they attributed to the capitalistic world. Moreover, when faced with a technological revolution which even the genius of Marx could not foresee in all its magnitude, they are hesitant as to the ideals they should propose to man. The portrait of man—or of the Marxist Superman as it is sometimes drawn nowadays—is very different from that outlined by communism in its early days. What is more, an increasing convergence tends to bring together, at the limit, the expectations of the Marxist, convinced that the recasting of societies carried to their maximal cohesion will make it possible for mankind to master the universe, and the schemes of the technocrat, so convinced of the effi-

113

cacy of his plans. Therefore the opposition detected as early as 1925 by Berdyaev between the atheism of the Aufklärung, which promoted the cult of a reason which is considered to be capable of ensuring the indefinite progress of man, and the atheism of our period, which is still fighting against the claws of nihilism, is becoming less pronounced. At the same time Machiavellianism is reappearing, forging an inhuman society where leveling down, "proletarianization of the masses," conceals the unlimited power of the hierarchies and, at the very top, of individual or collegial tyrannies.

Facing this society that is organized to "last," confident in the opportunities time will afford, it was unavoidable that Christianity should—if not change its doctrines, which are mainly oriented toward other goals—at least investigate the most effective ways it could be fitted into the temporal. We will not attempt to conceal the dangers of such an endeavor. For this world imposes conditions on spirituality which hinder its free expansion. This temporal road is marked by values which are not authentic, and ideals are dangerously thwarted by the deforming prism they impose upon us. And yet, we can less and less turn our backs to this world and ignore the technology of which it is so proud, and it would be both unfair and useless to condemn it. In this connection, we recall the luminous pages in Bergson's *Two Sources of Morality and Religion*.

But we will try to go even further. There has always been in Catholicism a very definite line of cleavage between two equally legitimate trends.[4] While one current was expanding and gaining in magnitude—in particular during the eighteenth century among the priests who claimed to be "enlightened"

[4] Cf. in particular our works: *Saint Augustin: temps et histoire* (Paris: Editions Augustiniennes) and "Théologie de l'histoire et antihistorisme de saint Augustin," *Cahier Recherches Augustiniennes, Donoso Cortès, théologien de l'histoire et prophète* (Paris: Beauchesne, 1956).

114

because they did not hesitate to trust man and wanted to help him to master his "alienations" so that, when Christ came back at the very end of time, he would rule over an authentic human community—another current remained wary and cautious of our nature, which it considered to be deeply perverted. There were still many writers, philosophers, and poets who remained convinced that, were it not for transnatural or even supernatural interventions in history, the regression of our wretched mankind toward more monstrous forms of animality would be even more pronounced. It is only too obvious that the opposition between these two trends has increased today to the extent of generating an open conflict embittered by misunderstanding, prejudice, and mutual mistrust. Yet one cannot question the sincerity and the nobleness of the beliefs of both parties, the first being convinced—with good reason— that charity, without which evangelization is inconceivable, must have precedence over everything else, the others that there is a supratemporal truth that conditions any attempt at conversion. Therefore, never more than at this time would the presence of a Saint Augustine—or of an A. Rosmini—be more necessary to remind us of the intimate relationship between truth and charity. Indeed, we do not hope to solve this painful conflict in this book; at the very most, we will try to outline the middle course marked by the work of some philosophers as well as by the calls of the poets, for the manifold interactions between present-day philosophy, poetry, novels, and drama cannot be ignored.

Strange indeed was the life of Nikos Kazantzakis! Born in the island of Crete, he was in fact a Turkish citizen. His childhood was shadowed by the indelible memories of succesive revolts and ruthless reprisals. No one therefore knew better into what depths of the visceral sensitivity of peoples history can be inserted, and how useless is the call of reason when the permanent atavisms of ancestral hatred rise to the surface! In an

115

instant, men who hitherto had been living in apparent harmony, who were united by the same daily cares and by an identical alternating rhythm of joys and sorrows, who used to meet in the street, in the market place, on the steps of their friendly houses, these men will be transformed into beasts of prey. Let the magic cry of "freedom" ring out, and weapons will be taken out of their hiding place and the insurrection unleashed. What scenes of cruelty and horror in *Captain Michel!*[5] Rape and disembowelment of women in front of their terrified children, while young boys and able-bodied men flee to the mountains, to the shelter of the monasteries where the cutthroats will find them. But when life resumes its normal course, resentment, this disease that is even more tenacious than Nietzsche and Scheler would have us believe, will remain buried in all hearts. Henceforth the distance between neighboring houses will be greater, and mistrust appears in all eyes. Until the hour of liberation comes at last and the sacred land once more belongs to Greece. How many tears are wiped away, how much sorrow is repaid, how many crimes are justified by this divine moment! In appearance at least, for things never really change, the struggle goes on, and sometimes yesterday's liberators become tomorrow's executioners.[6]

But the child will leave his home and discover a world in all ways similar to this Crete which is merely its microcosm. Is it not true that this island filled with harsh contrasts conceals amazing mysteries?[7] Not far from the sea, hurled to the ground by historical as well as telluric convulsions, lay the pillars of the temple of Minos. This ancient religion, in which

[5] An English translation is published by Simon and Schuster, under the title *Freedom or Death*. Cf. also *Fratricides* (New York: Simon and Schuster, 1964).

[6] In the island of Cyprus, where two communities live side by side without being able to reach agreement.

[7] *Report to Greco* (New York: Simon and Schuster, 1965).

116

the day and the night are struggling around the Bull—the Minotaur—will always haunt Kazantzakis' imagination. The labyrinth is nothing but the inextricable tunnel in which Dostoevski's underground man is struggling. This myth is very ancient indeed! It goes back to the very origins of mankind. Driven by his anguish, man is descending an endless staircase. Ariadne is the unerring womanly instinct, unwinding the thread of her own mind, of which the "labyrinth" is but the projection; she is human consciousness before the trials reflecting the various levels of the universe were confused by reason.[8] But Theseus, after his victory over the Minotaur, will turn away from Ariadne; he fears that the thread that guided him will also weave the net that would imprison him. Besides, it behooves the hero to solve his own problem, a problem that recurs with every generation. It was first necessary that the Minotaur fall, that he yield to the strength that was bending him. Kazantzakis drew some useful lessons from the dreadful insurrections of Crete; premature pity, unwillingness to face the ordeal, would merely call upon the irresolute warrior the scorn of the vanquished, who, because of this scruple, have become his victors. But victory does not solve anything if the man who gained it does not make it meaningful by mastering himself. The Minotaur is this inferior brother we must enlighten; for he too was imprisoned in the labyrinth, the victim of his own "alienations." Thus Kazantzakis' Theseus ends with a splendid lesson.

Silence has followed the clamor of the dreadful struggle;

[8] We have seen the role played in Nietzsche's philosophy by the myth of Ariadne. For a more detailed study see our: *Pour connaître la pensée de Nietzsche* (Paris: Bordas, 1964). Very recently, in the *Cahiers* devoted to this philosopher, Messrs. Deleuze and Quinot have examined this enigma in turn and proposed somewhat different solutions, pp. 213–217. Cf. also: Deleuze, *Nietzsche et la philosophie* (Paris: Presses Universitaires de France).

and now, leading the conquered Bull, the hero appears in broad daylight. Tamed, the Beast follows him; it will, at last, speak a human language.

"Freed from the Beast your face is again serene, pure and divine; how long were you fighting, elder brother, to free yourself from the Beast? For how many centuries were you bellowing in the darkness, in shame, in agony? An immortal soul, atrociously concealed behind a repulsive muffle, was sighing within you and calling for help."

The emergence of man from the labyrinth of his frenzied desires, this is the mission entrusted to the hero. A surrealist poet, Marcello Fabri, will also examine the long history of mankind and, like the Greek poet, will consider to be unfinished the task of the "humanimal" we have remained. The ruthless universe in which we are immersed, the atrocious murders committed during recent civil wars, all prove to us the precariousness of man's fulfillment. Theseus confronted with the Minotaur, Oedipus forced to solve the ever-renewed problems of the Sphinx, are these not parallel figurations of the somber destiny of man? Gustave Moreau depicted the fearless hero solving all the enigmas and wresting himself from the claws of the human-faced monster that was already clutching his side.[9] Here again the inspiration of the playwright, of the poet, and of the painter is identical.

The little room in the Collège de France in which Bergson taught was, at the beginning of this century, the guiding beacon for young people from all over the world who were less hungry for knowledge than for understanding. There Kazantzakis was to meet Alain-Fournier, Jacques Rivière, Péguy, and T. S. Eliot.[10] But he was also to discover Nietzsche, about whom a student spoke to him one evening, in

[9] Cf. the lines Marcel Proust has devoted to him in Contre Sainte-Beuve.
[10] For T. S. Eliot, see the end of our Chapter 6.

the Bibliothèque Sainte-Geneviève.[11] In Nietzsche's massive work, which he devoured in a few days, he deciphered the message of the half-god, whose gigantic shadow he would later see outlined on a rock of the Caucasus.[12] Had not Prometheus protected the ephemeral against the wrath of Zeus? By giving him fire, had Prometheus not made it possible for man himself to become a god someday? This is the promise we read in the serene expression of the Beast when, delivered from the shackles of anger and envy, it appears to King Minos as the prefiguration of a bright future. We now understand the meaning of the dialogue between the old king and the young hero:

MINOS: Speak with respect, this is a solemn moment; at your feet, O prince of Youth, there yawns an abyss; the same abyss yawns at my old man's feet and a merciless Destiny hovers above us.
I have learned to make necessity my will, this is the only thing on this earth we can call *freedom*.
THESEUS: To compel necessity to do as I wish, this is my idea of freedom.

And this tragic debate has not yet been settled. Is there a solution? And where does wisdom lie? In this daring affirmation? In the courageous acceptance of the inevitable? Or, as Camus will say, and so many others with him, in a constant refusal and a permanent rebellion? For the ancient Greeks, it was not the spirit of God and light that hovered over the unfathomable abysses but a Destiny which we carry within us! And thus our victories will always be precarious and threatened. Was it merely carelessness that caused Theseus to hoist

[11] Cf. *Report to Greco* concerning Nietzsche.
[12] When he went there to negotiate the liberation of Greek prisoners.

the black sail on the ship bringing him back to Athens? Or, by condemning his father, did he wish to abolish a past he had already rejected? Oedipus is no more without enigma[13] than Theseus; man, even in our times, remains a conscious sleepwalker.

How uncertain is the long voyage, punctuated by all too brief stops. Like the road passing under the Gateway, it led the writer from his native Crete to another Greek city where he was to remain until his death, Antipolis, Antibes. It marks out his spiritual progression on a sinuous road, along which Plato, Nietzsche, Buddha, Saint Francis of Assisi, Christ . . . and Lenin arose like gigantic archetypal figures, leading to the eternal wanderer—to the hero of this Odyssey to which he will write the sequel—Odysseus.

"My youth had been nothing but anxieties, nightmares, and questionings; my maturity nothing but lame answers. I looked toward the stars, toward men, toward ideas—what chaos! And what agony to hunt out God, the blue bird with the red talons, in their midst! I took one road, reached its end—an abyss. Frightened, I turned back and took another road; at its end the abyss once more. Retreat again, a new journey, and suddenly the same abyss yawned before me anew. All the routes of the mind led to the abyss. My youth and maturity revolved in the air around the two poles of panic and hope, but now in my old age I stood before the abyss tranquilly, fearlessly. I no longer fled, no longer humiliated myself—no, not I, but the Odysseus I was fashioning. I created him to face the abyss calmly, and in creating him, I strove to resemble him. I myself was being created. I entrusted all my own yearnings to this Odysseus; he was the mold I was carving out so that the man of the future might flow in. Whatever I yearned for and was

---

[13] Oedipus Without Enigmas is the title of an often confused though always profound work by the poet Marcello Fabri.

unable to attain, he would attain. He was the charm that would lure the tenebrous and luminous forces that create the future. Faith moves mountains; believe in him and he would come. Who would come? The Odysseus I had created. He was the Archetype.

"The creator's responsibility is a great one; he opens a road that may entice the future and force it to make up its mind."[14]

Thus the Superman is essentially the Creator; but this creator, in order to sculpt himself, must examine the past of mankind and model himself on a certain image of man; he must achieve that which previously was merely sketched. Everything is constantly called into question anew; Theseus will have to endure one day the derision of a young hero full of his own strength; Penelope, in her palace of Ithaca, weaves during the day a cloth she unravels at night; the fire that animates all things creates and destroys in turn. The fate of the "ephemeral" is a harsh one indeed; he must pull himself away from the comfort of home, from the prayers of those he loves, from a certain type of wisdom, to try to blaze the perilous trail that runs, high above the abysses, toward a future he is eager to face. Are we even sure of actually going forward? Are we not just running away from ourselves and our dizziness? Pascal wondered if the most free of all men is not the man who knows how to stay quietly in his room. The future of the wanderer remains enigmatic and finally amounts to seeking himself in his most distant past, like a flying fish falling back into the ocean after its daring leap.[15] Thus our individual consciousness rises to broad daylight only to plunge back into a deep night where Ariadne will no longer be there to guide it.

And thus Kazantzakis will forever oscillate between the Christian solution and the earthly, temporal solution proposed

[14] *Report to Greco*, pp. 487–488.
[15] Cf. *Report to Greco*.

121

in two differents keys by Nietzsche and by Lenin. Is it through its solitary heroes, through its saints "who are saints only by themselves and for themselves"[16] that mankind is progressing, through these individualities which at the very moment they begin to sense their power become merely the playthings of pride? Is it carried along by the impetus of fanatic masses, at the cost of the destruction by these monstrous aggregates of all originality, of all true resonance? Must we search the past for the prefiguration of the future, or, like the blue bird with red talons, like the arrow defying gravity, must we trace as we go the unpredictable course of the future? Great is the distance separating Buddha and his teaching of nonresistance to evil, of fusion of the atman and the brahman, of accession to the absolute void of the nirvana, from the revolutionary who, with his own hands, molds the human clay and changes its appearance. And very different also is the wisdom of Alexis Zorba, full of common sense and humor, from that, full of aspirations toward a Transcendence, of Bergson and of Schweitzer, whom Kazantzakis will meet in Alsace, while, in Assisi, Jörgensen will propose to him the example of Saint Francis.[17]

All his life Kazantzakis will hesitate between these diverging ideals, between wordly and suprawordly goals. He will be very much attracted by the absolute simplicity of Saint Francis, but how can one deliberately deprive oneself of such great riches? Everything, even God, is made perhaps of the rich though changing stuff of time. Would it not be man, in his flight, who lights up the sky with stars and even draws in it the face of the Eternal that is merely his own idealized face? One day, on a rock overhanging the sea, Kazantzakis went to see the hegumen. And the holy man told him his secret. It is in ephemeral life that eternity is dwelling, but only a few

[16] Cf. Baudelaire, *Journaux intimes.*
[17] Kazantzakis himself was to write a life of Saint Francis of Assisi.

chosen men can discover it there and gather its drops in their hands. God had pity on the other men; he consoled them with the comforting illusions of religion! "It is not God who will save us"—such is Kazantzakis' conclusion in *The Saviors of God*—"it is we who will save God, by battling, by creating, and transmuting matter into spirit." And in an even more explicit text: "Plants, animals, and men are the steps which God creates on which to tread and to mount upward."[18] God therefore does not exist, he makes himself, and just as Theseus saved the Minotaur, at each stage of a difficult ascent it is up to man to ensure his true fulfillment:

"My God is not Almighty. He struggles, for he is in peril every moment; he trembles and stumbles in every living thing, and he cries out. He is defeated incessantly, but rises again, full of blood and earth, to throw himself into battle once more."[19]

At the limit, Superman and God would coincide, just as the features of Theseus are very similar to those of the Minotaur. But the threat of eternal recurrence is hanging over this universe in gestation. And this struggle in which ideals laboriously and painfully take shape must always be taken up anew. The great Platonic myths play an important role in the mind of the Greek author. His lucid reason is trying to control a team in which two horses are competing: One looks toward the earth, unable to forget the pleasures of the flesh, while the other, animated by noble instincts, aims at the loftiest ideals. It is certainly not easy to sacrifice one to the other, so great are the delights of the flesh. But we must chisel everything anew so as to ensure the birth of a being who will deserve at last the name of man, so that the "call of the future" will be heard in this man.

[18] *The Saviors of God*, pp. 106 and 93; cf. also *Fratricides*.

[19] *The Saviors of God*, p. 103, §29; also p. 103, §31: "My God is not All-holy. He is full of cruelty and savage justice, and he chooses the best mercilessly. . . ."

A painful gestation, a tormented birth. "Monkeys must have felt the momentum of the universe inside them in this same way, urging them to stand on their hind legs, even though the pain made them howl, and to rub a pair of sticks together to produce a spark, even though the other monkeys derided them. . . . This is how the indestructible, merciless force kicked against our breasts as well: in order to save itself from man, and continue beyond."[20]

We are now almost halfway between Nietzsche and Teilhard. Kazantzakis also feels that man is an unfinished being. We are headed, by means of man and through him, toward a world that is beyond the human. Man is but a stage toward that which appears to us—depending on our perspective—as a creation or as an evolution. But the heroic deed of Theseus, in whom action and thought support and strengthen one another, must be repeated incessantly; otherwise, the movement would stop and man would be thrown back into the drifts of his past:

"I remembered something Zorba once said: 'I always act as though I were immortal.' This is God's method, but we mortals should follow it too, not from megalomania and impudence, but from the soul's invincible yearning for what is above. The attempt to imitate God is our only means to surpass human boundaries, be it only by a hair, be it only for an instant (remember the flying fish)."[21]

Thus finally, this God who had been so close, so present to the Greek author when, in Assisi, he encountered his most humble disciple, is no longer, for Kazantzakis as well as for Marcello Fabri,[22] but an idea, a symbol.[23] We must fix this

---

[20] *Report to Greco*, p. 496.

[21] *Ibid.*, p. 466.

[22] Cf. especially the *Cryptograms* in which all civilizations are reviewed.

[23] He will even sometimes think of Lenin as a sort of modern Christ (cf. *Fratricides*).

124

idea; we must, so to speak, become saturated with it in order to free ourselves from the gangue in which we are imprisoned; we must project into the future the image of the Creator in order to become creators ourselves. Little by little the disciple of Odysseus—and of Plato—synthesized the contrasting figures and teachings of Nietzsche, Bergson, Buddha, and Lenin. And Kazantzakis, this Greek so saturated with ancient wisdom, turned away from the contemplation of the invisible world to toil in the world of becoming; or rather, an osmosis occurred between them. The great Archetypes are set in motion, myths are brought to life by the rough hands of the proletarian Alexis Zorba. To mold the clay like he did, like him to support with the arch of a fearless body the collapsing walls of a mine and thus found a community of men and put an end to the isolation of souls,[24] to help these poor beings in endless gestation to free themselves from their servitude, here again is the same ideal of victorious freedom that Theseus opposed to the resignation of Minos. Mankind should be sent toward the future, like an arrow, like a bird; thus, because be darts above the water, the fish will be endowed, by this very aspiration, with the wings he was missing; the wonderful bird will frolic in the sky, having escaped from the hold of gravity. Icarus, more surely than Theseus, will escape from the labyrinth.

Unknown to himself, Kazantzakis revives the Pythagorean myths; and yet, according to him, in order to be born man must not surrender life and, like Sappho, throw himself into the sea from the top of the Leucadian rock, but in this very world he must aim at a better future. The Superman leads a reticent mankind toward goals that are so distant as to appear inaccessible; like a bird of prey he hovers, breathless, above the abyss. His destiny will be fulfilled only when from time itself he will have wrested eternity.

[24] There is an almost identical example in Merleau-Ponty's *La Psychologie du comportement.*

And yet, in Kazantzakis, the tension will ease sometimes; there are moments of rest and trusting surrender. We can sense in him—and this contributes to the charm of his extensive works—a hesitation between the moment of sacrifice and that of a thoroughly enjoyed simple happiness. He will never forget the shores of Crete, so beautiful in their desolation, the string of islands spread out over the sea, in which there is such a sharp contrast between light and shade—the diurnal light of Apollo and that of Athena, which is even more propitious to clear-sightedness. Throughout his voyages, Odysseus, the most subtle and intelligent of all men, aimed only at mastering himself. Only when his deepest being had been liberated could he find his way back to Ithaca. It is indeed the oracle of Delphi that he is obeying. He gained a more and more exhaustive knowledge of himself, discerning in himself both the most simple and the most universal features. It is by becoming himself that he perfected his human nature, wresting it from the darkness that concealed its features from him. And he will be rewarded with the faithfulness of Penelope, for whom action and understanding are also equivalent. We thought we had left our native land, and then one day we find ourselves back in it, like Selma Lagerlöf's Dalécarlien. It is in one of Antibes' narrow streets, near a market place brightened by bunches of familiar flowers, that a Cretan, at the close of his long life, will discover his only eternal present. For Kazantzakis, as for Pasternak and Selma Lagerlöf, heaven is an unblemished corner of this earth, untouched by the scoriae of sin:

"I boarded a caique which called at the graceful Aegean isles of Santorin, Naxos, Paros and Mykonos. I have said this and I say it again: One of the greatest pleasures man is capable of being granted in this world is to sail the Aegean in springtime when a gentle breeze is blowing. I have never been able to conceive how heaven could be in any way different. What other celestial or mundane joy could be more perfectly in harmony

with man's body and soul? This joy reaches as far as exaltation but it does not go beyond—praise the Lord—and thus the beloved visible world does not vanish. On the contrary, the invisible becomes visible, and what we term God, eternity, and beatitude board our caique and sail along with us."[25]
Is this not what the hegumen was saying when he claimed that eternity is already present in the heart of time? The divine Savior has boarded the caique, and already, unknown to ourselves, we have entered into the invisible world.[26]

Kazantzakis had set out with Odysseus for a long crossing, which turned out to be nothing but a long journey through a land he never left. Don Quixote is the navigator guiding Miguel de Unamuno in his heroic dream; but this Don Quixote, who has survived his author, is very different indeed from the laughable and burlesque character handed down to us by tradition. If it were not for want of space, how tempting it would be to extend the parallel between authors who were haunted by the image of the poor hidalgo. Flaubert will merely transpose into his century the image he had already formed in his youth of his favorite hero—this hero with whom he felt a close affinity due to the contrast between his chimeric impulses and his critical mind—and "bovarism" will become synonymous with "quixotism"—the romantic fiction of which the nineteenth century was so fond, being the counterpart of the romances of chivalry. Pirandello's wit is of the same stock as that of Cervantes, originating in this same contrast between the imagination and the irony that follows it step by step, that controls it, and, by its very excess, makes it sterile. Cervantes is thus his model, a Cervantes who laughs at himself and at the naive enthusiasm that led him to fling himself recklessly

[25] *Report to Greco*, pp. 466–467.
[26] We should also mention the pages devoted by Selma Lagerlöf in *Jerusalem in the Holy Land* to the vision of Dalécarlien on the eve of his death. In the deep water of a well he sees the lost paradise.

into the dream of the crusades. A lost arm, debts, the scorn or the indifferent pity of "successful" people, and, in the end, prison, this is the fate awaiting the "weary hero."

Another reincarnation of Don Quixote appears in the work of Milosz: the hero of *L'Amoureuse Initiation*, at once piteous, moving, and burlesque, the Count Pinamonte, the last of the Brettinoros:

"I then examined the babbler carefully; though gaunt and stooping, he seemed fairly well built, but his features, wrinkled by age and in which the memory of his worst experience seemed to have become fixed in a sort of bittersweet grimace both tearful and laughing, made me shudder with pity and disgust. Anxious wrinkles crisscrossed on a bloodless face, on which the love of adventure had left its mark: the peculiar twitchings of a huge nose, swelled with circumspect arrogance betrayed the habit—characteristic of nomads—of sniffing the winds of many countries. The vile ferrety eyes . . . would at intervals remain set in a sort of burning and vile fixity that chilled one's blood."[27]

This sorry character has his Dulcinea, Circé de Mérode, a courtesan who provides him with the coarsest pleasures but reveals the unsatisfactoriness of the delights of the flesh to this soul that yearns for the absolute, so that, finally, having reached the lowest depths of degradation, he will find the road to salvation.

But it is not like Unamuno to dwell on such images in which Milosz' humility delighted. For him also there has been a synthesis, or rather a blending of the softness of the mist-covered landscapes of his native Basque fatherland and the arid Castilian plateau, between his Catholic and Carlist heritage and the fierce republican ideal that set him up against

---

[27] O. de L. Milosz, *Oeuvres completes, L'Amoureuse Initiation* (A. Sylvaire).

tyranny. A fierce love of independence was the result of this amazing crossing. At the confines between Galicia and Castile, riding his hack through steppes cut by fissures at the bottom of which dark waters are flowing, he met Don Quixote and his faithful Sancho. And in his soul his lost faith has left the same fissure, the same dissonance, the same yearning. Crosses are still standing on their steles, but they no longer shield man from the certainty of his useless destiny; the tragic sense of life fills him with bitterness. Honor, when confronted with nothingness, becomes impatient and exasperated; it tends to become what it will be for Montherlant: the point of honor that demands a gratuitous self-sacrifice. The flame still burns in the darkness, but it hardly casts any light and is no longer warm; and the air vent gapes open above the souls toward which no more help is descending.[28] Mysticism lingers on but despairs of ever finding its object. Desire, carried to a paroxysm by its impossible fulfillment, still aims beyond this earthly life at a personal eternity; but his cold reason sees only a mirage in this eternity for which he yearns. This persistent longing for that which can in no way be proved is at the source of his painful division. Unamuno belongs thus to this race of thinkers "for whom meditation on the condition of man has assumed a pathetic import."

Numerous are those in whom he recognizes his intercessors: Marcus Aurelius, Saint Augustine, Pascal, Rousseau, Leopardi, Vigny, Kleist, Amiel, Kierkegaard, and also—since characters live their own personal life—René and, above all, Sénancour's Obermann. He is the philosopher of "nostalgia": nostalgia for a vanished world in which heroism would be the common rule, for a Spain that no longer exists, for beliefs that have been dispelled by the critical mind. He could have made his

[28] I am alluding to the painting by Jerome Bosch that hangs in the Palace of the Doges in Venice.

own this quotation from Sénancour, which Camus set at the beginning of his "letters to a German friend": "Man is perishable. That may be; but let us perish resisting, and if it is nothingness that awaits us, do not let us so act that it shall be a just fate." His fellow traveler would have been Giovanni Papini, the author of *L'Uomo finito* and *Crepuscolo dei filosofi*. But Papini was to become converted. This theme of the absurdity of life that was first developed by the Italian philosopher at the beginning of this century, he will take up again with such vigor that the existentialists will have nothing to add to it. But there is a ray of hope stealing through the air vent: "Life is absurd, but of an absurdity that allows us to hope for a meaning; the trouble is that this meaning is beyond our reach."[29]

In any case we must not hope to find this meaning in history, since history only skims the surface of life; for Unamuno it is nothing but a scholastic study, one of these arbitrary reconstructions of the human mind which cause people to let themselves be guided by secondhand concepts only and not by reality. For only the individual desire of man, who finds himself—to quote Pascal—"thrown into this world," "embarked without having wanted it," is real. This is indeed the tragic condition of man: Life demands securities, it requires at least some expectations; reason denies them to her. All the rest, God, freedom, the other world, are built upon the unprovable assertion of the immortality of the soul, which is a necessary "vital lie." But thought dispels these illusions without which, if man were consistent with himself, he could no longer go on living. This is indeed the "paradox": the greater his consciousness, the more man rises toward the higher forms of life, the greater the gap between his aspirations and the conclusions of his cool-headed analysis. There is but one hope,

[29] *The Tragic Sense of Life.*

though not a very strong one: "Our reason, our mind, our spirit are too limited to really understand completely that which they are trying to grasp."

The contradiction nonetheless remains in the very heart of man; it transforms his existence into a pathetic tragedy, an endless agony:

Tragic doubt (very different from the methodical Cartesian doubt which does not undermine the very forces of life) "inhabits a house which is continually being demolished and which continually it has to rebuild. Without ceasing, the will, I mean the will never to die, the spirit of unsubmissiveness to death, labours to build up the house of life, and without ceasing the keen blasts and stormy assaults of reason beat it down."[30]

The model of this struggle in the very depths of darkness is Don Quixote, not the Knight of the Rueful Countenance whom Cervantes brought to life only to laugh at himself and at his times but a fearless hero who rose from the tomb where his temporal Creator claimed to have buried him forever: "The real Don Quixote resurrected himself, for himself and before himself, and he goes through the world, following his calling."

Like Pirandello,[31] Unamuno believes that characters are more real than persons; they go deeper than the froth of history, through unexplored abysses, imposing upon all their "significant" destiny, realizing in their singularity the union of the individual and of the universal. They somehow "mark down" all individual adventures. Don Quixote teaches us that though reason and faith are invincibly opposed to one another, it is faith we must trust and we must believe in the "paradox." We must follow this daydreamer whose profile stands out, eter-

---

[30] *Ibid.*, p. 108.
[31] In *Six Characters in Search of an Author*.

131

nally, in the sky of "values;" we must join his crusade—or that of Ignatius de Loyola.

"Don Quixote wanted to make those men, whose mercenary hearts knew only the material kingdom of wealth, acknowledge that there is a spiritual realm, and thus redeem them in spite of themselves."

His lessons therefore remain inscribed in the heart of every man who is tormented by justice and who, though he knows that like truth it is inaccessible, nonetheless becomes its champion—in the heart of every unsatisfied and upright man "who would be more than man."[32]

Unamuno is irritated by the lack of understanding of which Don Quixote is the victim, by this inaccurate idea people have of him. By laughing at him we try to avoid his appraising look. Our conscience shirks away from the great warning voice. He would like us to be knighted and go through the world as eternal protesters driven by an unwavering heroic will; neither fear nor interest would succeed in making us forget our vow never to tolerate injustice and dishonor in any guise. This watch of arms that has been so ridiculed by some—and perhaps Cervantes himself had invited them to do so—what is it but the birth to a higher life, our ascent to a superhuman order, that very one of which Bernanos determined the rules and the code in his *Diary of a Country Priest?* Ignatius de Loyola also had his watch of arms:

"As he had read in books of chivalry that maiden knights used to watch their arms, he, as a maiden knight of Christ, in order spiritually to imitate that knightly rite and to watch his own apparently poor and fragile, but really strong and gorgeous, arms, which he had put on against man's natural enemy, all that night, partly standing and partly kneeling, remained

---

[32] Two great mystic poets, Armand Godoy and Louis Ruy, share Unamuno's views in their eulogy of Don Quixote.

watching before the image of Our Lady, offering himself to her with all his heart, bitterly weeping for his sins and promising to mend his ways thenceforth."[33]

Let us not however misinterpret this confrontation between Don Quixote and the great mystic. If reason, like a corrosive, has dissolved the object of faith, the only thing that remains of faith is the desperate impulse toward a reality that is not temporarily but permanently inaccessible. A now cold flame is unable to brighten the gathering darkness. The nightmare has become worse and the agony continues. Goya's specter has returned from beyond the grave but, his finger pressed on his icy lips, he does not reveal its secrets. There remains only one affirmation on which heroism can be based: that it is noble and good to give one's life for lost causes.

We must run the risk of belonging to this army of "spirituals" whom the "carnal" shun with derision and the intellectuals—the technicians—satisfied with the job they perform with careful dexterity and skillful at juggling with numbers, call "madmen," "dreamers," "mystics."[34] It is true that they cannot prove what they suspect and intermittently discern— that there is another world within ours, that mysterious pow-

[33] From Rivadeneira's *Life of St. Ignatius de Loyola*, Book I, Chapter 4. Quoted in M. de Unamuno, *The Life of Don Quixote and Sancho* (New York: Knopf, 1927), pp. 22–23.

[34] We are very close to the distinction between the three Orders which Pascal, with good reason, considered to be discontinuous and without common measure, very close also to the myth of Phaedra. Even more than of the "carnal" man who still senses certain calls permeating through the opacity of his desires, we must beware of the intellectual, of the cold technocrat (it was he Unamuno had in mind), overly fond of plans and calculations and convinced that only that which can be proved can actually exist. Though the "spiritual" cannot justify his intuitions, he nonetheless sees further and succeeds in surrounding the "mystery" all around us; it is only with the heart that one can see rightly.

133

ers slumber in the midst of our mind, awaiting the call that
will awaken them.

Don Quixote is, for Unamuno, much more than a symbol,
and also much more than a type, since he is the leader of all
these spirituals who are willing to fight in loneliness and agony
for what most men would call chimeras. He is for him, to
quote Papini, "the human spirit that becomes great only in
pity, in surrender to destiny—the successor and the companion of these valiant idealists, of these knights full of mysticism and love who were the grandeur of Spain."

Here again, the words of the great Castilian poet find an
echo in those of the French humanist Albert Camus. "We
live only of contradictions, and for contradictions," says Unamuno during his exile in Paris;[35] "life is a perpetual tragedy
and struggle, without victory and without hope of victory; it
is basically obscure and unintelligible."

"About the essential problem," Camus will answer, "I
mean, about all those for which one might die or those which
might decuple the passion for life, there are probably only
two ways of thinking: that of La Palice,[36] and that of Don
Quixote."

How then must we imagine the humanism that will arise
after this long night? Which values will mark out the road of
a man destined to surpass himself in the midst of desolation
and ruin, after an atrocious agony?

Once more, on the roads through the forest in which ancestral fears are unleashed, we see the profile of another Knight;
but he is guided by despair alone and it is only in the certitude of nothingness that he finds the strength to go on,

[35] "Paris," he will say, "is the city in which the present is made up
of definite and accumulated past, of a near and reasonably planned
future."

[36] A well-known children's song relates the adventures of Monsieur
de La Palice in a flow of truisms.

fearless between his two companions: the Devil and death.[37] We will not yet leave Spain where, following El Greco, Kazantzakis first led us. El Greco also had left Crete when he was very young; in Venice he met Tintoretto, who revealed to him the extent of the effort of spiritualization of which the soul is capable. He then had his first vision of stylized and elongated bodies rising like flames. In Toledo, Kazantzakis had the opportunity to admire the diptych of the *Burial of the Count of Orgaz*. It is through the eyes of faith, driven by a need that reason contradicts in vain, that we discern confusedly that without which our existence would be unintelligible: the higher plane death will open up for us. The soul wants to terminate elsewhere a destiny that encounters all sorts of unsurmountable obstacles here on earth, it wants to witness the birth of a "reciprocity" between consciousnesses that are now walled in. God, for Unamuno, is the guarantor of this fulfillment which alone can save us from absurdity. When, in 1936, Kazantzakis met the author of *The Tragic Sense of Life* in Salamanca, he found him worried and disillusioned. He feared that youth would turn away from the absolute, that, comfortably settled in the relative, it would

[37] But if faith is lacking, the scientist's reason will painfully realize its inability to make the world intelligible. This is the case—dramatic in its touching sincerity—of Jean Rostand. In his view, man is a "diseased animal, an accident among the accidents, with no justification or purpose to his existence, and going through life in the terror of death." This "miserable lord of the planet" can boast of "no essential attribute that does not also belong to the world of the living; he can only blame his greater share of torments to the hypertrophy of his intelligence and of his affectivity."

It was a moving encounter indeed, that of a very great poet and of a very great scientist. Neither believes in man; but the first overcomes by the desperate wager the obstacle of "total" absurdity, while the second raises his will so as to bear it (cf. *passim*, Chapter 10).

135

consider as chimeras and utopias the goals of Don Quixote
and Ignatius de Loyola.[38]

It is to remain faithful to these "utopias," to shield her
father from such mockery, that Mariana will sacrifice her
earthly happiness, which she realizes would only fall in her soul
like a handful of ashes. Antigone also, Anouilh's Antigone,
cannot imagine herself getting old at the side of Hemon; she
will not accept the ridicule of a great love fizzling out. Better
go and bury oneself in the silence of a monastery or in the cold
of the grave than to feel thinning within oneself the flow of
life that is about to irrigate other bodies. For Unamuno,
man, either too conscious or not conscious enough, was but
a rational automaton or a diseased animal terrified by the
ghosts arising from his futile desires. The Castile of Don
Alvaro and of the Cardinal of Spain and the Portugal of Don
Pedro will be even more arid. On this sometimes scorching,
sometimes freezing, windswept plateau, Montherlant will see
hatred arising from ideologies, and order and freedom destroying one another. The mutilated bodies hanging in the trees
and, in the village streets, the guns ready to fire at the slightest
provocation remind him of the horror of Goya's drawings.

In a daring effort, Unamuno had cast away the image of a
ludicrous Don Quixote. Let the doubts and negations of a
critical mind increase, let, in the same man, the contrasts
between "carnal," "intellectual," and "spiritual" become more
pronounced, and the impossible wager will be lost. The accen-
tuation of these contrasts in Montherlant has often been
attributed to his upbringing, divided between divergent influ-
ences: on the one hand, an ill mother whose delicate sensitivity and craving for happiness could hope to find solace only

[38] Kazantzakis describes his encounter with Unamuno in *Spain*
(New York: Simon and Schuster, 1963), p. 74: "I know these young
people of today very well," said the Castilian writer. "They hate the
Spirit."

in the compensations brought to her by an excessively spoiled child and later an adored and pampered adolescent; on the other hand, a puritanical grandmother who was convinced that the flesh must at all times be repressed and punished. But these tensions could have been overcome, thanks to the teaching of a professor of philosophy, Paul Archambault, whose lessons were strongly influenced by Blondel's views. Montherlant could then have understood the fruitful exchanges that occur between thought and action when they are both directed toward the same vivifying truth. Now, in Montherlant's drama, action and thought follow diverging paths; there is a sharp line separating them. "Reasons" do not penetrate to the core in which decisions first see the light. How could the gentle Inez have suspected that the forthcoming birth of her child would draw upon her not the loving concern but the wrath of King Ferrante? Everything is obscure, illogical, in the underworld where causes are fermenting. The roundabout ways of grace itself, in the drama of Port-Royal, appear to be due to this alogic rather than to a free gift of God. What a difference between this ambiguous progression and the light Bernanos describes slowly invading the little nun's soul!

Thus, through an inexplicable paradox rather than because of the presence of Apelles' stroke, lessons that should have ensured the intimate fusion of divergent forces left in Montherlant only the regret for an Absolute that would have satisfied him; they increased his inability to be at ease in this relative, which he felt at times could not fill the emptiness of his soul. And in a sort of challenge, to the lofty flame of spiritual life he substituted the recantations of Guiscard, the delirious passion of Pasiphaé—a sister of Kleist's atrocious Penthesilea—and later, the self-satisfied coarseness of an aging Don Juan. We are far from the progression of Milosz' Miguel de Manara. And yet, in his best plays, in *Le Maître de Santiago* as in *Le Cardinal d'Espagne*, and perhaps even more in the arid but at

times sublime *Port-Royal*, in which faith visits and abandons
as it pleases—I almost said, in its whims—humble creatures
who turn to it for consolation, we see a poignant regret for his
inability to rise to these peaks where the steep and strenuous
road of life becomes brighter. But while the finger of the saint
points imperatively to heaven, Goya's specter is raising the
tombstone and the dismal remains of knights tell their tale
of useless service and of sacrifice performed "for nothing."[39]

Thus the persistent need for the Absolute only discloses
the nothingness of existence, while the cool lucidity of reason
denounces the mirage of another world. Henceforth all hope
is extinguished; the flame that flooded Kazantzakis with its
crimson splendor, the light that still shone for Unamuno at
the window of the inn where ephemeral travelers linger in the
invading twilight has now completely vanished. The hero Don
Quixote is now but a ludicrous shadow riding the shadow of
a hack across the darkening plains.

It is true that one is not inclined to laugh when, in spite of
everything, there still remains in man this will to surpass himself. Here and there, a word of Don Alvaro, a confession by
Doña Inez, evoke the greatness of Polyeucte or the gentleness
of Berenice.

> ALVARO: God does not want anything or seek anything; he
> is the eternal calm. It is by wanting nothing that you will
> reflect God—snow drops are descending as did the tongues
> of fire on the apostles. Did you know that it was mostly
> during Whitsuntide that new knights were dubbed. (He
> unhooks from the wall the great cloak of the Order and,
> his hand on Mariana's shoulder, wraps the huge cloak

---

[39] We had to abandon our plan to quote *in extenso* this remarkable
confession, which is called *Chevalerie du Néant* (Chivalry of Nothingness) and is truly worthy of appearing in all anthologies.

round himself and his daughter.) By my hand on your shoulder I knight you. And now, let us go to a country where there is no shame, let us fly with the eagles, my little knight! . . .

MARIANA: Let us go to die, feeling and love. Let us go to die.

ALVARO: Let us go to live. Let us go to be dead, and the living are among the living. [*Le Maître de Santiago*, last act.]

It is in vain that this double imploration, this two-part canticle, rises toward the silent eternity. In vain the exaltation of a useless sacrifice is growing. It is indeed a matter of loyalty, but of loyalty to oneself—the loyalty of the man who does not want to fall, who wants to model himself at all cost on the noblest image he can form of himself.

"I soon heard a voice whispering to me the words of Sigismund in *Life is a dream*:

I am dreaming and I wish
To act rightly, for good deeds are not lost, though they be
*   wrought in dreams.*

"What does this mean? I now choose to understand: life is a dream, but doing good is not wasted in it. No matter how useless—useless to society, useless to save our soul—because it is to ourselves we have done this good, it is ourselves we have served, as it is ourselves who have crowned ourselves, and the only crowns that are of any value are those one gives to oneself . . .

"I looked at the earth, and it was all emptiness and nothingness . . . at the sky and there was no light in it.

"I have only the idea I have of myself to support me on the oceans of nothingness." (*Service inutile*)

To sacrifice oneself for a faith in which one no longer believes, to wager on that which one deems illusory because that alone is of value, how can we laugh at the man who carries

139

self-sacrifice to such extremes? He is a weak but still effective
reflection of the Superman.

But if man is overwhelmed by the agony of a will that is
divided against itself, of an intelligence that is torn between
an ideal of greatness and delirious obsessions, the pathetic
merely becomes ridiculous: This is how King Ferrante appears
to us, with his increasing obsession completely paralyzing his
generous impulses. Yet another step and we will see the ropes
animating the dislocated puppet; this is the case for Anouilh's
"Poor Bitos" and even more for Malatesta, whose hunger for
vengeance gives way to panic as soon as the Pope appears: As
punishment, he, the brave condottiere, will have to lead a
mere show army! The tragic still remains, for through all these
atrocious and burlesque scenes, Destiny unfolds an absurd
sequence of causes and motives; it scoffs at the best intentions: By trying to save her husband, the gentle Isota will
hand him over to his murderer. That which, according to the
norm of human feelings, should have saved Inez, will doom
her: Is there anything more ridiculous than a king incensed
at the birth of his grandson?

The theatrical works of Gabriel Marcel, though brightened
by redeeming grace, are also full of such illogical situations.
Attitudes are so ambiguous that we cannot be sure of Ariadne's intentions as she walks alongside the infernal abysses
in Le Chemin de Crête. It seems that in this century in which
man is more emancipated than ever before, there yawns
within him an abyss in which he might be swallowed up. And
the artist foresees these dangers which success conceals from
the technologist. Who can tell the deep despair of Cardinal
Cisneros, when—after the conversation in which the mad
queen appears to be more clear-sighted than he—he examines
his actions and the motives that inspired them? His loyalty
is that of these knights who battle against nothingness; his
service for his faith, for his country, for his king, is a useless

service. He foresees, or rather, he knows the betrayal that will reward him for his efforts, but he nonetheless continues on his way toward this self-fulfillment where death is awaiting him. How painful also is the destiny of Soeur Angélique, chosen by her companions as their guide in the impending trials; they think she is sure of herself, enlightened by the strength of faith. But now this faith abandons her at the very moment it has become her only support against the snares of the world and the temptations of an easier life. She finds herself helplessly lost in darkness. But at that very moment, the flame lights up in another soul, that of the weakest of the nuns of Port-Royal; though flickering at first, it gradually becomes steadier and soon shines above all human uncertainties. We would have to quote the whole scene, which remains, in spite of the ambiguity of the religious feelings, one of the highlights of dramatic art.

It is necessary—such is, unknown to himself, the message of Montherlant—that the flame consume everything, so that from the ashes of the carnal man, from the unsolvable doubts of the intellectual, the new man may be born: the unsatisfied spiritual man who "offers himself up to inspiration through self-humiliation." But there still oscillates in this perspective the image of the Superman engaged upon a dangerous road; his tense pride alone is keeping him up, forcing him to a desperate loyalty. This attitude sometimes lacks neither elegance nor strength. I am thinking of Swann's last visit to his Guermantes friends: He knows that he will soon die of an incurable desease. To obey the rhythm of habits, to play, without faltering, one's social role to the very last, is this not to be greater than fatality? In this life that is for us but a reprieve, freedom can assert itself only by interiorization. Lucidity itself is of no avail; it cannot alter events or actions. Since the mirage of another world has been cleared, time is running the ball we cannot leave till the very end; the Plague is the expected visitor who will be able to enter even through barred doors. All the will can still do is to refuse to yield to the ineluctable.

Characters appear on the stage, but very soon they are swallowed up again in darkness. On this earth that was once governed by order and measure, in which rituals and customs were regulated by the steady rhythm of time,[40] the ancient chaos has returned.[41] When hatred seems to subside, the poison it leaves behind in the heart accumulates toxins in it; "resentment" sows the seeds of new conflicts in our "tormented" and "unhappy" consciousness. Does our only hope of salvation lie in an entirely gratuitous grace? Can we not, by our efforts alone, succeed in undoing this "vipers' tangle" within us? He is strange indeed, this Superman who is capable of understanding the universe but remains unable to understand himself or to despise the feelings he condemns. Never have our moralists been so clear-sighted and so disenchanted.

Gisors' conclusion in André Malraux's *Condition humaine* is also full of disenchantment:

"We are all suffering, and each one of us suffers because he thinks. Deep down, the mind thinks of man only in terms of the eternal, and the consciousness of life can be nothing but anguish. One should not think about life with the mind, but with opium. If thought were to vanish, how many sufferings scattered in this light would vanish with it!"

And thus the caravan of men, constantly lured by new mirages, parched by a thirst that cannot be quenched by the too scarce and muddy water of the wells, would leave behind it a trail of dead gods. This "desire for eternity"[42] is also an ever-receding mirage, like the horizon of dunes on which the wind uselessly shifts the illusory sand.

[40] J. Anouilh, *La Grotte.*
[41] Montherlant, *Le Chaos et la nuit.*
[42] L. Alquié, *Le Désir d'éternité.*

And yet, in the desert, the vision of the Little Prince will be quite different. His native wisdom has revealed to him the origin of men's suffering:

"Good morning," said the little prince.
"Good morning," said the railway switchman.
"What do you do here?" the little prince asked.
"I sort out travelers, in bundles of a thousand," said the switchman. "I send off the trains that carry them: now to the right, now to the left."
And a brilliantly lighted express train shook the switchman's cabin as it rushed by with a roar like thunder.
"They are in a great hurry," said the little prince. "What are they looking for?"
"Not even the locomotive engineer knows that," said the switchman.
And a second brilliantly lighted express thundered by, in the opposite direction.
"Are they coming back already?" demanded the little prince.
"These are not the same ones," said the switchman. "It is an exchange."
"Were they not satisfied where they were?" asked the little prince.
"No one is ever satisfied where he is," said the switchman.
And they heard the roaring thunder of a third brilliantly lighted express.
"Are they pursuing the first travelers?" demanded the little prince.
"They are pursuing nothing at all," said the switchman. "They are asleep in there, or if they are not asleep they are yawning. Only the children are flattening their noses against the windowpanes."
"Only the children know what they are looking for," said the little prince. "They waste their time over a rag doll and

143

it becomes very important to them; and if anybody takes it away from them, they cry . . .”

"They are lucky," the switchman said.[43]

To know how to waste time, like children. Is this the highest level of wisdom and that which is most lacking nowadays? Yes—because time, for us adults, inevitably accelerates with the years, so that we can no longer linger to pick a rose or a daisy, to pluck off its petals, to unfold its mystery! Should we not at least impose upon time this "beneficial" pace, this ancient rhythm which made it possible to insert into it the "rituals" that punctuated life? We are in such a hurry that we have forgotten the slow and meaningful movements that made it possible to gather in the wheat and store it for bad days. The sweetness of stops, restoring its density to the instant, is now denied to us. Fabien will have to be lost in the storm and a corner of sky will have to appear to him between the accumulated mass of the clouds before—suspended between life and death—he will be granted a few minutes of contemplation:

"In a flash, the very instant he had risen clear, the pilot found a peace that passed his understanding. Not a ripple tilted the plane but, like a ship that has crossed the bar, it moved across a tranquil anchorage. In an unknown and secret corner of the sky it floated, as in a harbor of the Happy Isles. Below him still the storm was fashioning another world, thridded with squalls and cloudbursts and lightnings, but turning to the stars a face of crystal snow."[44]

And suddenly, after this dense second of an almost supernatural joy, Fabien realizes he is lost. We do not know whether,

[43] Antoine de Saint-Exupéry, The Little Prince, trans. by Katherine Woods (New York: Harcourt, Brace & World, 1943), pp. 71–73.

[44] Saint-Exupéry, Night Flight, trans. by Stuart Gilbert (New York: Signet, 1942), p. 103.

144

having reached this limit where no friendly look, no loving thought could reach him any longer, he shared in the joyful acceptance of the Little Prince. For the child knew that he merely had to abandon a little dust, a few atoms of flesh on this earth, to see again the love shining in the heart of a unique flower. Fabien will wander among the treasure of the accumulated stars before resolutely setting out for the world beyond. There was only one way out: to climb, climb again, keep on climbing, until the soul has proved and deserved its immortality by this deliberate act of heroism.[45]

[45] On Saint-Exupéry, cf. the work of Clément Borgal, appearing in the Editions du Centurion, and that of André A. Devaux, published by Desclée de Brouwer (in the collection "Les Ecrivains devant Dieu"), Paris, 1965.

6
In the Desert of Nihilism

One of the essential qualities that make man different from the
rest of nature is his awareness of the ephemeral nature of life, of
its beginning and of its end and, consequently, of the value of
time, a subjective and amazingly variable element that is completely governed by ethics, if one considers the use that is made of
it, so that a very small amount of time may represent a very large
one. The matter in some celestial bodies is so dense that a cubic
inch of it would weigh as much as twenty quintals on this planet.
And thus it is with the time of "men-creators." It differs in structure, density and fecundity from the easy-flowing time of most
people; and when he sees the great number of achievements that
can be fitted into time, the man in the street is likely to ask: "But
where do you find the time?"
. . . Man is free to sanctify time, he can treat it as a field that
needs to be cultivated with the greatest of care, he can consider
it as a field of activity, of incessant endeavor, of self-improvement,
of progression toward the fulfillment of his highest abilities and,
with its help, he can extract the unperishable from the ephemeral.

Thomas Mann[1]

*N*o writer, no existentialist philosopher has gone further
than Georges Bataille in yielding to dizziness, in the analysis
of the absurd, of nothingness.[2] Others who made a name for
themselves or even became famous simulated rather than
really felt this dizziness, which was but an idea for them rather
that something they actually experienced: the dilettantism of
horror is very popular these days.

[1] Cf. "Lob der Vergänglichkeit" (Eulogy of the Ephemeral) in
Thomas Mann, Gesammelte Werke, Bd. X (Frankfurt: S. Fischer,
1960), pp. 383–385.

[2] We will not deal here with the existential philosophers, such as
Martin Heidegger, in spite of the importance of their message. The
complexity of their analyses would require too lengthy an account.
We will spend more time on those who are influenced by Kierkegaard.

In the works of Bataille on the contrary, as in those of Julien Gracq, there are pages which cannot deceive us, though they may leave a strenuous, ambiguous impression. Bataille is thus somewhat different from the other "tormented" thinkers who were inspired by Nietzsche: first of all because of his interpretation of the *Joyful Wisdom* which he repeated on several occasions.[3] In his view, "the death of God" is the supreme sacrifice but a pointless sacrifice that makes absolutely no difference. It does not emancipate man in any way; he remains at the mercy of a necessity of which death is the undecipherable experience. What would happen if consciousness were no longer intermittent and memory could recover these successive existences obsessed with the will to be imprisoned henceforth in the Nessus cloak of individuality? It was in vain that Nietzsche tried to transform into joy that which can be nothing but an unbearable anguish, like that of Faulkner's characters when they are compelled to watch their life unfold *backward* from the moment it is about to leave them. Far from reproducing the carefree laughter of a child at play, this joy is but an atrocious sneering permanently set on our face by our suffering, a new mask which Ensor, the master of the ludicrous, will put on the face of Christ.

But Bataille brings us even lower, to the very bottom of the spiral. Pascal emphasized our "tragic" condition: We are "embarked" without having asked for it, so that this life and the consciousness that reflects upon it are not for us the result of a choice. Now, life involves more than itself and its ephemeral duration; we must "wager" for or against its meaning, for or against our "soul," whereas we only seek amusements and try to forget our miserable condition in the turmoil of easy entertainments or by being constantly on the go—like those travelers whose behavior puzzled the Little Prince. At least the

[3] Cf. his work on "Nietzsche."

"trial" we must face—to use the same word as Kierkegaard—can, according to the author of the *Pensées*, allow us to gain eternal beatitude. God remains the guarantor of the value of existence; we must be fully "man," but not "angel"[4] or Superman.

But if God no longer exists, we are driven to a useless heroism, unless, like Kirilov, we opt for suicide in order to prove to ourselves that we are free, gratuitously free. Calculate, says Bataille, the infinite improbability of our life in this world and the imperceptible moment our performance will last, from the crib to the tomb, and you will be stricken with terror. How infinitesimal was the chance—if one can call it that!—that "I rather than another should be endowed with the form and the feeling of my individual existence. Another second, a postponed encounter, and I would not have existed: "I," that is, that person who I am or think I am, who has become so fond of his differences as to want to be "for himself" and to mold himself! A ridiculous ambition if my existence is both indeterminate and determinant, if after depending upon an unlikely series of coincidences, it now imprisons me in a rigorous "ipseity." Time sweeps me along and neither my mind nor my will can hold me above it. I will have to "live" my death—which I see getting closer and closer—as a "personal" adventure in which all that exists, having been abolished all of a sudden, will be as though it had never existed; whereas society, by the words it uses, gives it an "anonymous" status: In the eyes of society I will be "deceased," cut away by a certificate from the world of the living, from those who will go on laughing, loving, suffering. At my birth a parenthesis was opened; it is waiting for the second stroke that will bring it to an end. At times of greater consciousness, the anticipation of this

---

[4] "He who wants to act as an angel, acts the fool." (*Qui veut faire l'ange fait la bête.*)

event toward which I am "hurled" fills me with "nausea."[5]

To depict this state that is mine, which remains incommunicable, since each one of us lives his own drama and that of other people remains—however close—unknown to him, Bataille uses striking formulas. The destiny of man, he tells us, is despicable. And yet "there has always been in some an inflexible will—though it may be deferred—to go further than is possible to man." Thus, apart from the mass that is resigned to its fate, from the herd that allows itself to be led to the slaughterhouse, there stands the lucid man, the Superman who wants, with an unbending will, to use these hours that have ended almost as soon as they began to reach his personal fulfillment. But what would be the purpose of this fulfillment? What is the sense in hurling oneself toward the future, in striving toward an exalted image of oneself, in forcing oneself to become—through a sort of heroic wager—for oneself and for oneself alone, a superior man or a saint, if this impetus is destined to fall back, wasted, like the water in a fountain. Will is illusory in its two conflicting efforts: that which carries it toward being as well as that which annihilates it in nonwill. For nonwill derives from the despair of not being able to surpass the others and rise higher than they; it conceals, behind its appearance of detachment, the positive will from which it originates.

No one has displayed the futility of this tormenting search for the absolute better than Bataille. Once more he takes up the theme of the "double," as Edgar Poe and Oscar Wilde present it with William Wilson and Dorian Gray. But he

[5] The analysis of "nausea" is something different for Jean-Paul Sartre. It is the sense of existing "for nothing," of being abandoned—left there like a useless object—which makes Roquentin feel "nauseous." And Sartre's novels abound in these useless or trivial gestures which increase in us this sense of utter futility. *The Wall*, in particular, is very close to Kafka's *Metamorphosis*.

149

carries it even further toward the absurd; the dreadful twin brother of the Abbé C. . . , his demoniac element which was separated from him only in appearance at the time of their common birth, seeks to destroy him, to enjoy his slow degradation. Even Kafka, except perhaps in the *Metamorphosis*, never went so low in the profanation of that which is noblest and most sacred in us: I am thinking of that dreadful final sweep. As for Monsieur Ouine, he was destroyed by his own spinelessness. Does he or does he not exist? The question arises at the very first page. But the sorry hero of Bataille delights in erasing from his brother's face that which he should love most. But is there something more in this essay than a play of "reflections," the struggle between two ghosts in the empty setting of a deceptive universe? Imprisoned by his consciousness, man casts his shadow in front of himself, he identifies himself with it, and, for a few moments, thinks it is alive. But let him be careful when ecstasy comes within his reach. This ecstacy opens up only onto despair: "It is in this tragic, artificial world that ecstasy is born."

But this ecstasy is only fictitious and art alone can grasp it. It is also in a world carried to the culmination of the tragic that the sublime vision of Goya will arise:

"Goya," says André Malraux, "proclaims a new right of the painter: that of madness. He himself is fascinated by it . . . and his intermittent deafness . . . is merely a forerunner of the disaster. What makes the voice of these madmen so authoritative . . . is that it is the ancient religious lament of wasted suffering, encountered for the first time perhaps by a man who believes himself indifferent to God."[6]

But, adds Pierre de Boisdeffre, this horror has degrees, steps which the artist, driven to madness by his purposeless lucidity,

[6] *Saturne*, N.R.F. Les Galeries de la Pléiade. "But the voice," he goes on, "that is beginning to fill his ever-deepening silence is not only his own; it is the long-vanished voice of Spain."

will inexorably descend. Little by little, Goya's devils will find their true form: "the atrocious." His "Caprices" will become "Disasters," and his "Disasters" will become "Disparates": the executioners have become ghosts, but the absurd is not exorcised—on the contrary. With his anthropophagous Saturn in the *Deaf Man's House*, Goya reaches the limits of his universe. Henceforth he will be haunted mercilessly by fear and by death.[7]

Bataille also heard these despondent voices. He too heard the specter's announcement: "*Nada*, nothing."[8] He is surrounded by the masks of death, those which Ensor depicted, huddled up around a cold stove in an attempt to warm their frozen bones:

"The distressing nature of death [this death for which time, for Bataille, is more than a symbol: the actual experience], shows the need man feels for anguish. Without this need, death would seem easy to him. . . . Man, by not knowing how to die, turns away from nature; he creates a world that is imaginary, human, fabricated by art: We are living in this tragic world, in this unhappy atmosphere of which tragedy is but the perfected form. Nothing is tragic for the animal who does not fall in the trap of the 'I.'"

It is perhaps this need to yield to anguish, which had finally become the very sustenance of his soul, that prevented Bataille from reaching another ecstasy: that which, in exchange for the sacrifice of what is most superficial in the "I," raises the soul beyond its finiteness.[9]

[7] Pierre de Boisdeffre, *A. Malraux* (Paris: Editions du Universitaires). Cf. also: Jeanne Delhomme, *A. Malraux*: "Temps et Destin," Essais (Paris: Gallimard).

[8] Cf. Baudelaire, *Quelques caricaturistes étrangers, Goya*, in his *Oeuvres*, Vol. II, p. 208.

[9] Cf. our work: *Les Dimensions de l'être et du temps* (Lyon-Paris: Vitte, 1953).

At times it seems that the thaw might set in. It would have been enough for him to relax, to enjoy what life has to offer when we allow it to invade us and invite us to be absorbed in beauty rather than in nothingness. After an illness, Bataille went to Italy to convalesce:

"I left Rome early and spent the night in Stresa. The following day was particularly beautiful and I decided to stay there. The great lake surrounded by mountains glimmered like a mirage in the spring light. It was lovely and warm; I lingered under palm trees, in gardens full of flowers . . . Suddenly, some infinitely majestic voices, both agitated and self-confident, burst forth, calling up to heaven. I remained stricken at first, not knowing what these voices were; a moment of ecstasy passed by before I understood that a loudspeaker was broadcasting the mass. In the harbor I found a bench from which I could enjoy the magnificent scenery that retained its transparency under the morning sun. I stayed there for the whole mass. The choir was the purest, the richest in the world; the music overpoweringly beautiful. The voices rose like successive and varied waves, slowly reaching incredible peaks of intensity, precipitation and richness, but at the very moment all seemed to be lost, they rose again by some miracle in a sparkling crescendo of shattering crystal."

And yet the crescendo of this song carried to its climax by the "tall flames of children's voices" will not lead his soul, freed at last from its tragic isolation, to a Transcendent which would reassure and comfort him. It only symbolizes the fleeting triumph of man:

"This was no Christian suffering but an exaltation of the gifts with which man overcame countless difficulties (in the technique of singing and of choirs in particular). The sacred character of the incantation merely added a sense of power, merely proclaimed more emphatically, to the point of breaking, the elating presence of man exulting at his own certainty and full of confidence in his infinite opportunities."

It is this same sense of a fleeting superiority, obtained this time by turning to the demiurgic powers, which we find in the finale of the demoniac Symphony of Leverkühn, the hero of Thomas Mann's *Doctor Faustus.* We have reached the extreme limit of a tension which it would be dangerous to maintain; desperately, the aspiration to another world is trying to escape from the infernal circles in which it is imprisoned. But hope dies away like a flickering flame, and only some sharp notes burst forth, trying to shatter the obscure wall of sounds. For Leverkühn as for Bataille, the "torment" will be eternal, and its coming, its imminence, is such that we wish for it to be postponed no longer:

"Life will lose itself in death, the rivers in the sea, and the known in the unknown. Knowledge is the gate to the unknown. Non-sense is the outcome of every possible sense."[10]

The buffoon imitating—supreme irony!—the wavering progression of the Superman casts him into the abyss by unveiling the mirage. Since Christian humanism, which had supported the rise of the steeple with the strength of the buttress, has been rejected, there is only one way out: renunciation of one's individual "I." Man must let himself be swallowed up in a collective aspiration. Then perhaps he may be enriched with all these converging forces. But Bataille dismisses this way out. For him, only the "individual I" exists, and this "I" is being invaded ever more by the nothingness from which it originated: Life is but the experience—both long and short—of this nothingness. Against this way out—or rather against this presence that is endured, though paradoxically also sought after—laughter, humor, are the ultimate means of liberation.[11]

[10] Bataille, *L'Expérience intérieure* (Paris: Gallimard), pp. 95 and 129.

[11] Cf. in particular the analyses of Julius Bahnsen, a disciple of Schopenhauer.

The stage and the spectators all fade away and vanish in their insignificance if we look at them through the wrong end of the glasses. Since we are born, at least let us not take life seriously. But is it possible to devaluate life in this way, and do we not see arising from this indefinitely increased contrast the desperate demands of our being. The recurrence of non-sense makes the search for sense even more desperate. It is in vain that we dismantle the mechanism and dissipate all the spells. We are still left with the "paradox" of a condition that cannot reach fulfillment in time.

What is of greatest interest to me in Sartre—more than the persuasive power of the rhetor and the skill of the dialectician who, through words, juggles with ideas, even more than the skill of the producer who knows how to make good use of the diversity of perspectives to reinforce his *trompe-l'oeil* effects, and also more than the ability of the dramatist to make ancient myths express present-day problems—is how, unknown to himself, the unexpressed signification of his works lies beyond his avowed intentions. This is of course true of all works of value: the future reveals the richness of their tone, the polyvalence of their meaning. But the contrast is more pronounced here between that which is brutally asserted to the face of an imaginary contradictor, "the bourgeois"—but where begins the "bourgeois"?—and that which remains veiled: an anxiety he will never confess, a sense of guilt that obstinately lingers on. One would not attack God with such violence were it *not suspected* that he had survived the blows of his murderers. It is too easy to replace him by his inconsistent prefiguration, a mere reflection of the reason of state, Zeus. If the look of other people invincibly transforms me into a "thing," deprives me of my freedom, petrifies me, and arouses feelings of hostility between us, if I myself cannot turn toward them without hitting back in a merciless duel, is it not because man has lost all humanity, because all ties are broken, as they

154

might be severed in a family where dissension between the parents is clear for all to see?

Saint-Exupéry strived to trace the intimate interrelations, the warm flow of persistent affinities, beneath the master-slave relationship, beneath this almost instinctive effort at appropriation which makes us inclined to use the other person as a tool. He was able to discern the true cause of an alienation of which we are all, at some time or other, the victim:

"I understand the origin of brotherhood among men. Men were brothers in God. One can be brother only *in* something. Where there is no tie that binds men, men are not united but merely lined up. One cannot be a brother to nobody. The pilots of Group 2–33 are brothers in the Group. Frenchmen are brothers in France."[12]

Communities are but the reflection of this universal community which tends to regroup around God. "As the inheritor of God, my civilization made men to be brothers in Man."

The house that is no longer welcoming, that has fallen back into itself, closed upon itself, as we sometimes see it depicted in children's drawings, has nothing much in common with the house built by the father of the family, in which traditions were observed, in which the family gods presided over the rituals: "Vast was my father's palace, with one wing set apart for the women and a secret inner garden where a fountain sang, the focal place of goings out and of comings in. . . . Else, a man is nowhere."[13]

[12] Antoine de Saint-Exupéry, *Flight to Arras*, (London: Heinemann, 1955), p. 151. "I understand the meaning of the duties of charity which were preached to me. Charity was the service of God performed through the individual. It was a thing owed to God, however insignificant the individual who was its recipient. Charity never humiliated him who profited from it, nor even bound him by the chains of gratitude, since it was not to him but to God that the gift was made."

[13] Saint-Exupéry, *The Wisdom of the Sands* (New York: Harcourt, Brace, 1950), p. 16. Cf. also p. 17; "I can hear the voice of the fool,

Where are we but nowhere in our cells that open onto end-less halls, cells from which we have but one desire: to escape, but to go everywhere and nowhere!

And yet, in order that a divided universe be transformed and created anew, all that is necessary is a little goodwill, a mere spark of love. Hostility then suddenly gives way and the snowdrifts begin to melt. This is what Henri Alain-Fournier is telling us in his "Miracle of the Three Village Ladies." Behind frost-covered panes, in the drawing room of a little provincial house, three highly respectable ladies are discussing their daily cares; but what really attracted the two visitors is the imminence of a scandal everyone is talking about, and their curiosity is sharpened by their friend's silence. How they would like to know where her niece is, this young girl whose misbehavior is causing more and more scandal! Suddenly there is a hubbub in the street that previously lay deserted under the snow. And the three ladies have rushed outside, sensing the cause of the disturbance. Indeed, on the window of another house, two silhouettes are outlined, one of them that of a naked young girl. But, as the ladies draw closer, the turmoil subsides; purified attitudes become fixed as in a stained-glass window, and finally there remains, in a universe restored to its original innocence, only the eternal symbol of love.[14]

In much the same way, Milosz' Miguel de Manara will be saved by the innocence of Girolame. We are very far indeed from the petrifying gaze of the Medusa, from the forbidding

saying: see how much space is wasted here, what wealth left unex-ploited, what conveniences lost through inadvertence! Far better were it to lay low those useless walls and level out those short flights of steps, which merely hinder progress. Then men will be free. But I make answer: Then men will become like cattle in the marketplace. . . ."

[14] The particulars of Alain-Fournier's story are slightly different from those related here; however, the spirit of the story is conveyed very well.—Ed. English edition

and secretive look, from the mask of hatred and envy on the faces in Van der Weyden's *Crucifixion!*[15] And also from Heidegger's dialectic of the "one," or the even more impersonal and objective "it" of Buber, in which the person sinks into the anonymity of indifference and scorn!

"Yes you are right, Girolame; I am no longer as I used to be. I can see better, and yet I was not blind; but there was not enough light, for exterior light is very little indeed. That is not how our lives are illuminated. You have lit a lamp in my heart; and now I am like a sick man who falls asleep with the burning coal of fever on his brow and the ice of defeat in his heart, and then suddenly awakens in a beautiful room where all things are bathed in the calm music of light."

Alas! the light that illuminates the world of Sartre is not that of the lamp near which our hearts are warmed and confidences are exchanged as our eyes are filled with pity and tenderness. It is not even the light full of spirituality in which the hills of Lake Maggiore fade away and from which arose one day, for Bataille, an ascending and triumphant chant. It is harsh electric light, tearing the eyes, baring the heart, and imposing its merciless presence! Ruthlessly it reveals all secrets that hitherto had been able to shelter in the darkness.

That life is sacred, this is clear to the fanatics; Dostoevski already said that certain crimes, in spite of an affected intrepidity, leave a permanent mark on those who perpetrate them. Orestes, even to the face of his creator, will testify to it. To the face of Zeus, he wanted to be God; he claims to have begun with his actions; his existence preceded his essence; he is as it has made him. In a dialogue in which we can recognize the voice of Nietzsche—though carried to the excess of deliberate brutality—he too proclaims the innocence of becoming;

---

[15] In the Prado of Madrid. Cf. also the atrocious *Bearing of the Cross* by Jerome Bosch.

he brushes away remorse as one would drive away "flies," with the back of the hand. Once the many-faceted mirror of his moral consciousness is destroyed, the emancipated man arises, alone and free. This man, free from all ties, laughs at the terrifying Erinyes:

"I would like," Mathieu will say, "to take only after myself."

But, on the contrary, as soon as man dwells upon his actions, as soon as he allows this Medusa's head to rise before him, he irremediably dooms and alienates himself; like the Baudelaire imagined by Sartre—a very different Baudelaire from the disciple of Swedenborg, from the admirer of the physiognomist Lavater—he lets himself get entangled in his past. Orestes refuses to be such a man; if he turns to his past, it is in order to master it; he is the man of his destiny only so as to impose his image upon it; he refuses to be "the man without immediacy" in whom "the slightest desires are already deciphered, already inspected before they ever see the light."

And thus Sartre goes even further than Gide, who, having discarded the level of moral consciousness at which the other people intrude upon us,[16] wanted to leave enough knowledge, enough lucidity so that the *nourritures terrestres* may still be enjoyed, to the full extent of the new desires. Sartre's man, devoid of essence and without original structure, also yields with delight to the call of spring, until his destiny catches up with him. Then Orestes will have to be Orestes but by a free choice. The Nietzschean themes have thus become more definite and have been enlarged: that of the gratuitous nature of the concepts of good and evil, for instance. The hero, the Superman must not allow these concepts to paralyze him; Goetz's misfortunes will begin as soon as he lets himself be hindered by scruples. Besides, in this absurd world, suffering can result from good as well as from evil. Fate often connives to make upright intentions lead to consequences that are far

[16] A. Gide, *The Immoralist.*

158

worse than those of deliberate selfishness. As for Franz, would he have wandered in the labyrinths of madness if some secret weakness had not caused doubts to rise in him which his father had never experienced? And Orestes, is he really as fearless as he claims? Is it really "precious," this burden he will have to carry? Pride still conceals from him the horror of the crime he has committed. But already the ludicrous "flies" that have set out after him have been transformed—through a "lapsus calami" of his creator perhaps—into the vengeful Erinyes. A contradiction is becoming apparent; a flaw undermines his affected self-confidence; the sense of a "guilt" that will upset his entire being will sneak in through this flaw. One day, Orestes, like the father in *Six Characters in Search of an Author*, will protest because people will see in him only the man of the fateful hour in which, obeying his destiny, he killed his mother.

Sophocles, with more insight and less faith in this absolute freedom, had called human laws, inspired by a more understanding "justice," to the rescue of Oedipus, who had been driven from his own country by a fateful crime. Oedipus, who punished himself for his belated lucidity, will find peace in Attica, where moderation has come to soften the decrees of the ancient Ananke. Will Orestes ever find peace, he who, because he wanted to be what he was, condemned himself to being "a king without a kingdom, without subjects"? And his alleged freedom, like that of Pirandello's characters, has it not been foreseen in the cycles of Eternal Recurrence?

In fact, the law is not imposed upon us from outside by a God who—like the Zeus of *The Flies*—would arbitrarily rule over the world; it is written in the heart of each one of us; conscience is this "accurate" balance which, as long as sin has not tampered with it, will tell us the true value of our actions. The anonymous artist of Niederrotweil understood this very well, witness his representation of the devils' vain attempt to drag

the souls of the just down to the abyss: The scale they are trying to pull down rises again on its own accord, and the fraud
becomes apparent.[17] Though Shakespeare, unlike Sophocles,
allows passion to be the mainspring of crime, those who have
yielded to it will be tortured by remorse and, like Hamlet
and Macbeth, pursued by ghosts. The fate of the prisoners in
No Exit or The Condemned of Altona will be even worse.
Hell, says Sartre, is created for me by the hostile presence of
other people. This "objectification" of which Berdyaev will
later detect the true source—egoism—is, according to Sartre,
only the inevitable consequence of the refusal of other people
to "accept me as a living and autonomous person." Hell therefore would be "the other people."

Merely by his contact the "other person" alienates me; he
takes away from me, by his presence alone, the portion of universe I wanted to claim for myself. It is true that Francis Jeanson has tried, with great skill, to tone down the brutality of
this assertion and claims that Sartre is in fact merely acknowledging the tendency in each one of us to appropriate as many
things as possible, to increase our property indefinitely, unavoidably at the expense of someone else—hence the attitudes
of permanent suspicion and constant hostility in a world that
has become a jungle. The society described in this way by the
existentialist Sartre would be the "bourgeois," the capitalistic
society, which the Marxists had good reason to condemn.
Once more Berdyaev will be more clear-sighted. In his view,
"embourgeoisement" is a "structure" of man which is already
apparent in his childhood and which no society can hope to
avoid.

The characters of No Exit are not dead, Jeanson adds, since
they are able to speak. But how can we be so sure that we
will not be able to speak in this universe in which we will no

[17] The Weighing of the Souls, altar in the church of Niederrotweil
(Baden).

longer be able to "act," in which we will remain as death caught us, in our last movement, our supreme attitude? This impersonal room in which three beings who did not know one another are condemned to live together without any hope of forgiveness or escape—if it is not hell, then it has very much indeed in common with it. It is true that sometimes jealousy and hatred lock us up, even in this life, in an identical prison; but up to the very last minute we are free to escape from it. Mercy was close by, ready to save the good thief of Calvary. Alas! the actions and the words of Garcin, Estelle, and Inez are are merely echoes; they are fixed in an "essence" in which lies their petrified freedom. It is in vain that each one of the "damned"—with the exception of Inez—will seek and beg for contact with the companions that have been forced upon him. A single minute of compassion and oblivion of their own misery would be enough to switch off the artificial light, while the flame that would transfigure everything would light up in their heart. But these prisoners will dwell endlessly upon the crime which they see reflected relentlessly on the "wall of apparitions."[18]

In these amazing monologues, from which a dialogue will never evolve, each one of these unfortunates is thinking only of himself. They will live—so to speak—side by side, exasperated by the projection of their monstrous egoism. But there are degrees of abjection: Dante's inferno had its circles; that of Sartre has its cells without jailer. Each person sinks into his own, indifferent to the suffering of others. Salvation is still within reach, but no one will ever say the redeeming word. It will not be Estelle, too preoccupied with her appearance; Garcin is floundering in his cowardice; Inez, who is fustigating

[18] We can sense here the influence of Pirandello. Mimi also, in *Tonight We Improvise*, is imprisoned in Verri's jealousy. And the shadows of the other people appear to her on a wall that is at times diaphanous like a screen.

him, is sinking even more irreparably in the swamp of hatred: "You're a coward, Garcin, because I wish it. I wish it—do you hear?—I wish it. And yet, just look at me, see how weak I am, a mere breath on the air, a gaze observing you, a formless thought that thinks you."

And thus the timid attempt of the weakest one of them will be rejected, just as Orestes cast away a repentant Electra who refused to recognize herself in a single temptation. Would Sartre's admiration go to the ruthless Inez? This woman who refuses the light, who rejects all help, whether human or divine?

> GARCIN (timidly): And now suppose we start trying to help each other.
> INEZ: I don't need help.

The jailer can go away; the door can open and reveal the endless empty hall lined with the cells of other prisoners. The culprits will not leave their room; they will go on tearing each other to pieces; they will perhaps acquire a taste for hating one another and live on this hatred, each one dwelling upon the crime he has committed. The conclusion, very different from that which Sartre would have us believe, will be formulated by the dreadful Inez:

> GARCIN: I died too soon. I wasn't allowed time to—to do my deeds.
> INEZ: One always dies too soon—or too late. And yet one's whole life is complete at that moment, with a line drawn neatly under it, ready for the summing up. You are—your life, and nothing else.

Is this the outcome of this "total" freedom with which we were born? By a strange paradox, the hell it would create, in this world or in the next, would be such that those who have to endure it would beg for another punishment; they would much rather the traditional forms of torture:

> GARCIN: Open the door! Open, blast you! I'll endure anything, your red-hot tongs and molten lead, your racks and prongs and garrotes—all your fiendish gadgets, everything that burns and flays and tears—I'll put up with any torture you impose. Anything, anything would be better than this agony of mind, this creeping pain that gnaws and fumbles and caresses one and never hurts quite enough.[19]

Finally, caught between his "existential" condition, an original status he did not choose, and a freedom he does not know what to do with, man has only one way out: to choose a "structure" that will allow him to fulfill his human destiny. For Sartre there is only one liberating choice: that offered by communism,[20] though it must be taken in a completely different perspective. Marxism is wrong in asking us to bend our will to an orientation that is already inscribed in historical becoming. Of what value would be a choice that entailed no risks? What would become of a freedom which would be considered valid and effective only if it chose to follow an evolution that would occur with or without this choice? The ethics of being must be replaced by an ethics of "praxis." We must build a better world in which men will become more aware

---

[19] Sartre, *No Exit*, trans. by Stuart Gilbert (New York: Knopf, 1947) p. 38, 58, 55. It would be interesting to compare *No Exit* with Selma Lagerlöf's *Ghost Cart*. There also we are dealing with a trip into hell. But the dead can still be saved, and, in the end, the holiness and the self-sacrifice of the woman who still loves him in spite of his failings will bring him back home, after a year's ride in the cart of Death.

[20] In a more structurally sound form of thought, an Italian philosopher, Nicola Abbagnano, set himself the same question.

of their rights and will be more free. It is only on this condition that existentialism will found a humanism, on this condition also that it will be able to propose to mankind guides with a clearer vision of its future. There is a constant correlation between the "I" and the universe, the "I" being merely "the inner quality which a freedom gives itself through the changes it performs in the world." Would Sartre's conclusion be that of Canoris, who reproaches his companion Henri with asking too many questions: "You worry too much about yourself, Henri; you want to save your life. Bah! just keep on working; salvation comes in the bargain."

To work, to be ready to sacrifice oneself for a "cause," would this be the last word of an existentialism which, though it claims otherwise, would find a solution in Marxism alone? Strange indeed is the fate of this freedom which claimed to be the beginning of everything. Is it not condemned either to fold up upon itself and feed on its eternal torment, or to renounce the initial gift it brought by surrendering to the collectivity, or rather also to depend for survival only on the risk involved in its generous wager? Imprisoned in a web of contradictions, Sartre's existentialism is of value only by the confession of its shortcomings. He thinks he can get out of the wood by calling those who criticize him "swine" or "slimy rats." But arguments on the meaning of "words" will not lend coherency to a rhetoric worthy of the sophist Prodicos!

There is less rhetoric and much more sincerity in the works of Albert Camus. For a long time their paths ran parallel; little by little they diverged, until the final polemic which was prematurely interrupted by the death of Camus. The tragic events in which he was involved left their mark on Camus— even more than on Sartre. Unlike so many others, he refused to take the easy way out and dissociate himself from them. The very fate of man was being settled. Man was at stake, or rather—and the drama had started with the atrocious Spanish war—he was at the stake. But Camus was to endure yet another suffering: that which opposed his Algerian land to the French mainland; it is because he understood the complexity of the drama better than Sartre that he did not think fit to adopt the easy solution of defeatism. He did not yield to the temptation of masochism. With his natural generosity, he endeavored to reconcile the irreconcilable. Sooner or later his call would have been heard. But what can be done when passions are unleashed? When the past that one thought could be enclosed in a narrative suddenly awakens at the level of behavior and reflexes? Is it not an illusion to believe that an insurrection—and the revolution that follows—can deeply modify the social structures generated by the tensions and conflicts due to human nature? Once the revolution is over and new institutions are set up, it all begins again, the only difference being that yesterday's lovers of justice have now become executioners. The state is the same, whether it is expressing the interests of a caste, of a class, or those of the proletariate. Thus Camus—and this will be the theme of his conflict with Sartre and Jeanson—will adopt Proudhon's main objection to Karl Marx. Alienation does not vanish because power has changed hands. The proletariate will in turn secrete its managers and its leaders—or the tyrant who replaces them—like the oyster secretes its pearl.

Now Camus could not tolerate injustice: He felt that a permanent rebellion was the only way to fight it. A useless rebellion, it was objected. At least, he answered, it preserves the rights which others defend only to better confiscate them to their advantage, invoking the state as their alibi. Once the revolution has succeeded, abuses will return, even worse than before; only the beneficiaries have changed. Officials will be even more numerous, making power even more inhuman, so that the condoned crimes will become merely statistics. But the legal crime in which resentment is given free rein is the

165

worst crime of all. This is what Camus tried to show in *The Stranger*. What must we think of these logical connections that are wound around the actions of a poor man who fluctuates at the mercy of his impressions? After the events, a series of motives is reconstructed where there was only a discontinuity of causes. This unfortunate victim of successive impressions or contradictory impulses is called on to account for his intentions! A person is condemned because it seems more convenient to assert his unity and identity, whereas he merely drifts at the mercy of his impulses. We want to transform an intermittently conscious sleepwalker—who forgets his sorrow at the sight of a deserted beach shimmering in the sun and who will later be made uneasy by the sudden glimpse of a shining blade—into a being who has premeditated his crime and has succeeded in carrying it out according to a careful plan! A stranger among other people, a stranger in his own family, a stranger unknown to himself, astounded at the pseudo-portrait society is trying to force upon him—such is the mediocre hero of this unhappy story reflecting only hesitation and uncertainty.

It is true—and Camus himself warns us of this fact—that the "seriousness" of his novels, and even more of his plays, is tinted with a certain humor.[21] Does this humor arise, as Pirandello claims,[22] from a more intense sense of contrasts, from the combination of an unbounded imagination and a critical mind that laughs and scoffs at its illusions? In this case it would only have subjective roots and at the extreme limit would be merely an idealism which dissolves consciousness and transforms the world into a simple play of representations —an insubstantial play in a mirror, reflections in a reflection.

[21] During an interview in 1958, Jean-Claude Brisville asked, "Is there in your work a theme which you feel has been overlooked by your commentators?" Camus answered: "Humor."

[22] Pirandello, *L'Umorismo* (Milan: Mondadori).

166

But this is not the humor of Camus; his world is substantial, though it may be opaque. It is composed of a set of realities, of objects against which man stumbles. The image of the cell, of the prison, arises quite naturally. The plague has imprisoned us in a city we can no longer leave. Alas! Oran was this city infested by a monstrous plague during which men were forced to die like rats, while the civil war was raging within its walls.

Did Camus have a foreboding of this drama when he wrote his novel? It is likely that he saw the first signs of the strange universe that was about to come. A cliff isolates Oran from the sea and compels it to look out toward endless expanses. This is why it appears to the writer as the symbol of the world in which we are imprisoned. Other cities have great harbors opening onto the expanse of the sea, an invitation to escape. Oran's harbor, separated from the city by a mountain, is but a casemate; Oran is closed, shut up in itself; there is nothing to encourage one to set out on the sea; it seems to be condemned to retire into its shell, waiting for an apocalypse or for the terrified flight of the rats.

But no more than Sisyphus succeeds in holding back his stone on the slope that pulls it down will man succeed in leaving the city where he is merely granted a reprieve. And even if he were to leave it, he would still find this same closed horizon! Even if he were to enlarge his prison to the limits of the universe, this cover about which Baudelaire complained would still be weighing down upon him! There is no possible escape or salvation in the sense of space-time—in which we are forever contained and which also lies within us since it is the very stuff of our corporeal being.

Camus will not draw all the possible consequences of this splendid intuition, since from the very beginning he seems to have excluded the other way out. He is obsessed by evil in its most unbearable form: that of the persecution of children. His

167

yearning for happiness cannot unfold as long as he is haunted by all the crimes that are perpetrated, all the injustices that are committed. One would like to go to the sea; it is there, quite close, in a glistening of foam and sea gulls. But a state of siege has been proclaimed. Kafka's architect wandered endlessly in the passages of a labyrinth, among indifferent or frightened people; one could sense the castle, one could almost see it, but it remained out of reach. The characters in *The State of Siege* are labeled; they are the victims of an inventory so carefully compiled as to make it impossible to escape it; the register office decides ahead of time how long they will live and what they will have to do. They are forbidden to live their own life, to exist by themselves; they are in the same position as Mathias Pascal after his corpse had been identified. Pirandello's little dog, on the contrary, is alive, since it is obliged to pay taxes. Pirandellian humor is both burlesque and ferocious; that of Camus is even more biting, hardly softened by a touch of pity: "Even in the dock," the Stranger will say, "it is always interesting to hear people talking about you."

Such is the disillusioned and cruel irony in *The State of Siege*, in the dreadful *Caligula*, and in the atrocious *Misunderstanding*, in which asphyxiation by horror is carried to its extreme. In these works we stumble against "that denseness and that strangeness of the world which is the absurd."[23] We are these unfortunate people who ignore one another, who do not know one another, who live without even being able to try and unite in a hostile universe, who accuse one another to discover a meaning for their suffering. Our greatness comes only from the useless refusal we oppose to that which appears to us unintelligible:

[23] Albert Camus, *The Myth of Sisyphus and Other Essays* (New York: Alfred Knopf, 1967), p. 14.

"I establish my lucidity in the midst of what negates it. I exalt man before what crushes him, and my freedom, my revolt, and my passion come together then in that tension, that lucidity, and that vast repetition."[24]

We refuse help; we are indifferent to the misfortune of others, thinking only of our own safety, ferocious as soon as we think it is threatened or when we are gripped by fear. This lack of communication is for Camus the greatest of all scandals. No analysis can reveal better the misery of a world without God. The coming of the Superman was supposed to be imminent, and see, man has become inhuman! How ridiculous to wish to become god when it is so difficult to live and to die! "The only original rule of life today: to learn to live and to die, and, in order to be a man, to refuse to be a god."[25]

Let us especially beware of excesses; they could lead us to madness as they did Caligula. Because he cannot own the moon, Caligula will try to prove to himself in other ways that he is free. To prove it, Kirilov committed suicide; to show it, Caligula becomes a monster for whom the most sacred ties are but shackles and who—supreme cruelty!—degrades his victims before killing them!

But, for Camus, the darkness is not complete. His rebellion originates in a disappointed love. A diffused light makes the darkness transparent. In *The Plague*, the atmosphere is transformed as soon as Doctor Rieux sacrifices himself to his patients and the journalist Rambert refuses to leave the city to return to his young wife, as he finally would have been able to. In *The State of Siege*, Olivier's abnegation, his refusal to yield to unjust laws, will destroy the structure of the state, that heartless monster; those he has saved by offering himself as a holocaust will be free to answer the call of the sea. Thus the

[24] *Ibid.*, pp. 87–88.
[25] Camus, *The Rebel* (New York: Random House, 1956), p. 306.

169

freedom of man imposing his right to happiness asserts itself to the face of a hostile world. Alienation comes from outside, from "the other people," when through our own fault their "alterity" becomes overpowering. It is up to me, by going toward them, to emancipate myself by emancipating them, to recreate in each one of us "this taste for man without which the world is nothing but a vast solitude."[26]

It is true that the weave of alienations is tighter than the Marxists would have us believe. Once the revolution is over, it will tend to return to its original shape. This is the burden under which Sisyphus is staggering. But let there be a little kindness, let the brightness of the summer sun gather people on a Mediterranean beach, giving rise to some simple gestures of tacit and joyful understanding, and all can still be saved! "To feel one's attachment to a certain region, one's love for a certain group of men, to know that there is always a spot where one's heart will be at peace—these are many certainties for a single human life."[27]

The true forefathers of Camus were the Greeks, whom his teacher Jean Grenier revealed to him at an early stage. Everything was simple and easy for them; man played his role so naturally that he seemed to identify with it. The body refused to be separated from the soul but joined with it in an identical effort of harmonious exaltation; Dionysus had to abandon his frenzied processions and yield to Athena's wisdom. Let us exclude from our lives this tendency to excesses which urges us to become gods. Contrasting with the conqueror who knows only how to destroy, there stands the artist, the only Superman who creates and unfolds in happiness:

"What the conqueror seeks right and left is not unity, which is first of all the harmony of contrasts, but totality

---

[26] Camus, Actuelles, I.
[27] The Myth of Sisyphus and Other Essays, p. 151.

170

which is the crushing of differences. The artist differentiates where the conqueror merely levels down."[28]

This dream of beauty will be the haven Camus was seeking; only there can man assert himself as greater than his destiny, only there will Sisyphus be happy. It is toward a renaissance in which human dignity would be preserved, in which the aspiration to truth, beauty, and justice would not always have to give way to error, deceit, and ugliness, that the author of *The Rebel* will turn:

"Art is an impossible demand given expression and form. When the most agonizing protest finds its most resolute form of expression, rebellion satisfies its real aspirations and derives creative energy from this fidelity to itself. Despite the fact that this runs counter to the prejudices of the times, the greatest style in art is the expression of the most passionate rebellion. Just as genuine classicism is only romanticism subdued, genius is a rebellion that has created its own limits."[29]

But once more humor arises from the contrast between the ideal of truth, justice, and beauty, which we cannot erase from our soul, and the universe that scoffs at it—between Sisyphus' aspiration to happiness and the cruelty of the unaccountable punishment to which he is condemned: a raillery that is full of distress, for it is very possible that this is the way the world is made, the state so strongly constituted and man so structured in his unchangeable nature that deceit, injustice, and ugliness will always prevail. Then all one can do is live in the luminous instant of joy or creation, or—what is even nobler— proclaim to the bitter end that we will forsake neither justice, nor truth, nor beauty: a desperate means perhaps, but a means nonetheless, of asserting the greatness of man, his constant will to surpass himself. For his greatness lies in the fact that

[28] *Actuelles*, I.
[29] *The Rebel*, p. 271.

he is "the only creature who refuses to be what he is."[30]
The essential elements of the Nietzschean heritage can be found in the works of André Malraux. Zarathustra's exclamation: how can we tolerate the existence of a God when we want to become gods ourselves? is repeated almost word for word in the following text:

"To be more than man in a world of men; to escape from this human condition, not only powerful, but all-powerful. The chimerical disease of which the will to power is but the intellectual justification, is the will to divinity. Every man dreams of being God."[31]

This will that tries to identify freedom and destiny at the cost of a heroic acceptance, which sets itself, in the face of death which it confronts and even defies, in a tension of the whole being in which is reflected a sort of desperate stoicism, is indeed the same as that extolled by Nietzsche; and Nietzsche appears also in the proud refusal to take shelter in a haven where one would give up trying to reach inaccessible horizons. Mankind cannot turn back once it has made the decisive choice that led it to reject as illusory the hope of another world, the help of the Transcendent. It is now obliged to make its way in the face of nothingness:

"To destroy God—and after he had been destroyed—the European mind annihilated all that could have been in man's way; once it reached the end of its efforts, like René before the body of his mistress, it finds only death. . . .

"It is true that there is a higher faith—that proposed by all the village crosses; it is made of love, and one can find appeasement in it. I *will never accept it*;[32] I will not stoop to beg of it the peace for which my weakness is yearning."

Would it then be a degradation to acknowledge this "mis-

---

[30] *Ibid.*, p. 11.
[31] André Malraux, *La Condition humaine.*
[32] The italics are ours.

ery of the Godless man" which Pascal conveyed so well, this uncertainty inscribed in the heart of man who, in a century during which the universe is revealing its secrets to the scientist, still remains "unknown" to himself. Does this call toward the being who supports our temporal existence originate only from our weakness? Or is it not rather from this love which could find in total communion alone that which would wrest it from its solitude? Must we reconcile ourselves to being, in this life that slips through our fingers like polluted water, "merely a marker left behind by the passage of a resolute genius"; to finally endure, without being sure of being granted a place in the Imaginary Museum, "the utter humiliation of man tracked down by his destiny"?

It is true that man's condition is dramatic today; he must accept the questioning of all the values in which he once believed; what am I saying? the questioning of himself on his ability to reach the goals he was rash enough to set himself. Once more, Goya, in a genial presentiment, had discerned the future of a being forced to keep going at all cost on a road that is now immersed in darkness. Walter Berger, during a wake, is questioning the past; he recalls that head of a young man in the museum of the Acropolis, in which are expressed for the first time the feelings of a man determined to see for himself and by himself:

"That day, man also shaped man from clay. The greatest of mysteries is not that we are thrown at random between the profusion of matter and that of the stars; it is that, in this prison, we ourselves draw images that are so powerful as to deny our nothingness."[33]

The worst is that we are hurled toward times of which we

[33] André Malraux, *Les Noyers de l'Altenburg* (*The Walnut Trees of Altenburg*). Cf. the entire text in which Malraux evokes the madness of Nietzsche, in a very different context from that of Thomas Mann (in *Doctor Faustus*), and then that part where Möllberg initiates a discussion during which several scientists try to define "a concept of man."

do not know whether they will be triumphant or catastrophic; we do not know if man will be capable of creating an image of himself that will allow him to face his destiny. For man, as the past has handed him down to us, is perhaps unsuited for the adventure that is calling him, imprisoned as he is in structures he inherited from a past that is both too stable and too short. He is immersed in a field in which opposite forces are threatening him, tragic contradictions which might leave him utterly helpless. But his intelligence has already expanded, and his sensibility has been transformed. Will he be able to raise his will to their level in order to dominate this excess of wealth that threatens to hold him back?

Let us however examine history where we can find precedents for the adventure we are now living, for the Imaginary Museum will yield some information on those periods during which man had to transform himself. But today we must definitively give up the idea of an indestructible permanence of unchanging structures:

"Just as a new concept of man was elaborated when there first appeared a past that did not fit into the Christian continuity, when the illustrious men first replaced the glorious knights, a new concept of man is now being formed, and we are groping no less toward it than toward our substitute heroes. The idea of the permanence of man (modified by some hierarchies or by progress) has always been based on a fundamental belief, on a religion, or at least, as in Rome and during the nineteenth century, on a fundamental concept of the world. But now our concept of the world, by its speculative nature, is tied up with a question about man, and not with a concept of man, a question that is fostered by the obsession with his dissimilarity rather than by the affirmation of his permanence."

In spite of several rashly asserted scientific hypotheses, it is not without reason that Malraux underlines the importance of the coming mutations—mutations which have no equivalent in the past. Will these mutations destroy "the eternal identity of man with himself" and force him to seek in art alone the intermittent markers pointing out the road he has followed through the centuries? Will they give birth to a "Superman" who will cast the humanimal[34] back into his obscure past, just as man supplanted the pithecanthropus or his more recent ancestor, the *homo sapiens?* Or will they, on the contrary, beget this monster whose coming terrified Bernanos, this computer capable of solving the most complex problems, a huge brain that is no longer paralyzed by the fantasies of imagination, the intermittence of memory, or the restless agitation of the heart? A perfect mechanism subjected to the very slow erosion of a time which is henceforth "cosmic" but no longer allows space for the requirements of the "spiritual" nor an opening for the rising of the soul. We must recall here the lines by Paul Valéry.

FAUST: Yes. For my magnum opus I want to make a study, and her [Luste] to take notes, of the Devil's reactions to all the exasperations which a visit to the new age cannot fail to excite in the infernal mind. . . . Think, Satan, think: this extraordinary transformation can affect you in your own redoubtable Person. The fate of Evil itself is at stake. . . . It may even you know, mean the end of the soul. The soul which impressed itself in each mind as an all-powerful sense of some incomparable and indestructible value, an inexhaustible will and power to enjoy, to suffer, to be oneself against all the odds of change, the soul has now sunk in value. The individual is dying. He is drowning in numbers. The accumulation of human beings is effacing all distinction. There's only a hairsbreadth of difference now between vice and virtue; the two are

[34] As we have already seen, it was Marcello Fabri who first used this term.

175

melted into the mass which is called "human material." Death now is just one of the statistical properties of this frightful living substance. Its . . . *classic* meaning and dignity are disappearing. And the immortality of the soul necessarily follows the same fate as death, which gave it its definition, its infinite significance and value. . . .[35]

But let one single soul survive, having eluded the clever chemical combinations, and the smooth-running mechanism might get jammed.[36] This is what happens in *Brave New World*, after the appearance of that man who can only be given one name: the *savage*, so archaic does he appear in a world in which everything is planned ahead of time. In Dino Buzzatti's novel,[37] we see the even more atrocious fate of the soul that has been resurrected only to be enclosed in the huge stone structure invented by a monstrous genie. It is condemned to remain there, panting, lamenting, and suffering, until one day it destroys itself together with its terrible prison.

And yet we are still surrounded by representatives of a past which we claim to be abolished; it is not only in time but in space that the witnesses of eras we believed to be over still linger on. The boomerang, the poisoned arrow, the amulet survive in this century of electronics; the future is read in cards and tea leaves as well as being the object of the most scholarly computations; because of superstitions or ancient social structures, there are still people living in the shadow of the totem pole, or in shanty-towns, while the most daring realizations of an art full of anticipation are rising near apartment blocks. It is therefore unnecessary to turn to the Imaginary Museum to discover these "steps" along a road which, after emerging from

[35] Paul Valéry, *Luste or the Crystal Girl* in *The Collected Works of Paul Valéry*. Vol. 3 (New York: Pantheon, 1960), pp. 37–38.

[36] Aldous Huxley, *Brave New World*, and more recently, *Brave New World Revisited*.

[37] Dino Buzzatti, *Il Grande rittrato*.

the night of time, will perhaps merge under the Gateway with that road leading toward a future whose uncertainties are impervious to the temptations of a science that claims to be "prospective."

And yet it is to the Imaginary Museum alone that Malraux will turn for consolation. It is true that this museum does not tell us anything about what man is but about what he is able to do; is it not true, though, that his being is identified with his power? It is on the will and on its indefinite capacity for aspiration, in spite of the nothingness surrounding it, that the author of *La Condition humaine* lays his emphasis. And here lies the unity of intention of his successive commitments. But these coming new times—or should I say: these times that are now assailing us?—are so different from earlier times, they require such crucial and rapid "mutations," that we can only wonder:

"If it is true that we are groping toward a universal humanism, in which a new stoicism is awakening to the consciousness of the great successive powers of man and of his permanence, if man, knowing that he can conquer in himself that which destroys him only by that which surpasses him, tries to find a basis for his fleeting greatness by seeking in his own nature that which he would once have called his 'divine' powers, as he also had discerned his demoniac elements (and though perhaps with an equally faint glimmer), then the Imaginary Museum offers to his first investigations what is perhaps the least ambiguous terrain and probably the easiest to grasp. Until mankind realizes that the heroes it remembers or invents, the truths it masters, and the forms it creates, govern it no less than the monsters that are haunting it, or until forms—once more—yield an unsuspected meaning."

What a magnificent way of saying it! But I am afraid that there is no answer to this question. Art, accumulating the "forms" of the past in which are inscribed the questions asked

177

by man and the history of his successive mutations, can certainly not provide it. In fact, man is threatened on all sides, and art, in a prospective that is very different from that of technology, expresses these dangers with great accuracy: the threat of disequilibrium or of dislocation in which man would lose his unity, the threat of an increasing uniformity in which all individuality would vanish. In Guy Tanguy's haunting painting *Multiplication of Arcs*, strange beings, more mineral than vegetable or animal, pile up on top of each other, above a petrified ocean. They are all alike, and everything is annihilated in a senseless will to climb always higher. What has been revealed to us by the witnesses of these times of crisis is the acuteness of the problems that Christianity must face. The fate of what up to now has been called man is truly at stake. Will he be compelled to yield to an almighty being, a mechanized giant for whom the soul would be merely a useless burden? Will he melt away, henceforth—with no other concern than that of his material existence—into a society in which order will prevail and in which everyone will be predetermined by his function, the space in which restless consciousness awakens having been filled? Or will he understand this universe with its ever receding horizons and its galaxies that drift away from him at speeds which can be reckoned only in terms of a time inscribed in the heart of space, and will the power of a mind enriched with all its latent potentialities establish his true, his authentic greatness in the face of this immensity? There are many Catholic thinkers, such as Antonio Rosmini, who feel that we must develop new structures in man so that he may rise, not to the vain solitude of power, but to the loftiest peaks of spirituality.[38] There are also many writers, such as Eliot, who express the hope that after the long night of doubt there will arise, not a civilization

[38] Cf. our study "Anthropologie et Ontologie de Rosmini," in *Revue rosminienne*, January, 1965.

entirely oriented toward well-being and matter, but a culture capable of satisfying the increased and multiplied needs of a new man at the intersection of time and eternity:

"The world," Eliot points out, "is trying the experiment of attempting to form a civilized but non-Christian mentality. The experiment will fail; but we must be very patient in awaiting its collapse; meanwhile redeeming the time; so that the Faith may be preserved alive through the dark ages before us; to renew and rebuild civilization, and save the World from suicide."[39]

[39] T. S. Eliot, "Thoughts After Lambeth" in *Selected Essays, 1917–1932* (New York: Harcourt, Brace, 1932), p. 332. We would have liked to devote a chapter to several English writers and thinkers: Virginia Woolf, Bernard Shaw, Joyce—and especially Eliot; however we were unable to carry out this plan.

7
Marxism and Technocracy: The Machiavellian

During all my childhood I saw chairs being re-seated in the same spirit and with the same love and the same hands as those with which this same people had built its cathedrals. . . . Everything then was rhythm and ritual and ceremony, from the first ray of dawn. . . . Everything was an uplifting of the soul and a prayer, the whole day, sleep and wake, work and rest, bed and table, soup and cattle, house and garden, door and street, yard and doorstep, and the dishes on the table. . . . In those days, when any old woman said something, it was her race, her very being, her very people that were speaking.

Charles Péguy[1]

Man is a strange animal indeed! At the very moment he appears to be most fenced up in his selfishness, at the first call, at the first hope of a better and more human future, there awaken in him unsuspected potentialities of devotion and sacrifice. If Marxism had been, as some of its most informed interpreters claim, only a new method, eliminating all subjectivity from the interpretation of social events, descending to the very basis of the relationships from which conscience is derived—the phenomena of production and barter—it would not have exercised such a great and lasting influence. Whether we like it or not, the scientific apparel with which it skillfully adorns itself makes its message more weighty. In fact, it brought two promises: the promise of justice, which would put an end to the multiple alienations afflicting man— all men, for property owners are alienated by their possessions

[1] *L'Argent*, quoted by Georges Cattaui, *Péguy, témoin du temporel chrétien* (Editions du Centurion), p. 47.

just as much as those who, because they own nothing, are dependent on the wealthy—and the promise of full control over the world, which is impossible as long as we are paralyzed by doubts or scruples and especially as long as the fragmented and antagonistic structures of our societies will not allow us to unite our incoherent and dispersed efforts toward the achievement of a common task. It is true that the advocates of Marxism apply themselves to refute those who reproach them with resurrecting Campanella's utopia, this *City of the Sun* that would flourish at the end of time thanks to the free activity of all. They claim not to be in a position to determine the conditions under which progress will take place and the conflicts will finally disappear, when the state has gradually fallen off like an unnecessary organ and the remaining hierarchies no longer reflect unjustly obtained positions but the diversity of merit and talent. Some of them—but are they really orthodox?—do not even exclude the possibility that the human adventure will end, after a lengthy emergence, in a twilight in which all energies will gradually fall apart.

But it is clear that this eventuality must be set in parentheses if we wish to arouse the élan of present generations toward a dawn that is bound to become brighter and brighter, while the irrevocable course of history, which must necessarily lead us from socialism to communism as it has led us from capitalism to socialism, causes a sort of dizziness in the defenders of an obsolete regime. Why stand up against what is bound to happen whether we like it or not; why not run without attempting to put up a useless resistance toward this future that is inscribed in the core of economic realities? As the sphex paralyzes its victims, Marxism annihilates all will to fight or even to criticize in its opponents. The most specious arguments are accepted as legal tender. I will cite as an example Henri Lefebvre's strange conclusion to his otherwise very clear and intelligent little book on Marxism:

181

"In this sense," writes this subtle dialectician, "and to end this study with an apparent paradox, we can ask the following question: how can we surpass a conception of the world which includes in itself a theory of surpassing? and which refuses to remain stationary because it is a theory of movement?—and which, if it changes, will change according to the inner law of its evolution?"[2]

But the whole question is precisely whether "the internal law of development of Marxism" coincides with the internal law of development of man, if it really urges man to surpass himself according to his deepest demands and his loftiest aspirations. A skillfully worded affirmation is not a proof.

Besides there is nothing very new in Marxism. We could easily find in d'Alembert, Holbach, Diderot, the same belief in the unlimited abilities of man as soon as he has broken away from his shackles; the word "alienation" alone is new. Marx's famous phrase: "We must not try to understand the world, but build it," is close to that of Descartes: Man, provided he remains loyal to his natural rectitude and to the method that would ensure this rectitude, would, according to the author of the *Principes*, "become the master and owner of nature." Careful analysis soon reveals the two main sources of Marxism: the Enlightenment of the eighteenth century and the Encyclopedia where all its trends are recorded—which, in spite of their diversity, endeavor to form a new image of man emancipated from his slavery—and Ricardo's theory of economics combined with the pessimistic views of Malthus and adapted to a more objective and more elastic evaluation of the processes of production, distribution, and barter. This gave rise to two different concepts, between which Marxism has always oscillated: Sometimes, following the principle that "the end judges the means," it seeks justification

[2] Henri Lefebvre, *Le Marxisme* (Presses Universitaires de France, Collection Que sais-je? 1963).

in the surmounted contradictions of a capitalistic society doomed to end in catastrophy and in in the emancipation of the proletariate; sometimes it turns for justification to the conquests of a mankind uniting all its resources to master nature and take possession of the universe. For a long time these hopes seemed to be intimately related. Emancipated from slavery and from the multiple religious, political, and economical alienations of which he was the victim, freed from the dialectic of master and slave that had previously prevailed in different fluctuating forms (castes, classes, monopolies), man could hope to become, to use Michelet's words, "his own Prometheus."

Little by little however, the always postponed realization of the final phase of socialism: the advent of a "classless society" in which everyone would be free to realize within himself the "total man," combined with the more and more pronounced divergence of the two coveted goals—to provide for the workers who had become their own master a greater and greater share in the collective wealth, an increased distribution of consumer goods, and a vast increase in the power of machines and in technological achievements in order to surpass the capitalistic states—had given rise to doubts. One gets weary of a hope that is constantly postponed and wonders about the value of the sacrifice he is making. Should one sacrifice several generations, who also have a legitimate claim to happiness, to a future paradise, even if it were—as is now admitted—only temporary and relative? Is there more justice in communistic societies than in the capitalistic ones? And did not "embourgeoisement" appear in the light of their evolution as an element intimately connected with causes that are as deeply rooted in man's nature as "socialization"?[3] Is it not true that the state is weighing more and more heavily on the

[3] Cf. the very pertinent analyses by Berdyaev, our study in *Archives de Philosophie*, April-June, 1958, pp. 196–231, and our work, in Spanish, N. Berdaïeff (Buenos Aires: Éditions Columba, 1965).

masses that are resigned, following each new "court" revolution, to incense their new masters? Is not power, like the ever-reborn phoenix, in the hands of a new ruling caste which, though it has come from the people and claims to represent them faithfully, consults them only after skillfully concealing its real aspirations?

Proudhon has already opposed to Marxism an objection which has never yet been refuted. It is not possible that the masses exercise the power; they can only delegate the real but inorganic omnipotence that lies within them. Alienation does not vanish because the state is no longer the instrument of a class. The state will always be a body or a subterfuge behind which a ruling minority takes cover. It makes little difference whether there is but one man or a group at the top of the pyramid, since the man who claims to be ruling alone as the guardian of the secrets of the doctrine depends in fact on the team to which he must delegate his power; what is more this team only seems to manipulate the control levers, since the more or less stable equilibrium of the dominant forces determines their application. The masses are satisfied for a while because they have not yet discovered their new masters, this occult power which is all the stronger for being hidden.[4] As for the rulers, they have at their disposal stronger means than ever before to anchor the deceived herd in its credulous confidence. Consciousness is now violated almost everywhere.

It would be senseless, however, to deny that the hearing Marxism has received is due not only to its success in many fields, but to its analysis—much more accurate than that of the earlier economists—of social conditions, to its major discovery of a constant reciprocity between social relationships in which economics play a fundamental role and the conscience they structure and whose evolution follows their own transforma-

[4] This power sometimes comes to light: recently, for example, with the elimination of Khrushchev.

tions. It follows that Marx and Engels—for they cannot be separated—propose to us a certain image of the man of tomorrow, of the direction in which he must head in order to surpass himself.

Dialectic, according to Hegel, should follow the unfolding of the Idea in the Empyrean in which its primary antagonisms —that of being and that of non-being, uniting in becoming— first arise; it should then always obey the triadic play of thesis, antithesis, and synthesis, whose abstract appearance does not succeed in concealing the tragic nature of the conflicts at the successive levels of the mind, of nature, and of history, until it triumphs over its own contradictions by solving the last and most concrete of them: the conflict in modern states between power and freedom.

For Marx, the role and the mission of dialectic is to follow closely the course of events in the ever-changing economic, social, and cultural context in which they occur. It is thus— and this was also Benedetto Croce's view—more a method than a doctrine. We know that Marx reproached Hegel with setting the pyramid which symbolizes the miscellaneous inter-relations forming our human societies on its vertex: the Idea, whereas it should be set on its basis: the relations of production, the insertion of human labor into always fluctuating economic structures. Ideology, therefore, is only a superstruc- ture—not a mere reflection, it is true, but the projection in the mind of the vital needs. If man had a false idea of himself for such a long time, it is because he let himself be dominated by dreams and illusory beliefs, like a hallucinated man whose actions are all distorted, whose efforts are all thwarted by false pretenses. It is time for him to realize the origin of these mirages, to reinstate within himself a strength that has not been put to good use because he has bestowed it upon ficti-tious beings to whom he granted full power over him. Thus will be born this superior man, this "total" man who will combine full lucidity with an irrepressible vitality. It is true that the Marxists offer only an outline of this total man: because it is only little by little that his features will become clear, as, triumphing over the obstacles, he will create his own habitat and, by his work, improve his living conditions. Unlike the "great" man who represents the past, who remains fixed in the attitudes imposed upon him by the traditions of his class, the "total" man is flexible, pliant, always capable of adapting and transforming himself.

What Marx has also pointed out is that any reform is bound to fail if it is inspired only by ideals which are not compatible with the ever-changing social conditions. There must first be a preliminary action that takes into account the carefully analyzed contradictions and differences. An example of such an analysis—whose actuality is beyond question—is provided by the study of the conditions of French farmers in the middle of the nineteenth century. The French Revolution, which had seemed to emancipate the French peasant, had in fact—through the increase of parceled property—handed them over to other forms of slavery:

"During the nineteenth century, the city usurer replaced the suzerains, the mortgage replaced the feudal dues for the land and the capital of the bourgeois took the place of the estates of the nobles. The parcel of the farmer is but the pretext which allows the capitalist to draw from the land profit, interest and revenue, and to leave it up to the farmer to find an income for himself. Parceled property, whose development inevitably imposes this state of slavery with respect to capital, has transformed the bulk of the French nation into troglodytes."[5]

And Marx then gives an objective account of the rural habitat and of the living conditions of these, often large, peasant

[5] Karl Marx, The Eighteenth Brumaire of Louis Bonaparte, 1852.

families, forced to pile up in slums, herded up like cattle, exposed to the dangers of calamities and disease. It is true that the picture would have to be touched up today. But, if there have been improvements, the risks of depreciation and of underdevelopment are still there. In order to pay his bills the farmer finds it necessary to keep on asking for subsidies, which the state, controlled by the industrialists and the businessmen—who are, in fact, ruling through the agency of the legal authorities—is very reluctant to grant. Land, which remains parceled, cannot yield to those who cultivate it more than a mediocre and threatened subsistence. The structures should of course be completely changed, but habit, as much as the indifference and the lack of understanding of the ruling powers, is opposed to it.

And thus Marx's prevision may well turn out to be true, and one day the farming class, which for a long time locked itself up in a fierce individualism and kept clear of the proletariate of the cities, will lend its support to the rebellion of a working class that is also tired of the working conditions imposed upon it. One may object that the Common Market opens up new vistas with the new exchanges it promises. But in fact, if it has been possible in the midst of this constellation of nations to harmonize interests to some extent in the fields of technology and industry, divergence persists in the domain of agriculture where the measures under consideration may well turn out to be inoperative.[6] This is where the contradictions that may be fatal to capitalism become most acute. For the countries who would think they can shut themselves up in a tight autarchy and would not know how to subordinate their goals to their potentialities would be condemning themselves to suicide. Here again, Marx was right in asserting that the will of the rulers is effective only if it is inspired by all the fac-

[6] We must add that competition, which is part of life, will go on, concealed by measures that will soon turn out to be ineffective.

tors that condition the life of nations and by all the increasing interrelations between them.

However, though the analysis of partial structures and the forecasting of the dangers they imply have been proved correct, though this intuition of an increasing atomization of previously stable groups was also accurate, the picture as a whole seems to be faulty in many respects. We all know this scheme: Classes would have arisen from the debris of the "castes," whose rigidity would have burst because of the increased mobility of exchanges; these classes would therefore form a new stage of evolution, an improvement on the preceding one because of their flexibility and their greater permeability, and also because of the progressive filling up of "social gaps." We then know how an increasing process of concentration of wealth in the hands of a few privileged people will raise tensions to the point where a revolution becomes unavoidable. Marx often said that his original contribution was not the discovery of "classes," nor that of the sometimes smoldering, sometimes acute, struggle between them—the "bourgeois" historians had said this before him (Sismondi, in particular)—but:

"My contribution consists of the following proof: 1. The existence of these classes is dependent only on certain definite historical struggles, connected with the development of production; 2. the struggle between classes will necessarily lead to the dictatorship of the proletariate; 3. This dictatorship itself only forms the transition stage toward the abolition of all classes."

Marx's principal mistake was that he failed to observe the overlapping of historical periods[7] and the persistence of the old types alongside the type that is destined to replace them. We will see that this is the case for the "Superman" type, for

[7] If we can use this expression which Croce is quite right in condemning.

the "total man" type. The "spiritual" survives while the "intellectual," the representative of the old "intelligentsia," is changing. History unfolds, not in a linear time in which a continuous process would take place, but in a pluridimensional human universe in which the past still affects the structure of a present that is activated by the ferment of the future.

In his still unpublished study of the problem of the origin of castes and of classes, René Grousset had no trouble in finding evidence of the simultaneous survival of castes and classes. For castes and classes do not have the same origin. The organization which led to castes was a certain structure based on ancient religious concepts: in this case, the wheel of existence, or the karma, and the beliefs deriving from it. As long as these ancestral terrors survive—this belief in an indefinite succession of reincarnations, each one of which is predetermined by the sins committed in an earlier life—no thorough reform will be possible; this is only too obvious when we look at the caste of the "untouchables," determined to oppose anything that might improve their miserable condition since their suffering will allow them to enter a higher caste. The same is true of the condition of women in Islam; it can change only if the strict observances imposed by monotheistic Muslimism are modified. But this does not prevent the coexistence with these castes—or in Islam with these great families which are unchanging because they are the keepers of tradition—of classes which reflect economical factors that are much more flexible and varied, just as there coexist, each one expressing a moment of history, the most varied types of "guides" and of "Supermen."

Nations—and within their frame, groups and even individuals—live at quite varied levels of culture, sometimes even torn between ancient demands and new imperatives: like the African student coming home to his hut and his totems. One might point out that no one civilization is better than another and that each one should be judged on the coherence of its structures. I am willing to concede this, but then let no one speak of progress. The word would be meaningless. And the Superman is then no longer a type aiming at expressing in himself the loftiest aspirations of human nature and trying to reach universality, but whosoever an upright or a deceived opinion considers to be such, the man to whom it hands over its destiny because he embodies its desires, its resentments, its claims, its ineffective thirst for power, or, at other times, the need for order, for a comforting stability. He is but an echo, a reflection, a medium.

But this remark implies others: First of all, it reveals that nationalism is not dead, contrary to what Marxism thought for a while when it claimed to transpose the obsolete conflicts between nations to a worldwide scale and solve, by revolution, by establishing the unity of mankind, the endless problems at the level of the interests of states. Chinese dialectic argumentation was able, with great skill, to exploit the too conspicuous contradiction between the communist doctrine—which only deals with the class struggle—and the permanence of national interests; but China is still not sincere for, concealed behind the Marxist-Leninist ideal, it is its will to power amplified by a frightening population increase that urges it to extend its sphere of influence on the vast Asiatic continent. It is also, alas! the resentment born from the degradation imposed upon it by the European conquerers; still smoldering are racial hatreds whose violence we underestimate. Marxism, convinced that all that is real can be rationalized, did not make sufficient allowances for this "irrational" which intelligence perceives and which the will is unable to master. History is rocked by telluric explosions that are as violent as those that once made entire continents collapse. Like the crust of the earth, reason is but a thin layer set on the abysses in which future seisms are smoldering.

190

Between America and Russia, on the contrary, history has not defined such lines of scission. They are very far apart, which makes confrontation difficult. Marcel Mauss has already pointed out that distance and the absence of common boundaries are favorable to peaceful relations between peoples. There has been too much emphasis, he says, on the complementary nature of civilizations; on the contrary, they clash as soon as their contacts multiply and as the "areas" they cover get closer. Add to this the prestige America enjoys among young people in view of its industrial equipment, the strength and the variety of its economic potential, the drive that pushes it toward spectacular conquests, and it is easy to understand that the risks of a confrontation will tend to decrease.

But there is more; and here again, Marxism-Leninism has overlooked certain fundamental elements. Any trend of ideas, any conception relating to economics, no matter how carefully elaborated, will inevitably fall into the rut of traditions and customs and will be influenced by them. Thus, it is in vain that one tries to dyke a river, to push back the ocean from the vast areas it covered. Let the work of consolidation ease off, let vigilance flag, and once more the water will spread over the insufficiently protected land. Communism did not follow the same course in Yugoslavia as it did in Russia, though it had been prepared to accept the colonization of the land by archaic structures and ancient practices. And the divergence of the lines of evolution became apparent very soon. The sudden Hungarian revolution betrays an even deeper unwillingness to give up the national ideal. Catholicism has left too deep a mark on Poland for it to accept for any length of time a tutelage that would seem oppressive if it were to interfere with its most instinctive habits and reflexes. Pluralism becomes necessary and will be increasingly necessary if one wants to preserve the same ideological orientation. But equilibrium is then unstable; and in each, now distinct, dynamic field, the

forces may soon combine to form a different state of equilibrium.

The worldwide unity of communist dreams also stumbles
against centrifugal forces that have preserved an unsuspected
influence. This is because, in a continuously oscillating motion,
two trends are confronting one another in the midst of all
human societies. The first urges men to form groups, to clus-
ter together; the "socialization" to which it gives rise actually
occurs at various levels so that the communities it creates
can vary considerably in coherence and stability: Man seeks
more the reassuring warmth of the flock, the exalting presence
of the others, the superficial convergence of reactions and
affections, rather than a deep communion, a gift that pene-
trates intentions and brings hearts closer. This trend leads
mankind toward the "brave new world" of Aldous Huxley,
rather than toward authentic communities:

"Alphas [those who are destined to become leaders and
therefore receive, even before their birth, a special prepara-
tion] can be completely socialized—but only on condition
that you make them do Alpha work. Only an Epsilon can be
expected to make Epsilon sacrifices, for the good reason that
for him they aren't sacrifices; they're the line of least resistance. His conditioning has laid down rails along which he's
got to run."[8]

We have reached a society that is even more perfect than
that of the Grand Inquisitor. All disquiet is banished since
everyone carries out, at the level that has been set for him, the
function that was assigned to him before he was ever born.
The proletariate, after secreteing its ruling class, keeps on
indefinitely producing the same type: that of the Epsilon, the
ant who is happy to build the ant-hill. Everyone is pleased to

[8] Aldous Huxley, *Brave New World* (New York: Harper, 1946), pp.
266–267.

192

see his neighbor doing the same things that he is doing, leading the same sort of life. Are we as far as we would like to think from this ideal of perfect quietude which Charlie Chaplin caricatures in *City Lights*? But there is always the Savage, the man who refuses to be assimilated. Is his appearance in a world that is completely shut upon itself due to an oversight? Does his persistent soul owe to a noneradicated microbe this incredible claim to freedom which it proclaims to the face of the stupefied herd?

In fact, it is impossible to eliminate the Savage. His character and even his final revolt are features inscribed in the structures of human nature. However malleable man's nature may be, however vulnerable to suggestion and to the incantations of pictures and slogans, it carries within itself a need which urges each man to develop his difference, to become conscious of the vocation to which he is called. Without this need, mankind would be nothing but a higher form of animality. Those whom Emerson called "the representative men" stand out from the herd. These nonconformists, these "innovators" who win disciples, admiration, or respect, soon become examples; the creative impetus that sleeps in each one of us comes out in them. But if, in my consciousness, there is the reflection of a universe that resembles no other, if I enjoy pleasures that I cannot, because they are so marvelous, communicate to others—like Marcel Proust's Swann—if I raise this personal taste to the highest level of creation, if I acquire a style that is truly my own, then I will be certain that—during a very short time, it is true, but an authentic one—I was something more than a number or a letter of the alphabet: a man who has set out to master his being. But alas! this being very often tends to vanish gradually, under the influence of everywhere identical tasks; a uniformity devoid of greatness is gradually spreading and genius no longer finds the fertile soil in which it can blossom. The aimless agitation in which a persistent dissatisfaction goes astray is due to these pressures which make us concentrate on our "appearance." The road is closed for us toward a true "surpassing" of ourselves which we cannot find "forward," like cattle driven by the stick, but always higher even if the horizon that is drawing us vanishes each time, like a mirage. The Little Prince, finding the desert too populated, sought refuge in his star. To defend his consciousness from the violation to which it was about to yield, the Savage committed suicide. But he carried away with him in his death that which is particular to man, that without which he would no longer be a man.

One might say that these comments completely destroy the Marxist thesis. I would be the last to make such a claim. Man, whatever the level to which he rises, develops and grows, molded by techniques, transformed by his machines, impregnated with the culture of his time. But, as technology develops and becomes more demanding, as specialization increases, as culture becomes uniform, the "superior" man assumes everywhere the same features. This is a new reason why societies of the "communistic" type and those of the "capitalistic" type are getting closer. The ruling class that arises in them is that of the technocrats, the scientists, the engineers, the businessmen. Look at this man who appears to us as the equal of the "hero" of antiquity: the cosmonaut, who has carried beyond all conceivable limits the virtues of endurance, of a persistent and firm patience, of self-control, to the point that his will has, so to speak, built him another body; it is impossible to tell whether he has been shaped by capitalistic technocracy or instructed according to the norms of the Marxist world. By this very fact, the hopes of Teilhard de Chardin are to a certain extent justified when he predicts the rapprochement, in a common adventure and in identical aspirations, of men who are separated by their recent education as well as by the ancient customs of their native countries, so that they will collaborate toward the same goals; it is as though, above them, a certain form of transcendence were inviting them to forget their quarrels, to overcome their disagreements. Their cooperation models them even more on the same mold, and even their reflexes are identical, bent on unpleasant duties they do not even notice, so great is their fascination with another world, however deceitful it may be.

At a lower level, the "manager" type, that of the American "executive" has more and more in common with the Russian "high official"; they must overcome the same obstacles, solve the same problems. In the American "seminaries" they submit to the same methods, to the same training, as in the Russian schools. Much more than docility to the imperatives of the doctrine, they are required to show natural aptitudes and the qualities that must be acquired to make best use of these aptitudes. They are both these "pioneers" of civilization which Max Scheler[9] ranks with the "sage," the "hero," the "saint" and the lover of the arts concerned with extracting from life all the joys it has to offer, among the "superior types" which the modern world proposes to us. The pioneer of civilization, the leader in the world of economics, is according to Max Scheler "bubbling over with an activity that is only too eager to be spent in order to constantly gain new profits; in the control of the economy, he is seeking power rather than sovereignty." Karl Marx said that "he takes the teaching of detachment very seriously, since he prefers the fetish of gold to the pleasures of the flesh."[10] The word "profit" may indeed sound surprising, but what difference is there between the "high" salary of the leader in the Russian economic world and the profit which the American businessman owes to his activity, except that the first is better protected against the risk of

[9] The French translation by E. Marny bears the inaccurate title: Le Sage, le Héros, le Saint (Lyon: Vitte).
[10] Ibid., p. 123.

failure? Can it be said that he is concerned only with the good of the community, that he forgets himself in the accomplishment of his duties? I am willing to believe that his personal interest is only secondary, but I cannot say the same for this will to power which is stimulated by success rather than by profit. To prove oneself superior to the others, to see one's forecasts turn out to be correct, to arouse admiration and emulation, these are, for both of them, the real stimulants to action. Besides, either one—and here again Scheler's comments are very pertinent—"thinks in terms of private rather than of national economy," which makes them unable to realize the full incidence of their decisions, to consider their problems from a broad point of view, that is, from their political angle. "Even when he [the leader in the world of economics] is very broad-minded in his realizations, he does not leave the narrow frame of his specialty. Moreover, *he is rarely good at psychology*, and even more rarely able to adapt to the mentality of other peoples or to that of their leaders."

Here again Marxists will say that they have at least removed the contradictions which transformed capitalistic societies into a jungle, that competition no longer comes into play between large trusts and monopolies. Who would dare make such a claim? Though it may be more latent, the struggle nonetheless continues, first because the various sectors are opposed to one another, and also because of the rivalry—prompted by an identical desire for promotion—between the "managers," who try to bring the political leaders around to their way of thinking. The elimination of Khrushchev is good proof of this. "Court" intrigues may replace the movements of the stock market, but the lofty or sordid goals that govern man have not changed. The "pioneer" remains everywhere an "adventurer" —the adventurer of modern times; he goes on without allowing scruples to hinder him; in his own way he is an idealist, since he is inspired by a project that is not realized and which

196

in many cases seems unrealizable. But, unlike the dreamer and the utopist, he strives to insert this ideal into reality, or to coordinate the conditions that will make its realization possible. It is in terms of the future that he builds the present, not by a sterile imitation of the past according to the rules of a cautious foresight, but by a sort of "wager" which considers as immediately realized the projects he has just conceived. Much has been said about the "acceleration of history": We have seen that it does not occur in all sectors of activity and that this discrepancy, if it is not controlled, gives rise to sporadic rebellions or, if authority weakens at all, to revolutions. In any case it is this "acceleration" which imposes a "prospective" vision of the world, a vision that tends to replace a "dialectic" that is more concerned with translating present correlations between facts than with anticipating the future. More and more, efficacy is becoming the criterion.

"He is not a technocrat," wrote Louis Armand in his *Plaidoyer pour l'avenir*, "the man who wants to begin with the actual data, to try and understand their meaning, and for this purpose attempts to make a synthesis. He is a man who loves life and wants to understand what he can do to make other people love it and to love it even more himself."[11]

But one does not become a manager, a daring technician, without formation, without having learned how to fit one's personal action into the work of a team. The claims of yesterday's individualists who believed themselves capable of solving all problems as well as the faith of the revolutionaries in the magical results of a sudden upheaval must be forgotten:

"The revolutionaries [of the traditional type]," wrote Gaston Berger, "want to change things so as to finish 'once for all' with the errors they are denouncing, . . . such a position is hardly tenable nowadays. . . . Once the revolution is over,

[11] Louis Armand, *Plaidoyer pour l'avenir* (Paris: Calmann-Levy), p. 230.

conditions keep changing so that the equilibrium that once seemed so final soon becomes precarious once more. Besides, even a violent revolution is too slow to produce the hoped for results. This is because a rebellion may be improvised, but not a revolution. Now, the time that is necessary to prepare it and then to carry it out is such that the goals one had set oneself at the outset have lost their relevancy by the time they are within reach.

"We must therefore learn not to undergo just one change but to transform ourselves incessantly so as to be always adapted. It is not so difficult to know how to be great as to know how to grow."[12]

This text and many others by Gaston Berger emphasize the importance of the "mutations" that are imposed upon man. These "mutations" are on the same scale as the third technological revolution, of which Marx, in spite of his genius, could not foresee the magnitude. Do they imply the birth of a new man with different structures than the old man, the man we still are? Will the chrysalis have to fall before the wings can unfold? It is true that we cannot foresee to what extent these mutations will change man. But we do see that they demand that contradictory qualities be developed to their utmost. Al Farabi counted eighteen such qualities which he believed cohabit only in one man: the Prophet. We would come very close to this number today. To the tenacity of an inflexible will, the business leader must add an extremely clear-sighted intelligence; he must, but with increased rapidity, be "as determined in his actions as he is careful in his deliberations";[13] he must be as capable of getting an overall picture as of seeing the details, as apt to fix the end as to choose the best means of reaching it, as farsighted as he is prudent; he must be acquainted with the motives that determine behavior without,

[12] Quoted by Louis Armand, *ibid.*, p. 164.
[13] Descartes, *Discours de la méthode.*

however, losing his respect for man; when dealing with familiar problems he must remain careful to stimulate his too readily flagging activity.

Just think of all a pilot or a captain must know and understand these days! And especially what remains the most difficult of all these requirements: to accept being only a cog, an articulation in a whole that sets a definite role for each member. For in business as in school, the members of the team are subordinate to the goal. Every day a nation assumes more and more the appearance of a pyramid converging toward a ruling team or toward an animator. This is what had already been forecast in the last century by the Italian sociologist Mosca.[14] He saw capitalistic societies evolving toward a "directorial" type of society. Does communism really evolve toward a classless society? Would it not also be heading toward a "directorial" type society? Mosca saw that a society in which all shared in government was unthinkable; he therefore felt that there would always be two classes: that which rules and that, much more numerous, which is being ruled—and which will be happy only if there is an increasing equality among its members. But if it is unthinkable that an unorganized mob should rule, so is it that an individual should be able to monopolize all authority and all initiatives:

"But the man who is at the head of the state would certainly not be able to govern without the support of a numerous class to enforce respect for his orders and to have them carried out; and granting that he can make one individual, or indeed many individuals, in the ruling class feel the weight of his power, he certainly cannot be at odds with the class as a whole or do away with it. Even if that were possible, he would at once be forced to create another class, without the support

[14] Gaetano Mosca, *Teoria dei governi parlementari* (1883), and *The Ruling Class (Elementi di Scienza Politica)* (New York: McGraw-Hill, 1939).

199

of which action on his part would be completely paralyzed."[15]

One might even say, adds Mosca, that "the larger the political community, the smaller will the proportion of the governing minority to the governed majority be, and the more difficult will it be for the majority to organize for reaction against the minority."[16]

Were it not for lack of space we would like to continue this analysis. Modern states are becoming more and more complex and activities more and more conditioned, so that both classes are becoming increasingly subdivided. A small group of higher leaders fills the key positions in our "directorial" societies, but beneath them, with a firm hold on the channels of power, there is a numerous and less well-known group. They all have the same features: hard workers, ambitious, not at all prone to compassion, indeed even with a tendency toward inhumanity. They have built themselves a mask of impassibility behind which they shelter their proud pretension, their sense of superiority! "Business is business," Octave Mirbeau said. But around them gravitate those whom very few people ever hear about: experts whose functions must remain secret and whose opinion, in times of crisis, will be decisive. Their task is to prepare reports, carry out missions, gather information; they are the ones who pull the ropes and only a crisis will sometimes reveal their names; but the curtain falls back on them very quickly and the anonymity behind which they hide will be raised only much later, by history.

However, there is another aspect of our times that cannot go unnoticed: the reappearance, in an even more cynical form, of the Prince, the Machiavellian Superman. Already the technocrat is prone, in his concern for efficiency, to overlook all moral criteria in his choice of means. If this is the attitude of those whose role it is to direct, to orient economic life, how much more pronounced will be that of the political leader,

[15] *The Ruling Class*, p. 51.
[16] *Ibid.*, p. 53.

accustomed to consider men as tools, as pawns one moves on a larger and larger board. Berdyaev has shown with great perspicacity that those who claim to improve the fate of men are often those who have least respect for them. They think they can operate all the workings that determine behavior; since they never meet the soul under their scalpel, nor God in space, they deny the existence of a higher order. To control reflexes that are hardly more complex than those of an animal, this is, in their view, the essence of the art of politics. They have learned that they can lie with impunity, for they know how quickly one forgets promises that were never kept: Two years is the maximum amount of time during which memories preserve an affective resonance. Once more Machiavelli is the master whose teaching must be perfected. Did he not say that when might is ineffective, one should resort to trickery?

But how can the relationship between individuals or between nations be founded on deceit and lies? The leader is only too prone today to consider himself a Superman whose will has the force of law. Deceived himself by temporary successes, caught in the snare of pride, all the more threatened by excesses as his field of action enlarges, how could he not believe in both the lawfulness of his power and the value of his mission? Moreover, it has become so easy to make people agree with you! The most specious arguments can be successful as long as they are presented in the right way. By appealing in turn to envy, fear, and credulous admiration, one can force one's way into the mind; one can handle it as one pleases. Prestige can be won at little expense: Epinal prints are now mass-produced. Never has Plato's definition of politics been more justified: "an art of flattery" which resorts to flattering appearances to induce into temptation, it is a poor imitation of medicine and gymnastics, seeking neither to heal nor to strengthen the body but to offer a semblance of beauty and health.

It is easy to resort to subterfuge. And how often it is done!

201

So as not to appear to condone the discredited formula "the end justifies the means," one now says that it "judges" them. But this is still Machiavellianism, and the author of the Essays on Titus Livius would have approved this transcription without hesitation. For him the "end that judges the means" was the liberation of his country from foreign occupation. Too weak, too divided, torn apart by endless factional quarrels, Italy badly needed to be united under the rule of a firm prince without scruples. Sinigaglia could have condoned if it had allowed Cesare Borgia to put an end to the rebellions of the mercenaries for whom money was the only ideal. Today the doctrine of communism claims to be the ultimate goal in terms of which all means should be evaluated. Thus any means will be not only condoned but praised if it fits into the course of events that will lead to this end, if it is able to make use of complex situations that are everywhere different and fluctuating. Any means indeed, since ethics, which some consider as the opposite of Marxism, is considered by the latter as the expression of the illusory ideals, of the misguided dreams of bourgeois consciousness. But the ideal which inspires Marxism is itself committed to time; it is of value only for this time, as the nationalistic idealism of Machiavelli was of value only because of the temporary decline of Italy. To this ideal, moreover, capitalistic technocracy opposes its own ideal; it was very quick in understanding that no one would condemn it for using questionable means if they led—if need be via devious routes and breach of promise—to the desired end. What strange relationships are those which are founded on the obstinate efforts of men and peoples to deceive one another! Gone are the days evoked by Selma Lagerlöf, when one had only to swear on the Bible in order to be believed! Nevertheless, it is necessary, so that some form of mutual trust may arise again, to ballast with the weight of an Absolute in which one no longer believes, values that are relative, uncertain, and threatened in the time that carries them along.

This is where the atheism of our times—"nocturnal" atheism as Berdyaev calls it—differs from the atheism of the Enlightenment. That "diurnal" atheism had faith in man; it believed that he would become more and more reasonable and thus more sociable, so that the relations of good manners and mutual respect that had been established between individuals would gradually spread to the relations between peoples. One should reread the letters which the Abbé de Saint-Pierre sent to the ruling powers to convince them to put an end to their quarrels and build peace on a solemn commitment. In those days only "just" wars were accepted. That of 1914–1918 was to be the last one; so that it might be ended without sowing the seeds of new hatreds, T. W. Wilson wanted to conclude peace in the spirit of the Kantian principles. These principles merely express, in an abstract and universal form, the demands of several centuries of Christianity.

In his famous *Treatise on Perpetual Peace*, Kant described the genesis of human societies whose relations have for a long time been determined by strength alone; he then shows these societies evolving little by little toward a juridical status, thanks to the progressive extension of moral laws governing the relations between individuals. We thus see appearing a society extending to all nations that are inclined to consider one another as "persons," a society which progressively models itself on a Society of minds, a spiritual community in which even the norms become more flexible, in which justice tempered by love becomes "equity." But in order to make decisive improvements, "cold war" must also disappear, cunning and deceit must not take the place of strength, the word of honor must be respected, promises must not, from the very start, be polluted with mental reservations, and most important, spying must be prohibited. Otherwise, with a veneer of civilization that will very quickly wear away, the law of the jungle

203

will reappear. This little book therefore is the ultimate attempt of Enlightenment to entrust man to his reason. For if the eighteenth century claimed to bring even religion within the limits of this reason in which, in its view, lies the greatness of man, it did not want to break the link connecting politics and ethics. It was their common human ideal that made it possible for the Abbé Pluche, for the Abbé Morellet, to consort with atheists, to attend the Baron d'Holbach's luncheons. The "enlightened" priests knew that this ideal would remain livable only if it was inserted in the Christian tradition; the atheists accepted this revelation only as the envelope which had for a long time protected the finally emancipated insect.

We could trace up to Teilhard de Chardin this current in which many different waters mingle: Some originate in Molinism, which refused to believe that man is irremediably perverted; others in rationalism, which was inclined to think that man is capable of being self-sufficient and that he would become better as soon as he was no longer unhappy. But, in the face of this somewhat naive optimism, a similar pessimism unites those who, despairing of man and believing him to be fundamentally bad, handed him over to the power of the Grand Inquisitor, whether he be the emanation of a religion more anxious to promote order than charity or the representative of a technocratic—or socialistic—state organizing a remarkable world enclosed in a ruthless hierarchy.[17]

This gradual vanishing of ethics, this acceptance of rules that are all inserted in an unstable becoming and subordinate to equally relative ends which claim to judge them, has been condemned by Albert Schweitzer, the most generous and most clear-sighted thinker of our times:

"The city of truth," he tells us, "cannot be built on the swampy ground of skepticism. Our spiritual life is rotten

[17] Cf. N. Berdyaev, *The Origin of Russian Communism*. We will have to avoid both excesses.

throughout because it is permeated through and through with skepticism, and we live in consequence in a world which in every respect is full of falsehood."[18]

Albert Schweitzer is thus strongly opposed to this new Machiavellianism. For Machiavelli and those who more or less openly claim to be his disciples condemn not only ignorance and flightiness, lack of energy and of "virtue," but also any concern and passion for ethics; they do not believe in the possibility of a religious regeneration, nor in the utopia of a peace founded on mutual goodwill and respect for the word of honor; at the very most, they believe in truces associated with a precarious equilibrium, which the art of politics must try to preserve thanks to an accurate knowledge of the elements in play. As for religion, it is, in his mind, this "opium of the people" which Marx and Lenin will have no difficulty in condemning: a way of maintaining, by fostering the hope of another world, the injustices and exactions of the present one.

Schweitzer refuses to join in this bankruptcy which he feels —together with Karl Jaspers—will lead to the annihilation of humanity or at least to the destruction of our civilizations that are exclusively concerned with technical realizations; desperately, he searched for this ethics our times are so badly in need of—an ethics that would allow man, not to surpass himself, but to fulfill himself. He thought he had found it one day when, going up the Ogowé river, a sudden illumination revealed to him that "reverence"—the purest of all moral feelings—should be applied not to abstractions such as moral law (Kant's categorical imperative) but to the most concrete of all realities, life in all its forms, even fragile and ephemeral. True, our Occidental conception of the world expresses a need for activity combined with a need for clarification. We prepare, not to withdraw from a world that is considered evil,

[18] *Out of My Life and Thought* (New York: Holt, 1949), p. 223.

to cast it away like a bad dream, to dissolve subjective consciousness in which this dream deceives us, but to leave our mark on it, to transform it, to subject it to the schemes of our creative will. However, if pursued too blindly, this goal creates a lack of balance:

"The disastrous feature of our civilization is that it is far more developed materially than spiritually. Its balance is disturbed. Through the discoveries which now place the forces of Nature at our disposal in such an unprecedented way, the relations to each other of individuals, of social groups, and of States have undergone a revolutionary change. Our knowledge and our power have been enriched and increased to an extent that no one would have thought possible. We have thereby been enabled to make the conditions of human existence incomparably more favourable in numerous respects, but in our enthusiasm over our progress in knowledge and power we have arrived at a defective conception of civilization itself. We value too highly its material achievements, and no longer keep in mind as vividly as is necessary the importance of the spiritual element in life. Now come the facts to summon us to reflect. They tell us in terribly harsh language, that a civilization which develops only on its material side, and not in corresponding measure in the sphere of the spirit, is like a ship with defective steering gear which gets out of control at a constantly accelerating pace, and thereby heads for catastrophe."[19]

Once the diagnosis is made—and how accurately!—one must find the remedy. There is no point in searching in the frame of another civilization—that of India, or even the present-day style of life—for the conditions of a more satisfactory equilibrium, for we would remain, whether we wanted it or not, engaged in the ways we had followed hitherto. Civili-

[19] Albert Schweitzer, *Civilization and Ethics* (London: Black, 1946), p. 2.

zations remain impermeable to one another. We have set ourselves an ideal of man, of the person, which we could not give
up without committing suicide. The values we will have to
establish are in the line of our development. They must only
be subordinate to a higher Value, both committed to time and
transcendent to it:

"In reverence for life my knowledge passes into experience.
. . . My life carries its own meaning in itself [*far from creating
it at will as Nietzsche claimed*]. This meaning lies in my living
out the highest idea which shows itself in my will-to-live, the
idea of reverence for life. With that for a starting-point I give
value to my own life and to all the will-to-live which surrounds
me, I persevere in activity, and I produce values."[20]

This moral sense, which alone can order our life, will teach
us how to offer to other people much more than passive compassion: effective help in their trials. It will allow us to make
clear for our times the message of Goethe.[21]

[20] *Ibid.*, pp. xvii-xviii.
Here is the essential text in which Schweitzer relates this sudden
intuition which revealed to him both the primacy of ethics and the
nature of reverence:
"Slowly we crept upstream, laboriously feeling—for it was the dry
season—for the channels between the sandbanks. Lost in thought I
sat on the deck of the barge, struggling to find the elementary and
universal conception of the ethical which I had not discovered in any
philosophy. . . . Late on the third day, at the very moment when, at
sunset, we were making our way through a herd of hippopotamuses,
there flashed upon my mind, unforeseen and unsought, the phrase,
'Reverence for Life.' The iron door had yielded: the path in the
thicket had become visible. Now I had found my way to the idea in
which affirmation of the world and ethics are contained side by side!
Now I knew that the ethical acceptance of the world and of life, together with the ideals of civilization contained in this concept, has a
foundation in thought." *Out of My Life and Thought*, pp. 156–157.
[21] Schweitzer does not hide his admiration for Goethe: "A spirit
like Goethe's lays upon us three obligations. We have to wrestle with

But I am afraid that the views of Albert Schweitzer are too noble, too generous. For the drama is that this sense, if only in the form of an instinctive impulse, of a mere velleity, is nowhere apparent in nature. Our ruthless wars are, it seems, but the extension of the merciless struggles that occur everywhere between scarcely individuated beings and even between species, on the earth, in the sky, and at the bottom of the sea: atrocious fights which our cameras have recorded! The only thing that succeeds in interrupting the carnage is the backlash which the devouring species must endure when its effects are too destructive. The laws of mathematical biology[22] fix, in the shape of oscillating curves, the ups and downs of this endless struggle.

Man, said Pascal, is *omne animal*; this wave of murder and aggression that follows the push of life extends to him; but he is even more cruel and ruthless than these animals, who at least are fighting for their life; he kills for the pleasure of killing, gratuitously, because of an inborn aggressiveness, a jealousy that can tolerate no superiority in others, whether intellectual or moral, or, what is even worse, for a mere divergence in beliefs or opinions. Must we separate these two worlds, the one governed by the law of the jungle, while the waves of charity are born and amplify in the other; one in

conditions so as to secure that men who are imprisoned in work and are being worn out by it may nevertheless preserve the possibility of a spiritual existence. We have to wrestle with men so that in spite of being continually drawn aside to the external things which are provided so abundantly for our age, they may find the road to inwardness and keep in it. We have to wrestle with ourselves and with all and everything around us, so that in a time of confused ideals which ignore all the claims of humanity we may remain faithful to the great humane ideals of the eighteenth century, translating them into the thought of our own age, and attempting to realize them today." *Goethe* (New York: Holt), p. 690.

[22] Cf. Vito Volterra's work on mathematical biology.

which acquired characters become fixed, in which a marvelous but sterile—since it only makes repairs and imitates—adaptation is perfected, and the other in which mimicry itself announces and prefigures, as Alphonse de Chateaubriant saw it,[23] the appearance—still timid perhaps—of the feeling which models the lover on the object of his love? Would there be in this life which proceeds according to the rhythm set by time— time that is both constructive and destructive—two ever more diverging directions: one which goes forward without making any basic changes in the structures that condition and limit our actions, the other that would lead to a world beyond, to a world above, demanding, in order to get there, the development of other structures which would no longer be merely rational][24] but spiritual? This is what we must now examine.

[23] Alphonse de Chateaubriant, *La Réponse du Seigneur.*
[24] Kant had accurately predicted the threat hanging over man: that of becoming a "rational automaton."

8

From Bergson to Teilhard de Chardin

Why is it, then, that saints have their imitators, and why do the great moral leaders draw the masses after them? They ask nothing, and yet they receive. They have no need to exhort; their mere existence suffices. For such is precisely the nature of this other morality. Whereas natural obligation is a pressure or a propulsive force, complete and perfect morality has the effect of an appeal.

Henri Bergson[1]

*T*hat man is the arrow climbing above and beyond the stable forms of evolution, that it is through man and through man alone that this evolution, instead of coming to a standstill in obsolete structures, progresses toward higher and higher forms of life, but that he carries within him the seed of an initial deviation that threatens to induce him to sacrifice his spiritual aspirations to technical achievements, this was the message of Bergson. The mineral order is ruled by combinations consistent with statistical probability; by using the chemical transformations they have perfected little by little, plants maintain a level of adaptation restricted to their survival and reproduction, without giving any evidence of an ability to innovate. It is true that instinct is more flexible, more dynamic, but it is still incapable of "interiorizing in knowledge," shedding only from within an intermittent and fleeting glow on a process

[1] *The Two Sources of Morality and Religion* (New York: Holt, 1935), p. 26.

210

over which, for want of reflection, it has no control; it therefore remains fixed in the same behavior; unless external stimuli compel it to modify some details, it is unable to open up channels for the creative impetus.[2] Man alone progresses by inventing. Because of him evolution, which hitherto remained unpredictable because it was determined differently at each stage, now becomes creative. But the initial orientation of his intelligence, as witnessed by the acceleration of his technological discoveries—what a change since the invention of fire and of the first computer!—as well as the structure of a language that is concerned more with finding, distinguishing, and using things than with understanding them, seems to hold back his progress and to determine the direction in which, very early, he has set out. An implement for fabricating implements, intelligence has progressed, assembling and disassembling, replacing living organisms by machines, solving by means of weights and measurements the problems which birds and insects can solve instinctively by adapting the movement of their wings to the air around them; but, by doing this, he is able to fly much faster and much further. Thus from his very first appearance, man was more interested in technology than in knowledge, he was more *faber* than *sapiens*. Karl Marx's belief that man should not contemplate the world to understand or to admire it but should aim at transforming it, therefore merely expresses, according to Bergson, a structure that was initially inscribed in human nature from the very moment it broke away from animality. It must therefore be corrected; other powers that are now slumbering in man must be awakened. They alone will open up for evolution the road toward this order of which Pascal said that it had "no common measure" with the order of the calculating intellect: the order of the spirit, the order of charity. Just as suitable im-

[2] Berdyaev will use this expression more often than Bergson. Cf. our work: *N. Berdïaeff* (Buenos Aires: Editions Columba, 1965).

pulses will correct the flight of a missile,[3] the nature of the
homo faber must be oriented toward spiritual life by incessant
appeals and suggestions. Bergson, as much as Schweitzer and
simultaneously,[4] realized the pitfalls of an unrestrained development of technology monopolizing all the faculties of the
mind. In societies, this plastic and practical intelligence carries its attempt at organization to the point of preparing the
juridical solutions capable of answering all questions; the rules
it formulates, the norms it sets, the strict obligations it pre-
scribes end up by shutting societies in upon themselves, satisfied with the order that has thus been established. Everywhere
mechanisms are set up in which invention is stabilized and
sclerosed. Bergson gave a very good description of this technological universe toward which we are heading:

"A body compact of creative intelligence, and, round about
that intelligence, a fringe of intuition, was the most complete
thing nature had found it possible to produce. Such was the
human body. *There the evolution of life stopped.*" (Note this
phrase; it is up to man to give life a new impulse.) "But now
intelligence, raising the construction of instruments to a
degree of complexity and perfection which nature (so incapable of mechanical construction) had not even foreseen, pouring into these machines reserves of energy which nature (so
heedless of economy) had never even thought of, has endowed
us with powers beside which those of our body barely count:
they will be altogether limitless when science is able to liber-
ate the force which is enclosed, or rather condensed, in the
slightest particle of ponderable matter."[5]

Thus the obstacle of matter has almost been overcome; it

---

[3] This comparison is naturally not due to Bergson! His work: *The
Two Sources of Morality and Religion* first appeared in 1932.

[4] Though it does not seem that they were ever in contact with each
other.

[5] *The Two Sources*, p. 301, italics ours.

will fall completely in a very near future. But in spite of his progress in mastering nature, in spite of his daring ventures in these infinite spaces which so terrified Pascal, man has advanced no further in solving the problem of his destiny. Even if he were to control life, having reduced it to a mechanism of which he would know all the workings, he would only have acquired unlimited means without being able to control their use. The warning of Socrates to the psycho-physiologists of his day, who were already eager to go down to the ultimate elements in order to be able to rebuild the universe as they pleased, must be issued once again, even more emphatically, now that men are so concerned with what they have and are so negligent of their being, which is dissolving and fading away. And neither have we succeeded in understanding the psychism of man, though its inner workings condition even the use we make of the ever more complicated machines we have at our disposal, nor have we been able to cure this "diseased" man from the complexes of aggressiveness, frustration, guilt, and hatred, which can so easily carry away the dams we are trying to build. In this atomic age, we have at our disposal to ensure the survival of mankind but a balance of terrors. Not only should man have become more lucid—for this increased lucidity can do more harm than good—but nobler values should have been presented to him or he should have been made to understand the importance of those which have been lighting his road like beacons since the beginnings of civilization. The disequilibrium between spirtual and technical powers is constantly becoming more pronounced. And there may not be enough time to remedy this situation:

"A spiritual impulsion had been given, perhaps, at the beginning: the extension took place automatically, helped as it were by a chance blow of the pick-axe which struck against a miraculous treasure underground. Now, in this body, distended out of all proportion, the soul remains what it was, too small to fill it, too weak to guide it. Hence the gap between the two. Hence the tremendous social, political and international problems which are just so many definitions of this gap, and which provoke so many chaotic and ineffectual efforts to fill it. What we need are new reserves of potential energy— moral energy this time. So let us not merely say, as we did above, that the mystical summons up the mechanical. We must add that the body, now larger, calls for a bigger soul, and that mechanism should mean mysticism."[6]

But it is not by dismantling the workings of his psychism and substituting a replica with controlled reflexes that one will give man the "bigger soul" he so desperately needs or that one will be able to arouse in man the reserves of spiritual energy and goodness which are so necessary, no more than one will be able to build a better organized, a "rationalized," society by molding characters to suit the needs, by correcting, even before birth, the position or the number of chromosomes so that as many children as each category requires will be born already conditioned to their function. The disquiet that is the sign of our greatness can be destroyed only by arousing an anguish which increases with our misery and, if this anguish falsifies the basic requirements for life in society, one may end up with the violation or destruction of consciousness; so that, finally, "men" would be merely contented puppets, automata reduced to their fabricated reflexes and to their inferior mind, and, on the social level, to gestures devoid of all intelligence and receptivity; this is indeed the universe of "objectification" described by Berdyaev.

Carrying the hypothesis to its extreme realizations, which even today no longer seem impossible, to the point that this vision of a "broken world inhabited by puppets," by disfigured or dislocated beings, is haunting the imagination of artists,

6 *Ibid.*, pp. 298–299.

Gustave Thibon imagines, in *Vous serez comme des dieux*, a time not far distant from ours in which, after an atomic cataclysm, men would be reconciled and would have solved the problem of their indefinite survival and that of their perfect mental equilibrium. They would have access to the furthest planets; love—a purely physical love—would blossom in peace and without fuss on a planet where the Little Prince need not worry about his "unique" rose, so great is the profusion of artificial flowers growing in the glass-houses. But in this world where all problems have been solved, where wishes are granted before they are even formulated, where time would extend by coiling upon itself, the image of a moving eternity—boredom, this dreadful boredom, would reappear and the exorcised specter of a death that is no longer feared but hoped for would arise anew.

Armande, the heroine of Thibon's play, and later Helios, her fiancé, because he loves her so deeply, will understand that, far from opening a door, science has closed them all and that they are imprisoned in a paradise from which there is no exit. The real door opens only for those who haved heard a call. This call, says Bergson, is addressed to us by mediators—the sage, the hero, the saint who is already at the limit of both worlds.[7] These "mediators" do not coerce, they do not even oblige us to follow them. Those to whom they point out the climbing road, among almost inaccessible crags and yawning abysses, are free, terribly free. Freedom increases at the point of evolution, and with it indetermination so that no one can say in which direction it will be settled. That which is offered

---

[7] "Let a mystic genius but appear, he will draw after him a humanity already vastly grown in body, and whose soul he has transfigured. He will yearn to make of it a new species, or rather deliver it from the necessity of being a species; for every species means a collective halt, and complete existence is mobility in individuality." *The Two Sources*, p. 300.

to us is not awaiting us in time, even if this time were indefinitely extended. A transfiguration alone would allow us to gain access to it. Does this mean that we should not trouble to make the required effort and become absorbed in prayer or inactive contemplation? Bergson did not think so, no more than Teilhard de Chardin. Far from being opposed to mysticism, technology can clear the way for it. By leveling out all obstacles, by making work easier, by increasing the amount of leisure, it makes energy available that can now be used to increase our lucidity and toward self-improvement. We are not free to toil for an ideal if we are threatened by poverty or if we have to fight for survival. The condition is, of course, that we do not waste these precious moments of leisure.

We have just brought together the names of Bergson and of Teilhard de Chardin. And yet it has often been said that Teilhard owed little to Bergson, that their outlook is entirely different. Teilhard himself underlined how his "evolution" differs from that of Bergson. Whereas the impulse of evolution would, for Bergson, diverge from its very first impetus—here brought to a standstill by too great a resistance of matter, thrown back or forced to remain fixed in immutable forms, there progressing for a while toward a more flexible adaptation, elsewhere following the tracks of instinct and intelligence, breaking through the thick wall of inertia, like a hand pushing away the iron filings around it—according to Teilhard it would converge, on the contrary, in more and more concentric waves from the initial attempts that were still shapeless and threatened with waste and regression, so that, amplifying first, then concentrating, reflecting back upon itself, it would progress along a cone to an ultimate point where it would be united and differentiated.

I am not sure however that these images are very convincing. It is true that Bergson himself often used a similar image: that of the jet of water rising in a scintillating sheet, then falling back, after a series of spurts, and dissociating into a multitude of drops pulled down and broken up by gravity and subject to determinism. But he soon sees the flaws in this comparison; he then lets other attractive forces come into play which, like the magnet attracting bits of iron, wrest intelligence from the threat of materiality, emancipating it from the closed world that is holding it back and launching it toward the world beyond: like Christ coming to open the doors of Saint Peter's cell so that he could accomplish his mission. This magnet is the mystics, the saints, who have only to exist and call out for us to go to them and for the new man to be born within us. And thus he goes beyond the conclusions drawn from the facts of the *Creative Evolution*. This evolution is given a new impulse: it now aims at a higher goal:

"On Earth, in any case [Bergson has been discussing the possibility of other types or individuals on the other planets] the species which accounts for the existence of all the others is only partially itself. it would never for an instant have thought of becoming completely itself, if certain representatives of it had not succeeded, by an individual effort added to the general work of life, in breaking through the resistance put up by the instrument, in triumphing over materiality—in a word in getting back to God. These men are the mystics. They have blazed a trail along which other men may pass. They have, by this very act, shown to the philosopher the whence and whither of life."[8]

Far from remaining within the conclusions of Teilhard, Bergson goes almost further, for he not only recognizes that it is up to man to bring creation to its fulfillment, that this mission shoots up like an arrow from a thrust that is nearly stopped, but he also senses the role of grace which is precisely to transform man so extensively that his very nature will be

[8] *Ibid.*, p. 246.

217

exalted. The call from above will endow the man who listens to it with the structures that are indispensable, so that, emancipated henceforth from materiality, he will be ready to receive a richer life. The loved one makes the lover capable of uniting with him.[9]

It is elsewhere—on the subject of "time"—that we find the main differences between Bergson and Teilhard. Bergson's starting point is inner experience. He starts with "the immediate data of consciousness"; among them he notes the presence of a qualitative time, which forms the weave of the phenomena of consciousness—a time which is sometimes distended, sometimes condensed, sometimes dispersed, sometimes coils upon itself, enriching its "present" with all the legacy of the past and with the anticipated wealth of the future. At its highest degree of synthesis, "duration"—enlarged like a snowball by all it picks up on its way—would gather all our existence in a unifying intuition; but those who are capable of such an intuition are very rare indeed, and even then it is only at exceptional moments in their life. But now in this essentially personal time, in this time of creation whose moments respond to one another, vibrating in the same tone in the intertwining of their leitmotivs—as in a Beethoven symphony—we see, after already thinning it out, the weave of existence that preceded and that will extend ours; nonetheless, at this stage it preserves, in its ebb and flow, in its impulses and its falls, its fluid and qualitative continuity.

Another step and time will thin out even more; it will no longer be qualitative but quantitative, breaking up into little pieces, dividing into a dust of discontinuous moments. Sub-

[9] ". . . the mystics unanimously bear witness that God needs us, just as we need God. Why should He need us unless it be to love us?" And: "Beings have been called into existence who were destined to love and be loved, since creative energy is to be defined as love." *Ibid.*, pp. 243, 245–246.

218

ject to the same rhythm, it will be projected from our consciousness into space; it will trace a path along which a moving body travels; the dense and consistent present, past, and future will be replaced by a moving "now" which will recede incessantly toward a definitively past "yesterday." A discontinuity of elements that are exterior to one another will have replaced this combination of affects, feelings, and ideas that are still rich in intimate experiences. Thus appears the empty time, that of the physicist, and later that of the mathematician uniquely concerned with rigorously establishing a simultaneity of events; the clock regulates this simultaneity which is made even more accurate by a series of corrections; this is the time which the computations of the theory of relativity deal with.[10]

The time of Teilhard de Chardin is completely different. No more than Bergsonian "duration" can it be represented by a line along which a moving body is traveling in an irreversible direction: That would be Herbert Spencer's time, expressing a mechanical evolution which progresses by addition or juxtaposition of elements. Teilhard's time is neither linear time —a succession of "settings" that are indifferent to the events that occur in them[11]—nor Bergson's "duration." It is cosmic time, or more precisely, the time of the "cosmogenesis."

"In addition to this space which fascinated Pascal, there is now time, not a receptacle time in which the years would fit —but an organic time measured by the development of global reality. We used to consider ourselves—and the things around

[10] Bergson explained his viewpoint in an extremely dense and inspiring work, *Duration and Simultaneity*, the conclusion of which, however, were not accepted by Einstein.

[11] "Until a quite recent era (till the last century in fact) time remained in practice, for men as a whole, a sort of vast vessel in which things were suspended side by side. In this indifferent and homogeneous field, each being was imagined capable of arising at any moment or place." Teilhard de Chardin, *The Vision of the Past* (London: Collins, 1966), p. 128.

219

us—as points closed upon themselves; beings now discover themselves to be similar to threadless sheaves woven in a universal process. And everything is hurling itself toward a future abyss—forward. By its history, each being is coextensive to the whole of duration, and its ontogenesis is but the infinitesimal element of a cosmogenesis in which the individuality and, so to speak, the face of the universe are finally expressed."[12]

Teilhard's time therefore carries within itself the structures of the cosmos, it is—so to speak—its stuff; inscribed in the heart of being, it evolves with it, caught in the simultaneously interwoven and diverging sheaves which are gradually gathered in the unifying movement of the phylum. Like a river, it is swelled with the water of its tributaries and flows, ever more majestic, between banks that are getting further and further apart; sometimes, however, its waters vanish underground and stagnate, motionless and dead, in hidden pools.

But now it triumphs and drains all sources toward itself, according to the more and more perceptible law of increasing complexification. It cannot be reduced to a rhythm or to a form; or rather, this form cannot be separated from its content. Saint Augustine had already said that time is not anterior to creation; it appeared *with* the creatures, when life first appeared in the original chaos.[13]

"In time," Teilhard de Chardin will also say, "forms lead to one another like branches along which certain characters (size, complexification or simplification of the teeth, modification of the limbs or of the shape of the skull) are regularly becoming more pronounced. Each one of these branches forms a whole, with its own type of individuality, of destiny;

[12] *Un seuil mental sous nos pas: du cosmos à la cosmogenèse,* (March, 1951), pp. 11–12.

[13] Cf. our *Saint Augustin: temps et histoire* (Paris: Editions Augustiniennes, 1956).

it is born, develops, becomes fixed and then disappears."[14]

Edouard Le Roy, who was Teilhard's collaborator for several years and remained a close friend, underlined also to what extent time is at the center of all present-day perspectives. For all people, whether they be philosophers like Martin Heidegger or Louis Lavelle, or novelists like Faulkner, Marcel Proust, or Julien Gracq, time—because we cannot break through the fluctuating horizon it unfolds before us, because neither our memory nor our intuition can master it—remains "the main cause of our imprisonments."[15]

Men did not have to wait till the nineteenth century, Teilhard will also point out, "before seeing how events, grouped in long series, were absorbed into the past. They talked of Time long before our day, and even measured it, so far as their instruments permitted, as we do now. But Time remained for them a homogeneous quantity, capable of being divided into parts. The course of centuries lying ahead and behind us could be conceived of in theory as abruptly stopping or beginning at a given moment, the real and total duration of the Universe being supposed not to exceed a few thousand years. On the other hand, it appeared that within those few millennia any object could be arbitrarily displaced and removed to another point without undergoing any change in its environment or in itself. Socrates could have been born in the place of Descartes, and vice versa. Temporally (no less than spatially) human beings were regarded as interchangeable."[16]

It is on this point that the contrast with Bergson is at its strongest. For Bergson, space and time remained separate: space is exterior to consciousness, it is a homogeneous medium

---

[14] Quoted by Jean Piveteau in *Teilhard de Chardin, Savant* (Paris: Hachette).

[15] Alain-Fournier first used this expression. Cf. our *De Renan à Jacques Rivière*, (Paris: Bloud et Gay, 1930).

[16] *The Future of Man* (New York: Harper & Row, 1964), pp. 83–84.

in which all objects are moving, in which we even project our earlier states, though they undergo a deep alteration in the process, for we are then expressing quantitatively that which is in essence qualitative.

For Teilhard, on the contrary, space and time are closely interwoven, they are imbricated in one another; time is like the stuff of all that exists; it is this sheaf in which chains and threads are tied up together; but, in turn, this sheaf is merely a thread in a larger sheaf, and so forth, almost indefinitely, "so that, Time acting on Space and incorporating it within itself, the two together constitute a single progression in which Space represents a momentary section of the flow which is endowed with depth and coherence by Time."[17]

But this Time that flows by, blending with the ephemeral duration of the species—or rather coinciding with their life which it carries only to abandon it later—is now being replaced by another current which rises more and more toward the level where the decisive step will be taken:

"There is no better proof that life is flexible and that it is progressing.

"In horizontal time, it goes forward or backward. In ascensional time, which is hidden from us, it is rising, but following certain lines only."

There is, therefore, an important division of time into two branches: "transformation or mutation on the one hand, upward thrust on the other."[18]

This decisive step—Teilhard has often repeated—is the

[17] *Ibid.*, p. 84 et seq.

"The universe," wrote Mme Barthélemy-Madaule, "appears to him as moving in a (hyper-Einstein) space-time whose particular curve is to arrange more and more all that is moving in it." In *Bergson et Teilhard de Chardin* (Paris: Editions du Seuil, 1963), pp. 68–69.

[18] This essential text is quoted by Jean Piveteau in *Teilhard de Chardin, Savant.*

appearance of man, after many unsuccessful attempts perhaps. Consciousness and the reflection of this consciousness upon itself—thanks to which man is not content only to know but, knowing that he knows, takes full possession of a knowledge which little by little becomes clearer—have weathered this dangerous cape,[19] and the ascending current of evolutive time, of the time not of the cosmos but of the cosmogenesis, is checked and amplified; it avoids the slope that threatened to pull it down and the waste products that were adding little by little to the contents of the entropy. This interiorized time takes a leap; it goes forward and upward, in concentric waves, higher and higher in the biosphere, and then emerges into the noosphere, uniting and differentiating at the same time. To use another image from the realm of music, we first have a single hesitant melodic line which gathers other melodic lines as it goes along and kneads them and integrates them into a more and more complex harmonization, until suddenly, in the intertwining of instrumental themes, there bursts forth the rich and unifying movement of a symphony. The phylum is made up of these various themes which rise along the stem to spread out in the branches that closely follow the curves, in turn divergent and convergent, of the time it is filling.

Does this time of evolution undergo metamorphoses by coiling upon itself toward the top of the cone where an ultimate and decisive transmutation is awaiting it and are there changes in its magnitude and in its rhythm? Saint Augustine thought so, but Teilhard, obsessed with the vision of a prodigious cosmogenesis whose phases he saw unfolding in a more and more ascending movement mysteriously oriented toward Man, did not dwell on such discussions. This was perhaps a mistake, for they are at the center of our present preoccupa-

---

[19] "The great apes also," Teilhard will say, "are swept along in this ascent. . . . They almost reach this wall that separates simple psychism from the reflective psychism, but do not succeed in crossing it. . . ."

tions. Depending on the solution we find for them, we will or will not provide for a slowing down of our own time under the effect of an increased velocity. Starting from geology and pale-ontology, Teilhard thought he had reached Einstein's four-dimensional universe and even the space-time curve drawn by the motion of a light which is itself governed by the laws of gravitation. But is time not even more complex, and can this time that sets the inexorable rhythm of our lives and encloses them in such narrow limits be reduced to cosmic time, a mere sheaf in the sets that contain it? Or does it have its own rhythm that is to some extent independent of an evolution that would blend with this cosmic time? Lecomte du Noüy, who studied this biological time, felt that its motion should be measured not by the regular rhythm of the clock but by the healing index of tissues, whence the feeling of acceleration we all experience as we get older. Do we not then feel that we are, to quote Jacques Rivière, "hurled toward our term," as though the current that is sweeping us along suddenly accelerated, drawn by the nearing falls, snatched up by the abyss that is about to engulf it?

But perhaps Teilhard's most serious mistake was that of reducing being to becoming, to the drift of time. With this presupposition he gets closer to Nietzsche and further from Saint Augustine. It is true that this becoming does not coil back upon itself, threatened from the very beginning by Eternal Recurrence. No Gateway joins the two roads: that going back into the past and that heading toward the future. At the end of its progressive coiling, temporal becoming, as conceived by Teilhard, encounters eternity and blends into it. But it is not, I think, in this direction in which the "forward" and the "upward" would coincide that we must seek an impos-sible fusion. For time maintains its own character, even if it becomes ascendant. It remains successive, and only thought which emerges from it can attempt to assemble its moments.

Thought is only carried along by time. Because it remains adherent to being, it dominates and transcends time. It cannot recognize itself in that which is happening. The present to which it would like to gain access is not the precarious present of becoming but a present that is in a sense eternal. This is what Louis Lavelle tried to make Teilhard understand, but the latter was suspicious of metaphysicians and wanted to stick to a phenomenological description.

Thus, in spite of several points of disagreement, Bergson and Teilhard de Chardin shared identical aspirations. "I pray for this remarkable man I venerate like a saint."

It is Bergson's last book, *The Two Sources of Morality and Religion*, that he thinks of as a model when vast projects form in his mind. He admires Bergson for giving a coherent form to a thought that is remarkably rich and close to his own. Bergson, too, opposes to the closed world of obligation the universe attracted by the infinite of "open" morality, transfigured by the call of the mystics. Bergson's last book appeared in 1932. Two years later, still under the influence of its reading, Teilhard said:

"Answering Msgr. Bruno de Solages, I once more point out to him that everyone in the Far East is awaiting a book on the *essence of Christianity* or on the *Christian point of view* (as opposed to Buddhism or Confucianism) which would be translated into all languages. But it would have to be something of the magnitude and serenity of Bergson's last book: a natural and well-constructed development of ideas. The genesis of a belief in Christ, starting from the simple belief in being, . . . from the passion for truth. Who will give us this *'Summa contra Gentiles'*?"[20]

But there is another writer who always comes to my mind when I evoke the constant orientation of Teilhard's thought

[20] Quoted by Mme Barthélemy-Madaule, in *Bergson et Teilhard de Chardin*.

or rather the very first reactions of his sensibility, and that is Baudelaire.

Both indeed turn straight away toward that which is solid, consistent. Both are in need of a structuring time, not this evanescent and fluid time in which all that exists is born, grows, decreases, and disintegrates. For Baudelaire as for Edgar Poe, this is the time of sin. He therefore evaluated progress in terms of ethical criteria, measuring it by the gradual vanishing of the traces of original sin, while he wanted beauty —avoiding the drift of time—to be fixed in the timeless. Whence his preference for stone, for the hard and translucent mineral; he refused to think about anything that carried within itself a threat of decomposition. Facing Lisbon, in the estuary of the Tagus where the cargo boat on which he was traveling halted for several hours on its way to the Orient that was to horrify him with its exuberant vegetation, he is filled with happiness for he sees rising before him an apparently indestructible city of marble in which only a few trees remind him of the rotting away to which the world of the living seems condemned. It is thus not to astonish but because of a natural inclination that he likes to describe, perhaps in the wake of the mystic Swedenborg,[21] lovely tidy kitchens in which neat rows of saucepans are softly glowing.[22]

Teilhard also, on several occasions, recalled his fondness for matter, even during his childhood, and the joy he felt then when holding a piece of flint or a metallic object, even a bit of iron whose flawless weight reassured him. But, contrasting with this fascination, he was haunted by a need for spiritual life, for unifying mystical effusions. He had, on the one hand, "the sense of the vastness of space, the sense of the depth— in which matter lies—the sense of the rhythm and of the

[21] Cf. Swedenborg's descriptions of the life of Dutchmen in the next world.

[22] Cf. L'Invitation au voyage en prose and La Chevelure.

number inscribed in it."[23] On the other hand, having been brought up in the midst of a traditionally Catholic family where his vocation to the priesthood soon became apparent, he felt "this need to experience fully within himself the reality of the spirit," to follow up to its ultimate flight a thought which he understood would not be satisfied with abstract reasonings but could blossom forth only in the burning light of love.

Such were the two ends of the chain; what lay between them eluded him. He could either have set them over against one another to the point of transforming them into an irreducible antinomy or have admitted that matter had deceived him with its false consistency. But he will renounce neither matter, whose composition and foundations he studied as a geologist, nor the spirit, which opens up a new orientation for the world. The concept of evolution appeared to him as the mediating concept between these two realities whose value differed but which he wanted to preserve and bring together. Actually, it is possible to distinguish two phases in his reflection. In the first, he sticks to the exact descriptions of the phenomenologist; rejecting both the conclusions of materialism and those of immaterialism, he sees matter and spirit "not as two things, but as two aspects of the same state, the inside and the outside of the same cosmic stuff, considered in turn in the sense in which it makes itself or, on the contrary, in the sense in which it comes apart."[24] In the second stage, he will see in Christ—making use of a daring image which calls for some reservations—"the burning heart of this matter," from whom flow the rays of a light of which the sun is but a

---

[23] "I was probably no more than six or seven years old when I was first attracted toward Matter—or more precisely toward something that 'shone' in the heart of Matter. . . ." Unpublished, from *Le Coeur de la matière*, les Moulins, August 15, Paris, October 30, 1950.

[24] Quoted by Jean Piveteau in *Teilhard de Chardin, Savant.*

pale reflection. Thus, the role of the spirit appears to him more and more decisive, present from the very beginning in this matter from which it will break away someday. This is where he disagrees with scientists whose views he first seemed to share,[25] since, like them, he rejected all dualism, seeing in change the very stuff of reality, in life the outcome of a more and more structured matter and in thought the higher expression of life from which it emerges.

We know that for Jean Rostand, for instance, the appearance of man, a mere accident due to a highly improbable set of circumstances, is the prelude to an adventure that was doomed before it ever began. The day will soon come—if we take the infinite of the time that sweeps us along as our point of reference—when this phosphorescence we call consciousness will fade away; then the stars and the planets will go on following their aimless course in the vastness of space-time. Another scientist, Jeans, said the very same thing: "What does life amount to? To fall, as by mistake, in a universe which obviously was not intended for it; to remain clutched to a fragment of a grain of sand, until the cold of death has returned us to raw matter; to strut for a tiny hour in a tiny theater, knowing full well that all our aspirations are doomed to fail in the end and that all we have accomplished will perish with our race, leaving the universe as though we had never existed. . . . The universe is indifferent or even hostile to any sort of life."[26]

Though he accepts an evolution that is almost identical to that of Jeans, of Jean Rostand, and of Julian Huxley, Teilhard de Chardin rejects such gloomy conclusions. It is true that he declines escape toward metaphysics and considers only the

[25] Whereas he was very harsh and sometimes even unfair to some Catholic philosophers, such as Louis Lavelle, Felice Battaglia, and even Gabriel Marcel, who did not want to give up the world of being.

[26] Jean Piveteau, Teilhard de Chardin, Savant, p. 118.

perspective of phenomenology; he nonetheless associates two groups of coordinates with evolution: The first, which governs a long sequence of adaptations in horizontal motion, leads to stable systems or to species subject to a rhythm of growth or of regression; as far as the spirit is concerned, it is therefore without purpose, without meaning, unintelligible. What strikes us is the inexhaustible number of possible combinations, the improvements in which nature delights with no other result than the slow degeneration or the useless survival of obsolete species from which no original branch has sprung out. But all of a sudden a new Order appears with the advent of Intelligence; a current rises in the midst of the general drift, uniting in a sheaf that which seemed to be irremediably divergent, so that we now sense the presence of a meaning, a meaning that is entrusted to man so that he will bring it to its full expression. And now a third envelope is enclosing the other two, along which widening waves are vibrating. And thus Nietzsche's assertion that "it is man who creates the sense" is now confirmed; for Teilhard, man does not create this sense in an arbitrary fashion but by discovering it; for he is not free to invent this meaning to suit himself; it is inscribed in the very first step of thought, at the end, whch it crowns, of a process of complexification-consciousness.

The first consequence of this would be that it is in man's power to reject this sense, to opt for meaninglessness, for the absurd, that is, for evil. Teilhard discovered this risk very soon —during the long winters of the First World War when, in the trenches of Champagne, he looked up at the moon, this dead star: It was then perhaps that he experienced most acutely the temptation of despair. This complete freedom that was granted to the intelligent being is indeed much more far-reaching, much more terrifying than that of the Orestes of *The Flies*, standing up in his vain pride against the now shaky power of Zeus. It can indeed be said that man is the being who, knowing that he knows, can, through his choice, ratify the course in which ascending evolution is engaged with him and through him, or replace it with complete non-sense, thus condemning himself and all this current that is henceforth adrift to vanish, to sink into the night with this universe that was prepared to receive him as a precious jewel. We therefore cannot deny that Teilhard answers the question that arises today on the subject of man, that he provides the means of founding a humanism which is more satisfying than that of existentialism, which confronts man with the absurd, or that of Marxism, which encloses him in a collectivity and defines him in terms of his function alone.

According to Teilhard—who like Pascal pulls us out of our wretchedness—we do not shoot up, like a flying star, from the emptiness of space in which we will be swallowed up again together with the societies we have built. Each one of our existences is prepared by a slow evolution which makes the earlier rough attempts of the inorganic and of the organic converge toward ever richer, ever more complex, ever more centrated realities. Thus fixed groups are replaced by the impetus of a matter that is already animated by life, a life that is already animated by thought. For Teilhard, evolution is therefore the answer to the enigma; it gathers that which if left stationary would remain fragmented, unites and differentiates that which would remain dispersed, complexifies the elementary and progressively coils around a single axis that which was moving independently around a multitude of different axes.

"As the star dust correctly located in the dome of the heavens assumes today, in the eyes of astronomers, the appearance of huge rotating spirals—thus the myriads of beings which we call Life tend to arrange themselves according to a very simple law of psychic concentration, culminating at the present instant of the world with Man. Beginning with man, descending toward the origins, consciousness appears to disintegrate, to diffuse to the point of becoming imperceptible. Toward Man, progressing along the axis of time, spontaneity awakens, organizes itself and finally reflects upon itself, emerging into the Personal."[27]

In a daring extrapolation, Teilhard extends to civilizations what he has asserted about life. These civilizations have appeared first at distinct, almost unconnected centers, in Mesopotamia, at the sources of the Nile, in China, in Central America; great gaps were separating them, then little by little and while developing each one in its own way, they spread their roots, grew closer together, and blended to the point of forming a culture that now covers all the globe. Gradual extension and an increasing complexity, these are once more the two directions followed by evolution.[28]

If Teilhard gets more and more enthusiastic over these signs that announce an acceleration of this mixing which promotes everywhere the triumph of a differentiating unity, he is nevertheless well aware of the dangers it entails; like Paul Valéry, he know that civilizations are fragile, unstable, precarious.

"That insatisfaction is our lot, that we must be resigned to live—and die—in anxiety and darkness, of this I am convinced. . . . This certainty regarding the vanishing of all human values unquestionably appears extremely gloomy to some and even to myself I must admit—but I think that it has to be accepted and 'channeled.' "[29]

We will not attempt to follow, step by step, along the end-

---

[27] *Esquisse d'un univers personnaliste*, p. 72.

[28] Marcello Fabri, whose intuitions are very often close to those of Teilhard de Chardin, uses the symbol of the "spiral" to describe this movement that is both converging and ascending.

[29] On the negative pole of the world, cf. *The Divine Milieu* (New York: Harper & Row, 1960), pp. 128–131, and "La Signification et la valeur constructive, de la souffrance," in *L'Energie humaine* (Paris: Editions du Seuil), pp. 61–65.

less geological periods, this slow maturation, with its share of unsuccessful attempts, oriented toward an essential threshold: that of the reflection of energy upon itself, of its concentration in the pole of consciousness. Reflection then, taking back all that appears as merely forming the prerequisites for its sudden appearance, turns evolution in a completely new direction; the law of complexification turns out to be a law of complexification-consciousness.[30] We note however—since many critics, even a Marxist such as Garaudy, seem unaware of this fact—that Teilhard completely rejects an idealistic starting point, so that he differs from Edouard Le Roy as well as from Bergson. For the idealist is bound to acknowledge that consciousness comes first; the world at the beginning exists only through and in each individual consciousness in which it is partially gathered, grasped by each one in its own perspective; it is only from its appearance that we can infer its being. Let consciousness vanish and the world vanishes with it. In this respect, existentialism could only give a more dramatic resonance to this irrefutable affirmation.

But, because he wants to remain a scientist and a phenomenologist, Teilhard is not hindered by the primacy of consciousness and of the *Cogito*. If he starts with sensations, it is to endow them with an objective value; we cannot question the fact that our existence did not rise from nothingness but that it comes from a branch whose origin is lost in the night of time. Science confirms what common sense dictates: My consciousness appeared at a certain stage of evolution as a mutation that may have been unpredictable but nevertheless cannot be isolated from the flow that preceded and carried it; the universe then centered around it, but it remains a fleeting instant of the process of hominization with which I must collaborate and which will go on for a long time after me. Like

---

[30] This law was first formulated in 1935.

the superimposed scales on the original stem of the phylum, it is enclosed in other consciousnesses; my memory also is but a cup in a memory that extends beyond it on all sides—the memory of mankind since its earliest origins; my mind is but a ray that is rapidly absorbed by the infinite if it strays from the source from which it receives its light. Originating in an initial dispersion, there appears a beginning of concentration, an outline of that much more complex concentration required by life. The atoms are grouped in more and more coherent systems to form corpuscles which, in turn, will become more complex until reaching the saturation point at which rudimentary organisms first make their appearance:

"To begin with, at the very bottom there is still an unresolved simplicity, luminous in nature and not to be defined in terms of figures. Then, suddenly came a swarming of elementary corpuscles, both positive and negative (protons, neutrons, electrons, photons): the list increases incessantly. Then the harmonic series of simple bodies, strung out from hydrogen to uranium on the notes of the atomic scale. Next follows the immense variety of compound bodies in which the molecular weights go on increasing up to a certain critical value above which, as we shall see, we pass on to life. There is not one term in this long series but must be regarded, from sound experimental proofs, as being composed of nuclei and electrons. This fundamental discovery that all bodies owe their origin to arrangements of a single initial corpuscular type is the beacon that lights the history of the universe to our eyes. In its own way, matter has obeyed from the very beginning that great law of biology, . . . the law of 'complexification.' "[31]

[31] *The Phenomenon of Man* (New York: Harper & Row, 1959), pp. 47–48. These views, which he first stated in *The Phenomenon of Man*, will later be taken up again in a series of studies and works between 1945 and 1953. We will only mention the most important ones:

"The Formation of the Noosphere. A Biological Interpretation of

We can therefore only be surprised to see a Marxist such as Garaudy classify Teilhard among the idealists; on this point, on the contrary, he clearly disagreed with his great friend Edouard Le Roy.[32] It would be impossible to stress too much

Human History" (January, 1947). Cf. *The Future of Man*, pp. 155–184.

"The Human Rebound of Evolution and Its Consequences" (April 20, 1948). Cf. *The Future of Man*, pp. 196–213.

"Does Mankind Move Biologically upon Itself?" (October 20, 1949). Cf. *The Future of Man*, pp. 244–259.

"La Réflexion de l'énergie," *Revue des questions scientifiques*, Louvain, October 20, 1949.

"The End of the Species," (February, 1953). Cf. *The Future of Man*, pp. 298–305. In this article he sets the crucial problem: Can man survive or will the human species have the same fate as all animal species? Here again Teilhard was replying to Jean Rostand:

"How could one believe," wrote the latter, "that the property of survival, that the right to an afterlife suddenly appeared at a certain level of the organic ladder, at a certain stage of evolution? No, if man is immortal, the pitheocanthrope must have been immortal also, and the great monkeys, and also the lower monkeys, and the mammals and the reptiles, and the fish, and the whole sequence of our ancestors as far back as the original cells. Each cell, each microbe, each virus, would then have to be endowed with a micro-afterlife, a micro-immortality." *Ce que je crois* (Grasset, 1953).

Teilhard claimed on the contrary that the psychic convergence that is becoming more and more apparent leads us to believe that death is destined to disappear. Moreover, this affirmation led to a new definition of Good and Evil:

"Is good all that which favors the ascent of life, creative transformation, and love that is the force born to take the place of blind energy.

"Is evil all that which hinders this ascent, all which tends to disintegrate this ascending energy, all which is against attraction, cohesion, and unity."

[32] On the subject of the friendship and the close collaboration between Teilhard and Edouard Le Roy, it is useful to read a note by Mme Barthélemy-Madaule in *Bergson et Teilhard de Chardin*, pp. 655–659. As for the idealism of Le Roy, cf. our study in *Portraits*: "La Pensée mondiale contemporaine" (Milan: Marzorati, 1963), Vol. IV.

that, as long as he is dealing with purely phenomenological descriptions, he seems to follow point by point the analyses of the Marxists. The discrepancy appears only when, suddenly broadening his vision of the world by a daring hypothesis, he unfolds up to the Omega point the ascending history of mankind, a history that he views as leading—perhaps after a final convulsion[33]—to the transfiguration of heaven and earth. Though they profess an energetics that is more vitalistic than mechanistic (without however admitting a telefinalistic arrangement of matter), the Marxists nonetheless refuse to admit a sudden change in the direction of energy that would henceforth be centered upon itself and in which "points" of reflection would multiply: "points" which are reminiscent of the dynamic atoms of Boscovitch, or even the "monads" of Leibniz—monads which would become more and more translucent and would have the power to "make themselves" while transforming the universe.[34] Though in full agreement with Teilhard regarding the more and more close and fruitful relationship established by work between the worker and the machine, between the artisan and the object he is molding, Marxism refuses to accept the idea of a "creative transformation": Teilhard used these terms to denote not only an adaptation to increasingly socialized tasks but an inner renewal by which man fulfills himself, "makes" his own soul, providing the universe with a new envelope, "the noosphere." In this

---

[33] Teilhard sometimes puts forward this hypothesis which is similar to that formulated by Joachim of Fiore.

[34] Cf. the following fundamental text: "Thus every man, in the course of his life, must not only show himself obedient and docile. By his fidelity he must *construct*—starting from the most natural zone of his own self—a work, an *opus*, into which something enters from all the elements of the earth. *He makes his own soul* throughout all his earthly days; and at the same time he collaborates in another work, in another *opus*, which infinitely transcends, while at the same time it narrowly determines, the perspectives of his individual achievement: the completing of the world." *The Divine Milieu*, p. 29.

grandiose prospective opening onto a bright future the Marxists will merely see a surrender to the dreams, to the egocentric
illusions of class consciousness.

This same disagreement will oppose Teilhard to his non-
believing friends and will become more pronounced in spite
of all his efforts to make them understand his point of view.
It is true that Julian Huxley, for instance, admits that man
made his appearance at the crucial state of evolution not as
the result of a series of accumulated modifications but by a
transformation that was sudden, unexpected, and coherent,
since it simultaneously affected all his organs by organizing
them in a different and unforeseeable manner; but, though he
agreed with his friend on this score and indeed went even
further—since he saw in nature thresholds that were reached
by "leaps," by sudden jumps—he refused to see in these
"mutations" the sign of an absolute beginning, corresponding, on a higher level, to a creative act. Besides, how could
Teilhard have convinced him? For him the two concepts of
"threshold" and "discontinuity" which Huxley accepts in connection with the human person are hardly sketched: At the
very most he will occasionally mention a "discontinuity of
continuities." It would have been necessary to define and formulate a law that would be as essential as that of arrangement
about a center and of continuous complexification in order to
show that everything happens as though the expansion of a
function—and even more its orientation toward other ends—
were determining the actualization of structures which had
been merely outlined until then. So that the structure-func-
tion relationship is not simple but reciprocal. That which we
call intelligence or thought covers an immense area; it involves
several potentialities: Thought can indeed either restrict itself
to the tasks of "lower" reason, absorbed in its effort of adaptation and prediction, or, by folding back upon itself, by reflection upon itself, it can rise to the peaks of meditation or of

inner knowledge, or absorb itself in the object to the point of reaching this disinterested contemplation which Aristotle considered as the highest form of activity, or finally, slowly, at the cost of uncertain trials, by means of presentiments, guided by warnings that are deciphered little by little, it can rise always upward toward the peaks of mystical revelation, above this time to which it was not destined.[35]

But this "upward" can at no time become tangential to a "forward." This time might unfold and coil upon itself without ever completing the skein it abandons to the past, without ever, by this double movement backward and forward, discovering the secret "dimension" that opens up onto eternity. As suggested by Plato's myth of the cave, we are here in the presence of two planes—as in El Greco's famous *Burial of the Count of Orgaz*—and these two planes cannot be put end to end: Time offers no means of access from one to the other. That which appears to us in the continuity of time, following a sequence which our need for intellection tries to make as rigorous as possible, merely expresses and translates the acts outside of time by which God creates the world, inscribing in it the indispensable corrections which will come to light as time goes on.[36] Thus history which flows in time reflects, in a perspective which unavoidably warps it, an eternal ideal history, to use Vico's expression.[37] No phenomenology can be valid if it is not backed up by an ontology; however, Teilhard wanted to be only a phenomenologist.

And this is also the reason for a divergence between him

[35] Cf. our work *Les Dimensions de l'être et du temps* (Lyon: Vitte, 1953).

[36] Taking into account, to a certain extent, the risk implied in the freedom granted to man, a freedom which is at the basis of another order but can cause serious disturbances in the lower orders.

[37] Cf. our work: *La Formation de la pensée de J.-B. Vico* (Paris: Presses Universitaires de France, 1943).

and Jean Rostand that will become more and more pronounced; in spite of so many common investigations, so many identical findings, they reach diametrically opposite conclusions:

"Between the pliocene world and the human world that followed," wrote Teilhard, "(a world that was so remarkably closed, . . . structured, . . . dominating all other forms of life), there is, no matter what has been said about it, not only a difference in degree, but a change of order (or if one prefers, a change of state). By its properties, by its methods of invention, by its autonomy, the human "noosphere" obviously represents a new envelope, *sui generis*, around the old photosphere."[38]

But this is not obvious to Jean Rostand, who may have missed some clues in his desire to stick to facts:

"For a naturalist," he writes, "everything in the living world mingles, blends, interpenetrates. Nowhere can he see a hiatus, a break. We must not forget that that which man adds to the animal is, in fact, very little, compared with what the animal already is, that the mystery particular to man is very little compared with the massive mystery of animality. We must not forget that the great problems which puzzle us arise in connection with *all* beings as well as with man: origin, evolution, adaptation, consciousness; these problems, it would be illogical and unfair to want to exploit them to the advantage of man alone, to endow him with a status which cannot be justified."[39]

Thus, where Teilhard announces an imminent awakening, the dawn of a glorious day, Jean Rostand sees only a nonprepared adventure doomed to failure. Can we be surprised at this when we think of the uncertainties of a language which,

[38] "La Réflexion de l'énergie," *Revue des question scientifiques*, 1949, p. 183.

[39] Jean Rostand, *ce que je crois*, pp. 58–59.

though it sometimes rises to the peaks of poetry, is only too often satisfied with formulas that are remarkably ambiguous, so much so that one wonders if evolution does not carry along all beings—including the supreme Being—in its drift, leaving it up to man to recreate them. As for God, one wonders if one should say that he is or that he *makes himself;* after slumbering for a long time in the heart of matter that was already made burning and luminous by his presence, then after animating the flow of life by rising in its branches, Being would gain access, thanks to man, to the midst of human communities and, in an exchange of love, to personal existence. Man, who was only imperceptibly different from the great apes, is now endowed with quasi-ultimate powers![40] Teilhard himself sometimes admits that only an act of faith can settle the insoluble debate between him and Jean Rostand. He then comes remarkably close to Pascal, for his choice can be justified only by a refusal to accept the unintelligible, or rather by feeling that it is impossible that a world in which intelligence has appeared should be doomed to absurdity:

"The answer to that uneasiness of the modern world springs up by itself when we formulate the dilemma in which the analysis of our action has imprisoned us.

"*Either* nature is closed to our demands for futurity, in which case thought, the fruit of millions of years of effort, is stifled, still-born in a self-abortive and absurd universe. Or else an opening exists—that of the super-soul above our souls; but in that case the way out, if we are to agree to embark on it, must open out freely into limitless psychic spaces in a universe to which we can unhesitatingly entrust ourselves."[41]

Thus two directions remain open, and it is up to our free-

[40] We would have liked to stress the excessive use Teilhard always makes of extrapolation and even intrapolation. In its own domain, science will resort to them only with the greatest caution.

[41] *The Phenomenon of Man,* pp. 231–232.

dom to make the choice that will influence our actions—two directions, but on neither side can we find "tangible evidence;" at the very most "in support of hope, there are rational invitations to an act of faith."

Did Teilhard maintain these cautious reservations? This does not seem to be the case. I read with great care and even with a secret desire to be convinced, the pages in which Henri de Lubac shows to what extent he struggled with the problem of evil.[42] But whereas in 1916 he was concerned about the danger entailed in an increase of power that is not compensated by an enrichment of the soul, he later yielded without reservations to an unbounded faith in the destiny of man; the achievements of the cosmonauts, reunited beyond the atmosphere, appeared to him as the omen of a universe enveloped, beyond a thin layer of respirable air, in a vast and deep noosphere.

Gabriel Marcel was surprised at this excessive confidence during a debate organized on January 21, 1947, by the "Science and Consciousness" group. The theme Teilhard chose for his paper was: "To what degree does the material organization of humanity lead man to the point of spiritual maturation?" In his talk, Teilhard underlined that technology is first of all a decisive effort to accelerate the process of spiritualization of matter that had already begun before the appearance of man. Collectivization, on the other hand, by creating a greater complexity, would give rise to a higher consciousness that would be more enlightened, more reflective, and more susceptible of reflecting the divine: Collectivization alone could bring about the maturation of man.

Not very convinced that a connection will rise spontaneously between the development of techniques—which first of

---

[42] Cf. the works by Henri de Lubac: *Teilhard Chrétien* and *Teilhard de Chardin: The Man and His Meaning* (*La Prière de Teilhard de Chardin*).

240

all aim at mastering the universe—and the process of spiritualization, Gabriel Marcel reproached Teilhard with exalting the Promethean man at the expense of the true Christian ideal. In fact, the discussion could have gone on indefinitely, without ever reaching a positive conclusion. Gabriel Marcel, aware of the waste of being that is undermining our "broken world," of the confusion of souls that are threatened by the most dangerous forms of "amusements," of the loss of the sense of the "human" which is forever becoming more pronounced, felt that the roads leading to inner enrichment are diverging more and more from those which aim at full possession of the universe: Man appeared to him as more and more concerned with increasing what he "has," and more and more indifferent to everything but his future in this world.[43] Teilhard, without in any way underestimating the obstacles which the world sets in the way of emancipation of the spirit, believed[44] that the times are gone when man, convinced that the end of the world was at hand, could afford to worry about his soul alone. Henceforth he must have the "sense of the earth." Because of this very evolution he is called upon to direct, not a single object, however humble, can be overlooked: We will save ourselves together or we will all perish, dragging down in our fall the whole universe, whose destiny is more and more tied up with the option of our free will. It is true that the soul is more important than everything else, but how can it be isolated from matter in which it has been present from the very beginning, which it animates and sweeps along more and more?

Unknown to himself, Teilhard had thus rediscovered—in a perspective of cosmogenesis—the conclusions of Avicenna. It is true, said the Muslim philosopher, that the soul is an

[43] Same notation as that used by Karl Jaspers; cf. *Man in the Modern Age*.

[44] And with good reason.

expatriate in this world; it is threatened by great dangers, but it must fully assume its role to bring back to the One all that which has been broken up, materialized in the multiple. In an indefinitely broadened perspective, the world, through the accelerated time of evolution, appeared to Teilhard as progressing toward Unity, a Unity which, far from creating uniformity, will differentiate. The decisive stage took place with the first appearance of man, centering around his own consciousness the whole evolutive course of things. From this transformation to the final transfiguration, there is but one step; it is up to us to make the world take it.

Thus the demands of the times in which we live call for daring solutions. This is what Descartes had already sensed when he assigned two apparently contradictory goals to man: to detach himself from all things in view of the eternal beatitude which is the end of the soul; to master and gain possession of nature. To show that these goals, far from excluding one another, actually condition one another is what Teilhard set out to do. In so doing he broke away from thinkers who were otherwise very close to him in their spiritual preoccupations: Berdyaev, for instance, for whom the danger of objectification affecting even the integrity of the person appeared more and more threatening; Louis Lavelle also, who reminded man of his obligation to remain anchored in his being, which is the only possible basis for his perpetual present. To all of them he objected that it is necessary to adapt to the conditions which are set for us to toil in a universe in which conflicts, though they may be acute today, will become constantly weaker, in which a movement of increasing concentration and convergence has already begun:

"We must understand this once for all. For us and our descendents, time and all psychological dimensions have definitively changed. Cosmogenesis is not only divergence and feeling: it is first of all a movement of convergence, of synthesis and of union. But how could God unite without immersing himself in the world, without sharing in the suffering of the world which is incomplete union?"

It is true that such sincerity deserves from us all an effort of understanding which Msgr. de Solages so eloquently claimed for Teilhard de Chardin. Must we not also agree with him that our perspectives have changed even more after Michelson, Lorentz, and Einstein than after Galileo? We are swept along by a current from which we cannot escape. It is therefore wiser to try to direct it. It seems that the dimensions of the God in whom we believe have increased together with those of a universe whose center, in space-time, is everywhere and whose circumference is nowhere. Will our mind, our will be able to rise to this level? Man himself must not only be surpassed but renewed, fulfilled in order to be in a position to deal with a world that has been entrusted to his care. Thus Msgr. de Solages will praise Teilhard for "showing, more than any other man, that evolution itself can only be finalistic, that it is advancing towards the spirit, that it can be explained only by the spirit, and that it postulates at the beginning because it postulates at the end, a transcendent God."[45]

The formula is valid, however, only because the word *transcendent* fortunately corrects the words *beginning* and *end*. For God is neither backward—in an act that would insert him in time, of which he would be the first moment—nor forward, at the end of a process during which he would fulfill himself. He is *above*, similar indeed to the apex of a cone, completely inaccessible to our efforts. He gathers and holds all that exists in an immutable consciousness in which all is simultaneously present. As for us, as Saint Augustine once said, we are carried along in the current of time which divides and destroys us,

[45] As quoted in Claude Cuénot, *Teilhard de Chardin: A Biographical Study* (Baltimore: Helicon, 1965), p. 267.

imploring the being in whom alone we can solidify and acquire some consistency. It is not within our power to fulfill ourselves and to transfigure the world.

Jean Hyppolite, after a lengthy conversation with Teilhard, was also amazed at the strength of a *Credo* which would not consider the possibility of any valid objections and, above all, at his claim to give it a scientific basis:

"We discussed existentialism a great deal at that time. From the first, I was struck by Teilhard's *optimism*—in this sense he was more Hegelian than I;[46] I felt more reserves than he on the crisis in the consciousness of Humanity. I insisted on the total risk; he recognized the threat, but answered me with comments about 'the light years' and the general curve in the future of Man—a philosophical and also Christian confidence. I think that Père Teilhard clearly went beyond existentialism in that poetic and prophetic vision of the future which he supported with his science. He agreed with me that the present crisis in consciousness was tragic, but this was for him only momentary. He was moving toward the future with a Bergsonian[47] confidence, with the certitude of a prophet and scientist."[48]

It is true that in this excessive optimism we must allow for an effort of the will which refuses to dwell upon the possibility of failure—a perspective that would be too depressing and would hinder its impetus, this impetus we must communicate to the world. But how can we resist the intoxication of such an exalting vision? And yet what would it avail man

[46] He believed that "All that is real is rational," thus excluding the possibility of a "heterogenesis of ends," of a "trick of reason."

[47] Cf. this other text: "The possible increments in total spiritual Energy are dependent on what Bergson called 'creative evolution'; they are therefore by nature unforeseeable." *L'Energie humaine*, p. 170.

[48] As quoted in Cuénot, *Teilhard de Chardin: A Biographical Study*, p. 255.

to have mastered the hostile forces of nature if he could not control the irrational forces within himself? Of what use would it be to extend his reign to the furthest planets, to get accustomed to weightlessness, to create—at distances that are at present beyond calculation—the conditions that would allow him to survive, if in all these conquered worlds he were to give free rein to his frenzies of frustration, aggresiveness, hatred, and envy? To extend to the galaxies this law of the jungle, which seems to get worse as civilization progresses, is this the way to ensure this need for spiritual life which our disquiet betrays? Gabriel Marcel was concerned, and with good reason, about the danger involved in the accelerated development of our technology, about the process of "dehumanization" rather than "spiritualization" attendant upon it. The Devil once offered Jesus the kingdoms of the universe. Christ was to face three temptations; the same ones are haunting us today and urge us to become "gods." The problem has not changed; man must know himself and fulfill himself in a universe which he discovers to be beyond him in all ways but which he nonetheless wants to subordinate to his own creative genius. His success or his failure will determine the outcome of a harrowing adventure.

9
From the Phenomenon of Man to Christology

I live at the heart of a single, unique Element, the Centre of the universe, and present in each part of it: personal Love and cosmic Power.

To attain to him and become merged into his life I have before me the entire universe with its noble struggles, its impassioned quests, its myriads of souls to be healed and made perfect. I can and I must throw myself into the thick of human endeavour, and with no stopping for breath. For the more fully I play my part and the more I bring my efforts to bear on the whole surface of reality, the more also will I attain to Christ and cling close to him.

God, who is eternal Being-in-itself, is, one might say, everywhere in process of formation for us.

And God is also the heart of everything; so much so that the vast setting of the universe might be engulfed or wither away or be taken from me by death without my joy being diminished. Were creation's dust, which is vitalized by a halo of energy and glory, to be swept away, the substantial Reality wherein every perfection is incorruptibly contained and possessed would remain intact: the rays would be drawn back into their Source, and there I should still hold them all in a close embrace.

Teilhard de Chardin[1]

*I*t is not without hesitation that I formulated some reservations about the phenomenology of Teilhard de Chardin. My reluctance to voice them is even greater now that I am going to try and follow him from "the phenomenon of man" to "the divine milieu," so splendid is the inner source, so enriching the meditation. I will try to be as understanding as possible, to penetrate as far as I can in the heart of this "intention"

[1] "Christ in the World of Matter. Three Stories in the Style of Benson," in Hymn of the Universe (New York: Harper & Row, 1965), pp. 53–55.

246

which is going to alter all the perspectives he had previously considered only out of concern for objectivity. Indeed, it would perhaps be better to speak of "intentionality" than of intention; a very special intentionality which aims at revealing what was hitherto concealed. It is the very core of the world that is revealed; it is the hidden source of reality that becomes apparent, the supreme mystery of the presence of Christ animating and promoting the real, orienting time toward its destination. It is still a phenomenology, but one which a daring extrapolation has carried to its final conclusions. It is thus neither that of Hegel, nor that of Husserl, nor that of Merleau-Ponty; we would rather think of Maurice Blondel, if Blondel were not always so concerned with giving his religious phenomenology an ontological foundation: that of Being and of the substantial tie with which this Being binds together and gathers in himself all the beings he has created.[2]

We must however be fair. Teilhard de Chardin is well aware that the most urgent problem our generation has to face remains that of the relationship between reason and faith; even more than yesterday, however much our vision of a world that is both past and simultaneously present in Space-Time may have broadened, we must avoid a double mistake: For it would be a mistake to compel faith to fit into the frame of a reason which aims only rarely at understanding and, in most cases, is satisfied to remain at the surface of reality, to "surround" it in order to make use of it; but it would be an even more serious mistake to oppose faith to reason, to the point of compelling this reason to accept that which seems absurd. This is why Teilhard invokes Saint Augustine—whose double formula he takes up again in the broader perspective of cosmogenesis: *intellige ut credas, crede ut intelligas*—and, even more often, Pascal.

---

[2] Cf. the thesis in Latin on the *Vinculum substantiale* and most of all *L'Etre et les êtres* (Presses Universitaires de France, 1938).

I do not think however that his essentially optimistic and conciliating nature would have allowed him to understand Pascal, though there is no denying that there are great analogies between his method and that of the author of the *Pensées*. Pascal remains the philospher of "antinomies." He makes use of them to "awaken" man, to oblige him to face his condition in the world; he reveals to him his "finiteness," equally distant from the two infinites he cannot hope to understand: the infinite of greatness and the infinite of smallness. It is true, he tells him, that "all our dignity lies in thought," but this powerless thought floats between principles that are invincibly beyond its reach and the ultimate consequences which are eluding it. It will therefore have to admit that it cannot, by its own means, satisfy the need for truth and justice which is essential to it. Teilhard does not experience so deeply the "tensions" which, already present in matter, become exasperated in our consciousness, or if he did experience them, grace was there to shield him. One must go back as far as the 1914–1918 war to find him crying out in despair. Then, meditating not only on individual death but on the collective death evoked by the ironical presence of the moon, he once wrote these lines that are as desperate as those of Jeans or Jean Rostand:

"Is it a challenge you are issuing, O Moon, you the implacable mirror of our future, or are you giving us your last lesson?

"If it is a challenge, we take it up. We will break through our limits, we will launch a boat on the ocean of space, letting the Earth sink behind us. . . . From planet to planet we will emerge; from star to star, as they begin to die, we will carry the flame of life. But to what avail? Would the last star be any less mortal than the Earth?

"What Titan could prevent Matter from folding back inexorably upon itself and closing upon itself? The day will come

248

when, like a great fossil, the Earth will also gravitate, all white. Movement will have vanished from its surface and it will have kept all our bones."

This text is of interest because it shows that at that time Teilhard had not yet seen opening up in the heart of evolution an ascending path in which matter, which had appeared to be doomed to immobility and death, will set out as though answering a call. But the discovery of the law of complexification-consciousness would not have been sufficient to overcome anguish and dizziness, which had become even more pronounced with the discovery of the quasi-unlimited dimensions of the universe, if a "marvelous" truth had not been revealed to him. What would be the use of going from star to star if these suns must die one after the other, after compelling man to undertake useless migrations? What would be the use of this ever-renewed sacrifice of individuals and generations if the species is condemned? What is the use of trying to find a way out toward some higher form of humanity, since this super-humanity would also be ephemeral? Teilhard provides a very subtle analysis of this anguish he then experienced. He distinguishes three types of fear:

a) The fear of being henceforth and forever reduced to immobility in a stabilized zoological group.

b) The fear of being lost in a world that is so vast and so full of indifferent and hostile beings that "the human seems to be of no significance at all in it."

c) The fear finally, the supreme fear of being shut up, imprisoned in an irremediably closed world "in which humanity will not fail to stumble against an impassable barrier."[3]

"Tomorrow," he will later write to the Abbé Gaudefroy, "tomorrow a sort of panic claustrophobia would grip human-

---

[3] "The fear that no one can hear us, the fear of not being able to move, the fixation of the universe in the form of a fixed set."

ity at the mere thought that it might be hermetically sealed in a closed universe."[4]

A threefold fear which expresses in the heart of each thinking element of the universe the same obstinate will to 'be differentiated, fulfilled, saved; current science cannot wrest this triune will from our heart, but by a prejudice of atheism, it transforms it into a triple despair.'

We must underline these essential words: *by a prejudice of atheism.* Teilhard appeals to a wider, to a *more comprehensive* science in contrast with this current science that sticks only to appearances. An unintelligible world will then be replaced by a world which will reveal its *sense.* The following letter is very important in this connection, as it indicates the essence of a demonstration that appeals both to reason and to faith:

"In the steps of Henri Poincaré and guided by a fashionable agnosticism or seduced by a semblance of stoicism or of higher detachment, many intellectuals imagine they accept without faltering the idea that Thought will last only a moment on this earth, and that, for this moment, we must give everything;[5] it is a 'flash in the night.' We feel that these people are deluding themselves because they have not gone to the very end of what is implied in the terms 'total death' of the universe. We are convinced that, unknown to themselves, they shy off before they reach the very bottom of the words they are using. They assume something will remain of this flash, something will be recorded in a consciousness, in a memory, in a look. Now it is this last hope we must discard if we want to reach the true concept (which is probably as absurd and the

---

[4] *Réflexions sur la compassion humaine,* published in 1953. Cf. *Trois choses que je vois,* 1948. (Here again we are reminded of Baudelaire: "*Quand le ciel bas et lourd pèse comme un couvercle.* . . . *Quand la terre est changée en un cachot humide* . . ." *Spleen.*

[5] Cf. the text by Thomas Mann which we quoted at the beginning of Chapter 4.

idea of Nothingness)[6] of absolute death. No, not even that (it would still be too much for the universe to have delighted, if only for a moment, eyes that would never shut). But all around us the dark and total night which will allow nothing of all these things we will have understood and conquered to filter through for anyone. . . . But then why go to all this trouble? Why obey the expectations and the calls of evolution? A supreme detachment? But there is no virtue in self-sacrifice when no higher interest is in cause! A universe that would continue to act and toil in the conscious expectation of absolute death would be a stupid world, a monster of the Spirit, a chimera! Then, since the world appears to us *hic et nunc* as a vast action, ever expanding with a calm confidence, it must be capable of providing indefinitely, in that which is born of it, for a taste for living that is ever more critical, demanding and refined, it must bear within itself the conditions for ultimate success. And thus as soon as Thought appeared in it, the universe could no longer be temporary nor have a limited evolution; it must, by its structure, *emerge into the Absolute*. Hence, in spite of the unstable appearances of life —in spite of its impressive ties with limiting spaces and decomposing forces—one thing remains more certain than all the rest (because it is as certain as the world): The spirit will always succeed, as it has so far, in overcoming all determinisms and obstacles. *It represents the indestructible part of the universe*."[7]

The first decisive step has been taken. The world had been oriented toward Thought and it is now oriented by Thought. Already, it is emerging through it; the psychic energies that will allow it to rise to the peaks where it will settle are accumulating in it. Nietzsche thought—since the number of combina-

[6] This is an allusion to Bergson's criticism of the concept of nothingness.

[7] In *L'Esprit de la terre*.

tions of elements and forces in action in the universe is finite
—that Time had to coil upon itself, enveloping all existence
in the Ring of rings and imitating Eternity with its incessant
recurrences. Teilhard sees an energy with unlimited power
building up the universe by centering progressively upon itself
to the point that it creates Thought. Now it is not possible
that having converged toward the Spirit, having emerged
through it into a new Order, it should now turn back; for
Thought after appearing in this way is now revealing a new
dimension which embraces the four-dimensions of Space-
Time; a new gravitational Center draws all things toward a
continuous raising. Another step and the nature of this Center
becomes apparent; it is this hidden structuration which, from
its very beginning, created the impetus and imposed convergence upon it. If we were to move indefinitely in space, if
after crossing the sound barrier, we were to come close to this
impassable light barrier, we would still not escape from our
prison. But we are discovering at last "the superior and boundless unity of the universe, the unique circle that embraces the
whole spirit and imprisons nothing."[8]

And our prayers rise toward this Center which gives a meaning to all that exists, which creates at the climax of the cosmogenesis a Thought that is attracted toward it: "O marvelous
center, O unique Sphere, O God. . . ." We are now saved,
since we know that "something exists beyond the circle which
restricts our view, something into which we shall eventu-
ally emerge. It is enough to ensure that we no longer feel
imprisoned."[9]

"It is incomprehensible that God should exist, and incom-

[8] *Cahiers P. de Chardin,* Vol. II, p. 48. "One thing is certain," he
says elsewhere, "without this Being which is as marvelous as it is
incomparable, there is no possible way out, no possible emergence.
Without him we are imprisoned."

[9] *The Future of Man* (New York: Harper & Row, 1964), p. 210.

prehensible that he should not" exclaims Pascal. But Pascal wants to arouse disquiet in us so that we will go and throw ourselves at the foot of the Cross in an act of faith and love. Teilhard reveals to us, in a universe in perpetual evolution, the living God of the cosmogenesis, the God without whom there would be no other perspective for mankind and for the individual than total death. But this is not a choice dictated by despair. There are so many signs, as soon as we get out of the "current" science, so many "traces" of God appear to us, that we cannot but believe. It would be absurd that, the world having evolved toward Thought, Thought would not be able to emerge from all-destructive time into a Time that is eternal; it would be absurd that it should have taken this decisive step without this Presence toward which it is ascending. Teilhard therefore rejects Pascal's wager. This wager bothers him:

"To determine man's choice, in his famous wager, Pascal loaded the dice with the lure of boundless gain. Here, when one of the alternatives is weighted with logic and, in a sense, by the promise of a whole world, how can we still speak of a simple game of chance? Have we the right to hesitate?"[10]

But Pascal did not weigh the dice, and his logic is remarkably more coherent than that which we are examining, strengthened by "promises" which can be read in the universe —promises which so many other scientists do not see in it! The wager, though it only plays a limited role in an apologetics aimed at pursuing the unbeliever to his last entrenchments, is nonetheless stated with extreme rigor. Its purpose is to shake these "libertines"—and there are many of them—who do not want to lose the substance for the shadow and who, well anchored in existence, will exchange it only for something certain—and for a greater "gain." Pascal then resorts to the calculus of probabilities; he shows that even if there were only

[10] *The Phenomenon of Man* (New York: Harper & Row, 1959), p. 232.

one chance in favor of a future life, it would win over all the others—which may be innumerable but are still finite in number—by virtue of the beatitude it promises. As soon as this future life appears possible, the mirage of the ephemeral happiness offered by this life is dispelled, and we cannot understand how we could have been satisfied with it, how we could have been taken in by the senseless agitation of "amusements." Of what importance is this time that is flowing by and hurling us toward nothingness as compared with this eternity in which we would set foot? Impressed, having lost his proud assurance, the unbeliever will now be prepared to listen to other proofs; he will now be ready to receive the truth.[11] The God he is about to discover, this God whose negation makes the world unintelligible, the one to whom we are led by the spirit of geometry, "the God whom our reason discovers and our faith senses . . . this God we know as we know the first principles of geometry and who is above the principles and not against them."

But we need a God who is closer to us, "a God the heart can sense." Pascal had himself experienced that the distant God, the God of geometric reason was not enough for him when he was first converted. A void has appeared in the heart of man, an emptiness which nothing can fill; it is in vain that one would throw all the riches of this world in it, the heart would remain unsatisfied. We will therefore have to look away from the universe "whose center is everywhere, and whose circumference is nowhere" and discover the living God we were

[11] This is what Pascal's brother-in-law, Etienne Périer, has pointed out: "He begins with a picture of man in which he forgets nothing of that which would make it possible to know him inside out, up to the most intimate movements of his heart, and makes him wonder at the amazing contrasts in his nature." (Etienne Périer's account of the conversation during which Pascal explained the positive aspect of his apologetics; cf. also the conversation with de Saci.)

seeking, who is more intimate, more interior than we are to ourselves:

"To those who do not have religion out of a sentiment of the heart, we can give it only by means of reasoning, until God (who is the source of the ultimate initiative as well as the first call) gives it to him out of a sentiment of the heart, failing which faith is only unhuman and useless toward salvation."

What a vigorous and yet delicate account of the ties uniting intellection and faith! Let thought always remember the proofs that convinced it of the existence of God, let the consenting will orient toward this essential truth all the powers of the soul, let it bend the "machine" so that this instrument that is too often led astray by imagination now becomes docile, and the illumination will come someday revealing a loving God to an ecstatic creature. No one has ever equalled this remarkable psychology of the *Pensées*.[12]

Though he is the God of the "heart," the God of Teilhard de Chardin is first of all the God of a creation of the world, of a "cosmogenesis." The question therefore will be to make the "God of evolution"—for whom "to create" is to make converge, to *unite*—coincide with the Christian God, the loving God; the first one is immersed in the world, while the second is transcendent to the world and "sensible to the heart." This is clearly expressed—but can it really be done?—in a letter which Teilhard wrote a year before his death:

"If it is true (and it seems to me indisputable) that we are no longer in a cosmic régime but in one of cosmogenesis, then the Christian God must necessarily be a God of cosmogenesis, i.e. a God of evolution.

"From another angle, if we admit (and experience, I maintain, proves it) that cosmogenesis is essentially a 'noogenesis' (we know this from study of the phenomenon of Man), then

---

[12] Pascal's final word remains: "*Ne evacuetur crux Christi.* Act in such a way as not to make the cross of Christ useless."

255

there is only one way in which the God of evolution can animate evolution to the very end (which, by definition he must be able to do): he must be (and so appear to *reflective* consciousness) super-personal, which means supremely loving and lovable. And so we come back to the Christian God."[13]

We can understand the hesitations of Blondel when he was confronted with this confusion between immanence and transcendence by a mind that was unquestionably generous but showed very little regard for coherence in the very handling of ideas. For a real conjurer's trick would be necessary to go from the God of evolution, from the God operating in the heart of matter, to the Christian God, to the superpersonal God. God himself must emerge at the end of times, at the ultimate point of a Union that differentiates. What does this mean, save that he must be projected into the Ultrahuman, after owing his actualization as superpersonal God to a slow genesis. Teilhard will reproach his opponents with clinging to obsolete concepts, with still thinking in terms of a stable world, contained in space and traversed by time, instead of the four-dimensional cosmos that expands and centers upon itself in a movement of incessant convergence. He will even say that Blondel does not possess "the cosmic sense, even less the sense of a universe in state of cosmogenesis."[14] Even Valensin will be accused of remaining imprisoned in a static concept of the cosmos.

Above all Teilhard will therefore try to fix the starting

---

[13] Letter dated January 28, 1954, as quoted in Claude Cuénot, *Teilhard de Chardin: A Biographical Study* (Baltimore: Helicon, 1965), p. 369.

[14] Blondel was familiar only with the formulas used by Teilhard in one of his very first essays, *La Vie cosmique* (1916): "God is vibrating in the ether; God is working in life. God can be seen through man and personifies in man. . . ." His thought certainly became clearer from 1916 to 1954, but the ambiguity remains.

point and the point of arrival of this huge drift of the cosmos, divided between two conflicting concerns. This attempt is in itself quite legitimate, since he is merely taking up again, in a different perspective, the similar attempt by Saint Augustine. The author of the *City of God*, whose concept of the universe was still static, had pointed out the starting point and the end point of a creative act revealing itself to us through more and more accelerated periods (cf. in this connection his original and actual interpretation of the Genesis):[15] God first creates an inanimate matter in which the "vibrations" of time can be imperceptibly felt; he then prepares the setting for the heavenly Jerusalem, the peaceful City he will organize and govern; the angels and the saints are there already, awaiting the elect; but it is only at the end of time that its definitive structure will be revealed. Only then will time—which will regulate, with different rhythms, the movements and the pulsations of all creatures until thought partially dominates and controls them—be inscribed in the original act which, from the very beginning, contains it.[16] For Teilhard also, Evolution oscillates between a point Alpha and a point Omega. We must admit that it was only when he opposed his converging and uniting evolution to Bergson's diverging and fragmentary evolution that he was explicit about the point Alpha;[17] he was much more willing to speak about the ultimate point—Omega —in which everything is fulfilled, differentiated in Union and transnaturalized.

In a "memoir" he addressed to Maurice Blondel, he tries to define this point Ω at the crossroads of the drift of time and the Being beyond time, tangential between the evolutive and

[15] Cf. the appendix to our study: "M. Blondel et saint Augustin," in *Etudes Augustiniennes*, January-March, 1965.

[16] Cf. our *Saint Augustin: temps et histoire* (Paris: Editions Augustiennes).

[17] Cf. Chapter 8.

257

the fixed, between the personal and the suprapersonal:

"If, for the sake of simplicity, we call O the natural term of human and cosmic progress and Ω the supernatural term (plenitude of Christ) of the Kingdom of God, there are three possible relations between O and Ω:

1. O and Ω are disparate terms.
2. O and Ω are antagonistic terms.
3. O and Ω are hierarchical terms."

Teilhard believes that the first solution is lame, that the second is ambiguous since it minimizes the role of man and the value of his work; he therefore chooses the third: The gap between the point O of natural natural evolution, of human progress constantly enlarging the noosphere, and the point Ω of the transfiguration is ever getting smaller. And a supreme effort can therefore fill it.[18]

But this option involves some serious difficulties. In this connection, Blondel's warning is very important. Teilhard does not seem to have taken any notice of it.

"Charity," Blondel wrote to him, "does not live on human passions; supernaturalization, if one thinks of what divine incommensurability entails, cannot be easily achieved. As much as I dislike Jansenism, I mistrust all devout humanism, all Christian scientism. It is just as forbidden to supernaturalize the natural as to naturalize the supernatural, if only in the manner one states and uses it."

In this text—as in many others—Blondel is indicating the narrow path Christian philosophy must follow: We must avoid with equal care the pitfall of Jansenism and that of Molinism; we must not be too severe on man and condemn him without reserve. This would amount to handing him over to the ruthless tutelage of the Grand Inquisitor and to the boundless authority of the state. But it is also important not

---

[18] The prepared insertion of Christ will fill this gap.

to set one's trust in him alone, considering him capable, through the sole enrichment of his mind and his progressive "socialization," to transnaturalize a universe he has raised to a new Order. The gap between the Orders must be respected and we should remain fully aware of what man is unable to do without the help of God.

One must read with great care the two memoirs which Blondel wrote in reply to Teilhard de Chardin's ideas which had been communicated to him by his loyal disciple A. Valensin.[19] He certainly approved of Teilhard's intention of extending the majesty of Christ to the confines of the cosmos, an intention that could claim to originate in the teachings of Saint Paul and of Saint John. We are too much inclined to restrict Christ to that place in space and that moment in time in which he became incarnate in order to redeem us. The historical Christ invites us to consider him present whenever we get together, wherever we are suffering, wherever we are loving; does it follow that we must make him descend to the level of matter to see him rise with the universe and through it, with Mankind and through it, to the point Omega where his mission would be fully revealed? Is there not a danger in this conception which we must avoid at all costs?

"The danger we must avoid," wrote Blondel, "is pantheism. Christ does not play in creation the role which pantheism attributes to the Soul of the world. Christ is not the Form of the multiple world. It is in the Logos that the world is created, is still being created; it is in Christ, Alpha and Omega, that creation receives beginning and end, existence and fulfillment. But the function of Christ is to carry creation to its supernatural fulfillment: the divinization of human nature, the adoption of the sons of man, an adoption which is possible only if man is willing to be reborn and become a new creature. It is

[19] These Memoirs were published in 1961 in the *Archives de philosophie*.

259

therefore not in a physical sense that Christ is the origin of creation and its Head; it is in a sense that is infinitely real and realistic, but supernatural.

"The greatest danger of all is to assume, without even observing it, that natural order enjoys a divine stability because it is a natural order, that Christ plays physically the role which pantheism or monism assign to the vague and diffuse God with which they are satisfied."

And Blondel concluded:

"A purely physical supernaturalism does not make sense. True pantheism must be carefully cleansed of all physical and pantheistic elements."

Did Teilhard head this warning that was issued with such great restraint—for Blondel always wanted to remain understanding and kind—though it is categorical in its content? He was already too busy trying to find a mediator between the God of the cosmogenesis and the superpersonal God not to proceed recklessly and see in Christ the culmination of a progressively transfigured universe. And thus he develops a grandiose vision, a poem to the glory of the world and of Man, which has never yet been equaled in this century. The wind of prophecy is inspiring the Announcer of universal redemption; before him, as before the followers of the Graal, the sacred vessel lights up with the double mystery of the Trinity and of the Eucharist. First there is the God of evolution, present in each point, each instant of a world in incessant creative transformation until, from its very beginning oriented toward the Spirit, it receives a new impulse from the Spirit. This God is omnipresent, we find him at the beginning of the genesis, in the middle of all that which exists, and at the final point of convergence where all the axes of spiritual energy will come to end, drained and channeled by human labor.

"The God we are trying to grasp with the tentative efforts of our lives, this God is as spread out and tangible as an atmosphere in which we are immersed. He envelops us from all sides like the world itself."

It is true that Teilhard uses symbols which would be difficult to reconcile with one another: A rigorous logic would soon prove them to be conflicting. But he is less concerned with coherence than with effectiveness. These symbols correspond to a frame of mind that is very common today. He wants to make palpable, tangible this God who is omniscient, omnipresent but whom Evolution conceals from us. It is within himself, according to Saint Augustine, that man finds God, a God who has withdrawn to the inner corners of his inner being only in order to compel him to search for him: he does not evade this confident search; he reassures those who question him: "You would not be searching for me if you had not already found me."

But today man is turned more outward than inward: He runs the risk of getting lost in the universe if he is not shown that if it were left to itself the energy animating this universe would disintegrate. We must therefore endow this world which man wants to conquer with a fifth dimension, a spiritual dimension. It is in the heart of the universe as well as along its boundary, all along the spiral along which it unfolds and concentrates, that we must teach the unbeliever to look for the infinite Being, "a Being which, by the omnipotence of its word, is capable of mastering and molding any matter that would be born."

Anxious to solve the preoccupations of his time, to be consonant with it, to espouse even the will to power that is animating it, Teilhard de Chardin will very soon see no divergence between the two directions in which man can set out: toward the world in order to master it, toward his soul in order to discover the presence of God in it; or more precisely, he will invite us to follow two courses of action which, for him, far from drifting apart will soon coincide, to follow two routes

261

simultaneously: one which turns us outward, toward the vast universe we are entitled to master, the other leading us to our soul, which we will discover to be surrounded by a Supersoul at the very moment we unfold the envelope of the noosphere around the universe. Merely by increasing our control over the universe, we will carry ever further this zone of spirituality which changes the appearance of the galaxies imprisoned in Space-Time. Simply by meeting beyond all areas that were hitherto explored, the cosmonauts will overcome their differences and enrich our societies. This coincidence of goals with divergent starting points will become for Teilhard an act of faith. More and more he will progress with his eyes fixed on this ultimate point toward which all Evolution is geared, the point Omega. In this respect, far from heeding Blondel's friendly warnings, he will lose sight of all hierarchies; he will eliminate the intermediary stages or remember only the final supernaturalization of the universe. In 1918, he distinguished, as we have seen, between two levels which he called O, the term of human progress, and Ω, the term of the transnaturalization of the universe. In *Mon Univers* he tells us that "O is subordinate to Omega, so that natural human effort and grace concur, *each one for its essential part*, to the development of the (human) spirit, which continues to develop in its natural substance, while at the same time God is raising it to the supernatural order." The world therefore is no longer only "a place of exercise (or of trial), it is a task to be performed."

Henceforth, the point O, the term of human progress, and Omega, the ultimate term of cosmic Evolution which has been oriented and indefinitely extended by this progress, are no longer hierarchical. They coincide, they blend as though, having reached its supersaturation point, the spiritual opened up like a flower, revealing the transnatural within. Everything is then set for the final culmination. Beatrice appears to Dante when, stage by stage, he has gone through the last circles of

Purgatory. The cosmic Christ appears when man has climbed the last rungs of his ascent toward the Ultrahuman. It is the Omega point which, in a sense, collects all the riches originally contained in the cosmos, which were then displayed in the initial stages of the cosmogenesis and later recentered, united, mixed, and, by this mixing, reoriented and recreated, while the arrow of human progress shoots upward.

We will quote only two texts; the first is from *Ce que je vois*:

"By this name 'point Omega' I have for a long time denoted and I still mean now an ultimate and self-contained pole of consciousness, sufficiently blended with the world to be able to collect in itself, by union, the cosmic elements that have reached the extreme limit of their centration, by a technical arrangement (?)—and capable yet, in view of its supraevolutive (that is, transcendent) nature, of avoiding the fatal regression that threatens (by structure) any construction in Space-Time stuff."

The point Omega is therefore defined: human progress reaches it by its own movement, sweeping the whole cosmos along in its wake as 'soon as this cosmos emerges from the more and more centered curves of the evolutive process; then the Space-Time stuff, the structure of the universe, comes to light, completely folded in upon itself, like these Byzantine mosaics in which the whole starry sky converges toward the gigantic figure of the Pantocrator.

A later text is even more explicit:[20]

"If we extrapolate in the future" (we will not dwell upon the hypothetical, even mythical, element in an extrapolation which exceeds by far what would be allowed by science at its most daring), "the technico-mental convergence of Humanity toward itself imposes (?) the forecasting of a paroxysm of co-reflection at some finite distance ahead of us in Time: a

[20] In a summary in *Perspectives phénoménologiques du monde* (1959).

263

paroxysm which cannot be better (or even otherwise) described than as a critical point of Ultra-reflection. We of course cannot imagine such a phenomenon (which apparently implies an evasion from Space and Time). However, certain precise energetic conditions which must be satisfied by this foreseen event (increasing activation in Man, as it gets closer, of the "taste for evolution" and the "will to live") compel us to think that it coincides with our final access to the Irreversible (since the perspective of a total death would immediately interrupt, out of despair, the process of humanization)."[21]

Thus the two roads will meet at the Omega point: that which the caravan of mankind is unwaveringly following in its drive forward, and that which opens upward little by little in the Space-Time Stuff transformed into a noosphere. To express this convergence and this fusion at infinity, Teilhard de Chardin sometimes used perilous formulas:

"The only God we can now adore 'in spirit and in truth' is, in a phrase that appeals to me, the synthesis of the (Christian) God of 'above,' with the (Marxist) God of 'ahead.' "[22]

One might say that we have deliberately chosen a text containing "debatable" expressions, since a Marxist would be very surprised to hear that he believes in a God "ahead," whereas for him God is but the illusion created by a supreme "alienation"! But the expression "in a phrase that appeals to me" (comme j'aime à le dire) would suffice to show that Teilhard often used this formula which, to say the very least, is not very clear. Besides, who would deny that it reveals a turn of his mind? Do we not see him enumerating the recent discoveries

[21] Teilhard has not forgotten what was revealed to him in the trenches, during the long nights he was watching a dead world (cf. La Grande Monade).

[22] As quoted in Cuénot, Teilhard de Chardin: A Biographical Study, p. 369.

of our technologies with enthusiasm and almost with fervor, viewing them as instances of a spiritualization of the real? The conquest of space, the discovery of new sources of energy —oil, uranium—the invention of cyclotrons in which matter is transmuted, the improvement of our living conditions, Teilhard delights in this enumeration of the remarkable achievements which prove that man is really the arrow that carries along the cosmos in its flight. Let us therefore go forward, resolutely and without fear, now that we have been freed from our ancestral fears, we who are no longer frightened by "the silence of infinite space," now that we sense and even know that in the end the Christian God of above, the transcendent God, the God of the Bible and of Islam, will be revealed to us.

What will we find "forward" at each one of the stages that bring us closer to Omega? Not the isolated, solitary man which was Nietzsche's idea of the fulfilled man but something which is beyond the present man, the Ultra-human, whose structures are already taking shape within us. We know that *The Dawn* and *Joyful Wisdom* were among the books Teilhard owned. He was no doubt also familiar with the Zarathustra poem. But that he should have preferred *The Dawn* and the gayest aphorisms of *Joyful Wisdom* is in no way surprising; *The Dawn* still contains a hope which the announcement of "Eternal Recurrence" has not yet killed. The desert of nihilism has been crossed and the horizon is illuminated by a marvelous dawn. A new world is unfolding before us in which all adventures are possible. Thus in Nietzsche, Teilhard did not hesitate to see one of his precursors; he approved of his breaking away from the static conception of a cosmos that would be stationary forever, for seeing that man is an unfinished being, for saying that this being under gestation must be "surpassed." He also approved of his reversing perspectives and subjecting the present—not to the past—but to the future, thus inventing a new science: *Prospective*, which he was himself to use so much.

But after throwing the door wide open to the future, Nietzsche shuts it again. He models his Superman on the past; he borrows his features from the heroes of Greece and from the Renaissance; perhaps even unknown to himself, he is inspired by the angelic vision of the Middle Ages, the process of personalization being confused with that of individuation. Each Superman is a closed universe, a great monad developing according to its own law. The adventurer of the future is like Columbus, who ventured on the tormented seas to discover new earthly horizons. Besides, how could Nietzsche have foreseen, in 1878, the dimensions which science and technology were to confer upon the universe, the gigantic mixing of the cosmogenesis and of the biogenesis? Moreover, his unwillingness to recognize the value of mutual help, of collaboration in the midst of a team,[23] and—through an increasing broadening —at the level of a united Mankind leads him to confuse the two divergent processes of individuation and personalization. For the person develops only through the multiplication of interrelations, by the intensification of communications.[24]

Quite different is the Ultra-human in which blossoms, at the superior stage of co-reflection, a more genuine freedom, a richer and more efficient thought. We are indeed witnessing here the appearance of a new type. Mankind emerges, molded by its own techniques at the end of the unifying convergence. The Ultra-human already existed besides in germ form in the heart of a reality which, by centering and diversifying, was to create man. The Humanity that will arise from an accelerated complexification from which consciousness will benefit will be socialized to the extreme. Everything will be ready for it to receive its ultimate animation from Christ; through Him,

[23] Cf. the play by Charles Morgan: *The Flashing Stream.*
[24] Cf. Emmanuel Mounier's *Manifest personnaliste.*

266

the Ultra-human will open up onto a perfect community. Here again, we are reminded of Dante's dream of a universal monarchy whose harmonious ordering would reproduce a community of minds. But for Dante there is still a hiatus between these two levels which grace alone can fill. Teilhard de Chardin, on the contrary, envisions this ultimate society as similar to Campanella's *City of the Sun:* It gathers and embraces the whole of mankind enveloped in the sparkling cloak of the noosphere that is following it in its peregrinations. United in a single block, this Mankind is transformed, by a sudden mutation, into this City of God announced by the prophets. Inserted in the context of evolution, the ancient message now takes on its full significance. But no destruction, no cataclysm will precede this advent.[25] The radiant apparition will arise in societies that have been extended through the collaboration of all their members.

In 1947, Teilhard heard a talk by Louis Lavelle at the Catholic Center of French Intellectuals. The theme of this conference: "What use is the world?" was bound to interest him. But for Louis Lavelle, the world is an obstacle rather than an adjuvant. Our finiteness is inscribed in it and it makes us aware of our dependence, so that we then turn to our soul. This is how the trial can be fruitful, but our true home is beyond; spiritual life can be born and develop within us only if we separate ourselves from exterior realities, preparing thus our awakening in this world of being which the screen of time is now concealing from us. This thesis, with its essentially Socratic and Platonic inspiration, could not meet with Teilhard's approval. He saw in it that which he most emphatically rejected: the affirmation that our present life is a "time of trial," of "exercise," as he used to say. The distinction between the two levels of being and becoming, because it affected evo-

[25] According to most texts. Sometimes however Teilhard forecasts an ultimate crisis.

lution with a negative coefficient, could not satisfy him either. It is true that he admitted that one slope of being is not touched by evolution since it already possesses its perfect Unity: This is where we find the God of the Bible, the God of the ancient cosmos. But, for us who toil on the other slope, being must be accomplished; it has, so to speak, been entrusted to us to be carried to its highest degree of unification. To be is to be united; to create is to unite. Beyond, through a supercreation, Christ will step in to superanimate and transfigure a creation in which we will have taken part.

If this is the case, how can we consider our life in this cosmos as a period of trial, as a passage, a painful pilgrimage, when through our efforts something is being achieved, something is being realized? How can we reduce the cosmos itself to simple representations, to the veil of Maya unfolded over a consciousness it is deceiving, when this world gives us, through its original *consistency* and *solidity*, a fulcrum without which our efforts would be in vain? Thus, after the talk, Teilhard will comment: "One cannot help finding in Lavelle a lack of interest in the world, which is considered too much of a means, in spite of the great breadth of view of his explanation."[26]

Once more he saw this idealistic orientation common to all university teaching and which he could not tolerate even in his friend Edouard Le Roy.

Unlike the idealistic philosophers, too eager to abandon this world and the arduous task it sets upon us, Teilhard was convinced that it provides the only authentic reality; it is up to us to give it its spiritual dimension, to surround it with the effluvia of thought and offer it, after a long and courageous effort which will have deeply transformed it, to the divine intervention that will then transfigure it. Therefore he often

[26] As quoted in Cuénot, *Teilhard de Chardin: A Biographical Study,* p. 254.

used the expression of which Nietzsche was so fond: *the sense of the earth*. It is true that he did not claim, like André Gide, that we could be satisfied with the *nourritures terrestres* and drift from pleasure to pleasure like prodigal sons. The earth contains a mystical ferment, the very one which Alyosha Karamazov and the Elder Tikhon considered as the instrument of our salvation. They found new strength in bending over this earth from which they were born, by adhering to it to give it a human face. The bread of the earth is already rich in spirituality. But this food which is sanctified by a hidden presence, it is together that we must eat it. In all Teilhard's writings on the subject of socialization, there always lingers the memory of the Last Supper. Humanity must gather around the Table; when its union will be perfect, when each one of us will see the other as his brother, then Christ will appear as he appeared to break the bread with the disciples of Emmaus.

Here is a text which Claude Cuénot is right to consider as decisive: "An important consequence of the unifying process which mankind is undergoing at the present time is that each one of us taken individually is less and less capable of being materially self-sufficient. We are constantly experiencing a series of new needs, which it would be childish and antibiological to consider as superfluous and artificial. We can no longer live and develop without an ever increasing ration of rubber, minerals, oil, electricity and countless sources of energy. No individual would now be able to knead his own daily bread. More and more, mankind is becoming an organism endowed with its own physiology and, as we say today, a common 'metabolism.' We may well claim that these ties are superficial, that we will loosen them if we so desire. In the meantime they are getting stronger every day through the combined action of all the forces around us; and History

[27] *L'Atomisme de l'Esprit*, Peking, July 13, 1941.

269

shows that, on the whole, their web which is woven under the influence of irreversible cosmic factors has never ceased to get tighter.

"Around our individual lives, *a general human life* is therefore irresistibly taking shape. Now, this is no mere 'symbiotic' wave ensuring through mutual support the survival or even the individual development of the members of the community. We can already see some 'effects' of this association which are specifically characteristic of collectivity. We do not even notice these effects; and yet there are countless examples all around us. One need only look at an 'airoplane,' or a 'radio,' or a 'Kodak' and think of all that is presupposed by the existence of these objects in the line of physics, chemistry, and mechanics; how many mines, laboratories and factories; how many arms, brains and hands. By its very nature, each one of these machines is, and has to be, the result of countless converging disciplines and techniques which no single workman could master in all their intricacy. The conception and the realization of these familiar objects presupposes nothing less than a reflective or complex organism, acting *per modum unius* (as a single being), as a single entity; it is mankind, not man, who creates them.

"Now this type of solidarity which is so evident in the realm of mechanics is but the tangible manifestation of an even deeper psychological unification. Where is Leibniz today, with his isolated monads? Henceforth, more than ever before, man cannot think alone. We need only look at our modern concepts in the realms of science, philosophy or religion. Is it not obvious that the more general and fruitful each one of these concepts, the more it tends to be a collective entity, a facet of which might well be mastered by an individual, or a fragment developed, but which rests in fact on a vault of buttressed thoughts. The concept of the electron and of the quantum or of the cosmic ray, the concept of the cell and heredity, the concept of mankind or even of God, no one individual can fully master them. And thus, through man and above man, mankind is not only working, it is thinking. It is inconceivable, by the very nature of the phenomenon, that this trend should not continue in the same direction tomorrow as it does today, ever stronger and faster.

"What conclusions can we draw from all this, save that in mankind taken as a whole the amount of activity and consciousness is greater than the sum obtained by simply adding up the individual activity and consciousness? We are faced with a progress in complexity which is expressed by a centric deepening. Not merely a Sum, but a synthesis.[28] Precisely what we would expect if, in the realm of the social, beyond our brains, the foreward motion of the universal 'moleculization' [sic] really takes place (as I claim it does). Before man, one might say that the goal of nature was to produce 'the unit or grain of thought'; in the direction of a 'thought of thoughts,' it definitely seems that, following the laws of some gigantic hyperchemistry, we are now hurled—always higher— in the abyss of the infinitely complex."[29]

We have quoted this text without any omissions not only because it summarizes and condenses the essential ideas of Teilhard de Chardin but most of all because it groups all his claims that are open to criticism; it shows in particular that the hypothesis from which Teilhard started, and which was to become stronger and stronger, is indeed that which Maurice Vernet summarizes so well, namely that "the laws of

[28] These are the arguments put forward by E. Dürkheim in favor of "collective" consciousness. This raising of individual consciousness to the higher level of a consciousness of humanity is the quasi-terminal point of Evolution.

[29] This important text is quoted without any special reservations by Claude Cuénot in his otherwise excellent book on *Teilhard de Chardin* (Paris: Editions du Seuil, 1963).

physics and the physico-chemical processes of transformation of matter apply to all life, including even consciousness."[30] In these pages Teilhard also expresses or assumes all the postulates he claims to be beyond question and which are subjacent to a system whose precariousness is concealed by its breadth:

a) The increasing complexification which goes from particles to molecules is presented to us as *sufficient* to prepare the appearance of life; the crossing of a threshold would ensure its unfolding, at least in its elementary forms.

b) In the same way, at a certain level of life, hominization would occur and consciousness would rise from a more "centered" complexification; after a few unsuccessful attempts, instinct would transform itself on its own accord into intelligence. Pascal, once more, was more perspicacious and saw in "instinct and intelligence" the mark of two different natures.[31]

c) The step from the human to the Ultra-human, which will precede almost immediately the final transfiguration of the world, will be taken in the same way by means of a convergence that would only be more pronounced and more accelerated, the perfecting of techniques being accompanied by a broadening of the noosphere; the spiritualization obtained in this way would gradually reach even the most refractory layers of matter.[32]

d) Finally, the personalization which we are already witnessing would lead to a "socialization" which would arrange and organize all the concurring parts of the social body with

---

[30] Maurice Vernet, *La Grande Illusion de Teilhard de Chardin* (Gedalge, 1964).

[31] So that where experience yields solutions of continuity, it is asserted without hesitation that we must assume the existence of intermediary chains which will be revealed to us someday (unless telluric convulsions have destroyed them).

[32] ". . . from the depths of matter to the highest peak of the spirit there is only one evolution. . . ." *The Future of Man*, p. 23.

a view to the formation of a Mystical or Christic Body. This is how the efforts of matter to organize and center upon itself would lead to the "reflective social."

This daring affirmation exceeds and contradicts all observations to such an extent that one wonders how it could be so readily accepted in so many circles. That which the Church calls "Mystical Body" or "Christic Body" has nothing in common—as Saint Augustine pointed out—with our human societies, and our "communities" are only very poor approximations of it. Some of them are merely "leagues" (*Band* is the German term used by Vierkandt) in which affective or even passional elements come into play, incommensurable with the very high spiritual needs Christ has aroused in us. The Italian social psychologist De Felice has studied this "effervescence" ruled by instincts, by cravings emerging confusedly from "preconsciousness," from these superimposed "underground passages" described by Dostoevski; only a pale glimmer, a vague phosphorescence, succeeds in reaching these abysses. As for the help we give one another, Merleau-Ponty has shown that it should certainly not be underestimated, but it does not rise on its own accord, by its own ascentional movement, to the heights of charity: "This is of a different Order," Pascal would have said.

In any case these small communities based on ties of blood or on affinities capable of creating "friendship" are always fragile and precarious, and a mere conflict of interests is often sufficient to destroy them.

Moreover, these "communities" are absorbed in societies which are getting larger and larger and more and more indifferent to our spiritual needs; what one *has* is more important than what one *is*; justice consists merely of setting the rules of the expedient, of distributing "goods" according to varying criteria, of reconciling ever divergent interests. Human groups are also the prey of antagonistic solicitations; some of them

273

raise these groups to the highest level of true community life accessible; others dissolve them and disintegrate them until they stumble against the resistance of the basic family or social cells from which the edifice will slowly be rebuilt. Thus a canvas woven at the price of a patient effort will come apart if a single thread breaks; the fraying will stop only when it meets a knot. As for "socialization" itself, it is far from automatically leading to an increase in "differences." The division of work has quite the opposite effect. And genius asserts itself only in opposition to this "conformism" required by "social order." Finally, the same conflicts, the same struggle for life which has accompanied the ascent of the species, are continuing in the midst of human societies and even more between nations. Teilhard himself will acknowledge this at times. He sometimes sees "milliards of germs and millions of adult growths jostling, shoving, and devouring one another, fight for elbow room and for the best and largest living space."[33]

If this is the case, we must admit that Evolution is not really an evolution and that a call which arises from our soul is constantly struggling against the bitter law of competition; it would be difficult to say that this soul, which has been entrusted to us so that we make it bear fruit, "must in one way or another have grown out of the general mobility of things."[34] Christ, always present not in the heart of matter but in each one of us, comes himself or through the mediation of his saints to lead us back to this humanity whose features might fade away in us and to remind us of our duty to fulfill our "nature."

[33] Quoted by Vernet, *Le Grande Illusion,* p. 29; *The Phenomenon of Man,* p. 109.

[34] In *The Phenomenon of Man* Teilhard also speaks of "the gradual conversion of the 'granule' of matter into the 'granule' of life," p. 82. As for the quotation on the soul, see *The Future of Man,* p. 13.

Conclusion:
Christ and the Cosmic Man

ALMIGHTY AND BELOVED FATHER,
The man who does not possess you, who lives without you and
without piety, does not know where to look for the support and
the purpose of his life. When he has exhausted the resources
of his sensuality—and for some even before this—emptiness is
within and around him, and this emptiness fills him with anguish
and anxiety. He then sees you as the only force that can fill this
void within him. He then tries to know you as his constant Creator. Then he knows you as his beloved father, and, little by little,
thanks to this quality of always growing which characterized all
knowledge of you, he feels that through the essence of his soul
he is getting ever closer to and partaking in your divine essence.
And thus he feels rising within him a boundless source of joy.
He is then born to the infinite plenitude of the joy and the immortal security you grant to him. His own present has become
your glory, and for him there is no hour that is not to your ever
greater glory. Your substance has become his living soil and the
only homeland of his destiny.

Alphonse de Chateaubriant[1]

*W*hen the process of socialization will be completed, when
this creation which will be Union has reached its term, then,
like the flower unfolding its petals to the fecundating pollen,
the circles of mankind will open up to make way for Christ
and then, lovingly, will close up around him. To find as rich
a Christology as that of Teilhard, we must go back as far as
Joachim of Fiore, Saint Bonaventure or Dante:

> In fashion then as of a snow-white rose
>   Displayed itself to me the saintly host,
>   Whom Christ in his own blood had made his bride,

[1] Cahiers: Le Bouquet de ma joie.

275

But the other host, that flying sees and sings
    The glory of Him who doth enamour it,
    And the goodness that created it so noble,

Even as a swarm of bees, that sinks in flowers
    One moment, and the next returns again
    To where its labour is to sweetness turned,

Sinks into the great flower, that is adorned
    With leaves so many, and thence reascended
    To where its love abideth evermore.

Their faces had they all of living flame,
    And wings of gold, and all the rest so white
    No snow unto that limit doth attain.[2]

When he rises to Christ, the burning heart of this mystical bouquet, in whom matter incessantly blossoms forth, Teilhard is lavish in his epithets. For Christ is not only present in a place of space, in a point to time, present in his flesh, Savior and Redeemer, he is not only the One who spoke to Peter and the Apostles, who struck Paul down on the road to Damascus, and spoke in the Gospels and the Epistles, he is also the Christ of Evolution, the divine mediator between his Father and men; as a superior soul, he is the "cosmic" Christ, the physical Focus of creation, he burns and glows in the heart of matter, he really—not only symbolically—supports the universe, raising all that exists to his own level; he is Christ "the Evolver," the ferment, the germ of life present in all beings, however humble; he is the supreme instigator of the cosmogenesis.

"In fact, the keystone which must be built already lies in our hands. There is no better way of performing the synthesis which our generation is awaiting between faith in God and faith in the world than to extract dogmatically, in the person of Christ, the cosmic face and function which set him up,

[2] Dante, *Paradiso*, Canto XXXI, translation by Longfellow.

organically, as the driving and guiding principle, as the 'soul' of Evolution."[3]

In his concern for man, whom he raises above animality, to whom he confers his dignity as a person, he is the "humanizing" Christ of whom Vico said that he alone can restore to humanity the world of the nations. The Principle of all existence, he is also the Supreme End, the Realizer of all the aspirations he has aroused, appearing at the point of convergence of the final anthropogenesis, where the Human is replaced by the Ultra-human; finally he is the Christ-Omega, the Universal Christ, since he binds all things together and makes them converge, since he is at the top of a cosmogenesis that is transformed little by little into a biogenesis, then into a noogenesis, the focus—virtual at first, and then gradually actualized—of "personalizing personality." We must not be afraid, in using such epithets, that we will "make the human reality of Jesus vanish in the 'superhuman,'[4] volatilize in the cosmic. . . . For the more we ponder on the basic laws of Evolution, the more we are convinced that the Universal Christ could not appear at the end of time at the apex of the world if he had not previously inserted himself in it *on the way*[5] through his birth as an element. If it is really the Christ-Omega who keeps the universe in motion, it is (in theory and historically) from his concrete germ—the Man of Nazareth— that the Christ-Omega derives all his consistency so that we may know him. The two terms are intrinsically interdependent and, in a truly total Christ, they can only change simultaneously."[6]

[3] From *Christianisme et Evolution, Suggestions pour servir à une théologie nouvelle*, Peking, November 11, 1945.

[4] To our knowledge Teilhard used the words "Superman" and "Superhuman" only three or four times.

[5] The italics are ours, for the expression may sound surprising.

[6] From *Christianisme et Evolution*.

The boldness of these formulas may be surprising, especially if we must take them literally, as we are asked to, and not consider them as approximating symbols—which they are since they refer to the essential act of the Incarnation. It was necessary that Christ manifest himself at a moment of history so that man should be led back to humanity, so that he should be saved from the fall to which his selfishness would have condemned him: "*bestione*," hardly different from the beast.[7] But this appearance had been prepared for a long time; long before the sublime Christmas when Christ appeared as the carpenter's son in this world that was to witness the worst of all scandals: the murder of little children. The slightest particle of matter, the most ephemeral creatures, everything, since the beginning of time, was preparing to welcome him. The convergence we read in the centuries preceding his birth was possible only through the convergence of the entire cosmos, preoriented toward him. Thus the historical Christ, far from concealing the cosmic Christ, Christ the Evolver, the Christ-Omega, urges us to discover him, present in the slightest fragment of matter to which he confers its real consistency. For the role of God cannot be restricted to his appearance in time. And his divine Son has saved mankind and the world by his Incarnation and his Redemption only because he was present in this world from the very beginning and because everything gravitates and heads toward his radiant figure. As early as 1925 Teilhard already used expressions which frightened Maurice Blondel:

"Glorious Lord Christ: the divine influence secretly diffused and active in the depth of matter, and the dazzling centre where all the innumerable fibres of the manifold meet; power as implacable as the world and as warm as life; you whose forehead is of the whiteness of snow, whose eyes are of

---

[7] Vico first used this word.

fire, and whose feet are brighter than molten gold; you whose hands imprison the stars; you who are the first and the last, the living and the dead and the risen again; you who gather into your exuberant unity every beauty, every affinity, every energy, every mode of existence; it is you to whom my being cried out with a desire as vast as the universe, 'In truth you are my Lord and my God.' "[8]

So far, the fervor of the prayer covered up all pantheistic undertones, but now there appears an amazing restriction. Teilhard wants to inscribe his prayer in the context of his phenomenology. It is beyond question that "intelligent, loving, active power" was there in the beginning, and it is also beyond doubt that this power will come at the end of time to crown the edifice, as the steeple crowns the church. But, in the meantime, Evolution concentrates upon itself, it complexifies, collects by the intimate fusion of sentiments, then by co-reflexion, that which was already convergent. And the mission is assigned to mankind to perfect the dwelling in which God will come to reside: "You who know why it is impossible that the Creator be born otherwise than carried by the stem of an endless Evolution." But the risk of pantheism is increasing dangerously and the historical Christ is being covered up by Christ the Evolver, by the "humanizing" Christ, while we begin to worry that man will be more anxious to capture the latent energies of the universe in order to satisfy his ambition than to abandon himself to God in a movement of trust and love. It is true that the hymn is so beautiful it reminds one of a Bach chorale. But is it now bringing us back to the starting point of an inadequate phenomenology? Its author was able to find reassuring stability and consistency only in the roughest and most opaque metal; then, experiencing demands of another order, so that that the granite should become translu-

---

[8] *Hymn of the Universe* (New York: Harper & Row, 1961), p. 34.

cent, he had introduced Evolution in the heart of all things, ordered matter with a view to life, oriented living beings toward the cosmic man. Under the new impulse of Reflection, nature opens up like a shining chalice to receive the supreme power; it becomes the flesh and blood of the Savior. And without being annihilated in the hearth of a mystical fusion, which is setting them all ablaze, making "even matter glow in them," the now diaphanous individual consciousnesses gather around a Super-person in a harmonious choir. It is true that this is the theme of the "Mystical Body" as presented by Saint John and Saint Paul. But this ultimate Transfiguration no longer requires the appearance of a New Earth and the destruction of our all too human Cities. It is in the midst of this world, set at its highest value, that the divine influx is acting; work is not only sanctified, it becomes the instrument of this trans-naturalization, endowed thus with quasi-unlimited powers. And God is really the burning heart that sets all that exists ablaze with its fire; Christ, the animating element leading the world to its fulfillment:

"The mystical Christ has not yet completed his growth, and therefore neither has the cosmic Christ. Each one of them both is and becomes; and the ultimate spring of all created activity lies in the extension of this engagement. Christ is the term of the Evolution of all beings, even if it be only their natural evolution." (Cf. *Hymn of the Universe*; in particular the *Hymn to Matter*.)

Far from becoming more subdued, Teilhard will state his position more emphatically as time goes on. Soon he will abandon all reserve and give priority to Christ the Evolver without realizing that he finally becomes a Christ tied up in Evolution, like Aristotle's soul swept along in the movement of the body. We hope we will be forgiven for giving only two quotations from his last work which is, in a sense, his testament and the ultimate expression of his faith: *Le Christique*.

"If the universe were static, no organic integration of the multiple in Christ would be possible. It would be impossible to understand Christic cosmocity. But if the universe is evolving and converging, then how can we not see that there is a unique, a singular position at the top of the temporal-spatial system, of the system of which Christ, without deformation or effort, literally becomes—with an incredible realism—the Pantocrator."[9]

If we really take these expressions to the letter, we would see a Christ engaged in matter, working and toiling with it, suffering in all living beings, becoming conscious of himself in man, perfected at the point of Evolution by human reflection and labor.

"Christ remains," says another text, "the one who bears the sins of the world, the Redeemer History shows to us, but he is also, and even more essentially, the one who structurally overcomes in himself and for us the obstacles to the spiritual which are inherent to matter. He is the one who bears the weight which unavoidably follows the construction of any species, of creation. He is the symbol and the movement of Progress."[10]

I think that in order to understand Teilhard's mysticism, we must evoke his first contacts with Oriental mysticism; the nobleness of this mysticism had struck him from his first arrival in India and in China. Later he will say that India was for a long time the religious pole of the Earth: a real "cyclone" raged on the banks of the Ganges. He reacted very soon however. This Oriental mysticism, far from promoting the advent of a person that is conscious of its difference and of its value, far from heading toward a differentiated Unity, tries to absorb all multiple and living reality in the undiffer-

[9] *Le Christique*, 1955, p. 10.
[10] *Christologie et évolution.*

entiated One,[11] in a Being that coincides with the absolute Non-Being: "Was it not," he wrote to the Abbé Monchanin, who had reproached him with being too sketchy and not taking the diversity of doctrines sufficiently into account, "a Japanese Neo-Buddhist who was telling Grousset that his religion culminated in 'the intoxication of emptiness'?"[12] The Brahman or the Atman—the apparently individual soul—is indeed swallowed up and we are left with total emptiness; the universe has been reduced to a weave of appearances and finally dissolves with the illusion of the "I." All action becomes impossible in this universal annihilation. Occidental mysticism is quite different; it is a mysticism of action, of creative unification, and of the "forward" movement of all individual

[11] In this work *Teilhard de Chardin: A Biographical Study* (Baltimore: Helicon, 1965), Claude Cuénot gives a transcription of the notes he took during a talk by Teilhard in the beginning of 1933, the theme of which was precisely: "Orient and Occident; Mystical Views on Personality," pp. 140–141.

[12] As quoted in Cuénot, *Teilhard de Chardin: A Biographical Study*, p. 142. The Abbé Monchanin, who led a life of contemplation and prayer in India, in the Diocese of Trichinopoly, pointed out, among other things, the opposition between the monism of Shankara and currents of pluralistic tendency, such as that of the "jnana-yoga," which is an asceticism of knowledge (every being is present as the unreadable number of an undifferentiated Absolute), and of the "karma yoga," which is an asceticism of action. Teilhard, while acknowledging the validity of these comments, answered: "Basically, if the religions of India are less negative than I said, the fact does not essentially affect my thesis, the purpose of which is above all to distinguish the two possible essential types of mysticism. . . . " it is true, he admitted, that these types can nowhere be found in the pure state. He nonetheless claims the right to consider "oriental mysticism as an example, as close as possible, of negativism," and to assert that "the oriental religions and oriental contemplation mean death to action," which is his main objection to them. Letter dated April 29, 1934, as quoted in Cuénot, p. 142.

and collective wills stretched to their breaking point. In 1932 he wrote: "These last few months I have been led to make a sort of sketch of the main ways in which mysticism has attempted to solve the fundamental intellectual and spiritual problem: How explain, and then surmount, the multiple, and arrive at unity?[13] It strikes me that there are two theoretical solutions (both of them attempted): the oriental (that we arrive at unity by dissipating—through evasion or suppression —the illusion of the multiple) and the occidental—scarcely formulated yet, I should say—(that we arrive at unity through the effort of extending, in their proper direction, the potentialities—*convergent by nature*—of the multiple). Mysticism of detachment from things, or mysticism of passage via things? I think (it is my whole life) that present-day Christianity is tending *towards the latter*, in which the salvation of humanity consists."[14]

Note the confession: "It is my whole life." During his whole life indeed, Teilhard experienced the intoxication of "action"; research too, research in the field, in the mineral world as well as in the world of long-vanished animals, is action. It is probably this "intoxication" that led Teilhard to seek the opinion and the advice of Blondel, who was then given the title of "philosopher of action"—which many considered to be no compliment. But action, for Blondel, was an ascent toward light; in turn enlightened and shedding light, enriched at each new exertion by all the contributions of individual experiences and collective life, it gradually binds us completely, though not without an incessant reflection, but it finally turns out to be completely ineffective; we have to

[13] In the line of neo-Platonism, Teilhard identifies Evil and the Multiple.

[14] *La Route de l'Ouest vers une mystique nouvelle*, Penang, September 8, 1932. Cf. Cuénot, *Teilhard de Chardin: A Biographical Study*, p. 141.

283

admit that we cannot, by our own efforts, reach the goal toward which it was aiming more and more manifestly. Because of its finiteness it could not sense the vivifying presence of the Being in which it was initially inscribed and therefore had to progress step by step, aspiring to a plenitude of which it is incapable. Most of all, it never would have occurred to Blondel that the action of the technician is of the same value as this interior action through which we seek to accomplish ourselves. Now Teilhard eliminates all interval; in every act he sees the presence of God:

"To begin with," he wrote in *The Divine Milieu*, "in action I cleave to the creative power of God; I co-incide with it; I become not only its instrument but its living prolongation. And since there is nothing more personal in a being than its will, I merge myself, in a sense, through my heart, with the very heart of God. This contact is continuous because I am always acting; and at the same time, since I can never find a limit to the perfection of my fidelity or the fervour of my intention, it enables me to assimilate myself still more narrowly, and indefinitely, to God."[15]

Who cannot see that the emphasis here is not even on the will, but on "the will to power," since every chance of using and increasing this will brings man closer to God? Let us become gods and we will be assimilated to God. Thus action is effective when it is efficacious, when it goes in the very directions of this permanent "creative transformation" of Evolution; *The Divine Milieu* is a hymn to the glory of the *homo faber*, for whom the universe will have no more mysteries when his will has penetrated and animated it.

His condemnation of Oriental mysticism would have gained by being formulated with more nuances; the detachment[16] it preaches is an indispensable palliative for us Westerners, who

---

[15] *The Divine Milieu* (New York: Harper & Row, 1960), pp. 31–32.
[16] Teilhard will acknowledge the usefulness of this detachment, though in a completely different sense.

are so intoxicated with the fantasic development of our techniques and forget "the sense of interiority" by throwing ourselves "forward," by scattering our efforts. in a multitude of projects. Once more, Albert Schweitzer will be more clear-sighted when he draws our attention to the imbalance created in us by the exaltation of the will to power; we get lost in the vast universe we are trying to master; it absorbs us and annihilates us like a speck at the very moment we think we have mastered it. Of what importance is this passage which does not even leave behind it the trail of a flying star? Silence closes in behind these space ships in search of impossible living places. The Little Prince was certainly more fortunate, for he could get back to his star after leaving the weight of his dust in the desert. He is now freed forever from his heaviness:

"An excessive amount of labour is the rule to-day in every circle of society, with the result that the labourer's spiritual element cannot possibly thrive. This overwork hits him indirectly even in his childhood, for his parents, caught in the inexorable toils of work, cannot devote themselves to his upbringing as they should. Thus his development is robbed of something which can never be made good, and later in life, when he himself is the slave of over-long hours, he feels more and more the need for external distractions. To spend the time left to him for leisure in self-cultivation, or in serious intercourse with his fellows or with books, requires a mental collectedness and a self-control which he finds very difficult. Complete idleness, forgetfulness, and diversion from his usual activities are a physical necessity. He does not want to think, and seeks not self-improvement, but entertainment, that kind of entertainment moreover, which makes least demand upon his spiritual faculties."[17]

[17] Albert Schweitzer, *The Decay and the Restoration of Civilization* (London: Black, 1947), pp. 18–19.

Cf. also Henri de Lubac, *Affrontements mystiques* (Paris: Editions du Témoignage Chrétien, 1950).

The Westerner confuses action and activity, he turns away from this quest of the spiritual which gives his actions their initial impulse; there occurs a dissociation which installs him in a shallow time, in "operational" time in which he elaborates successive schemes. This time does not offer us any secret passage, but only a "forward" and a "backward" dividing a present that always eludes us. The Fates unwind its skein, which the indifferent hands of one of them rolls up in a useless block. In this time, man assesses value in terms of success or status alone. This is the level Marcel Proust deals with in *Remembrance of Things Past.* As for collaborations which become closer with the progress of technology, they cannot promote understanding and love without an intention that would change their "sense." How many friendships which had seemed to be intimate will disintegrate as soon as common trials and suffering are forgotten! The more work is divided, the more it isolates those whose task it predetermines; people live side by side without knowing one another; only resentment can bring people together, and also the smoldering anger stimulated by a uselessly renewed effort.[18] Simone Weil, who took it upon herself to live this experience, describes with great accuracy, in *Gravity and Grace,* all the desolation it might cause if supernatural help does not come to alleviate it. Thus the most humble task raises and exalts us if it is performed in a spirit of humility and charity.[19]

There is, on the contrary, in Oriental mysticism a detachment, a renouncement, which may be excessive and based on an overly pessimistic evaluation of existence but which is nonetheless beneficial. If man considers his birth to an individual existence as an affliction, in breaking away from the exacerbated desire which is at its source he becomes sensitive

[18] On this point, see Jean Anouilh, *Pauvre Bitos* and *La Grotte.*

[19] Cf. also Charles Péguy, *L'Argent* and Georges Cattaui, *Péguy, témoin du temporel chrétien* (Editions du Centurion, 1963).

to the universal suffering;[20] he acquires this patience from which all virtues are derived.

It is between these two equally dangerous extremes that we must look for the road to salvation. Christianity is this road. It sanctifies work by reminding us of its true goals:

"The Indian idea of the divine is that it is pure, spiritual essence. It is the ocean into which man, tired of swimming, wishes to sink. The God of the Gospel of Jesus is living, ethical Will, desiring to give to my will a new direction. He says to me: 'Strike out courageously! Do not ask where your efforts will take you on the infinite ocean. It is my will that you should swim.' "[21]

Christ ordered the hesitant and discouraged Peter to go and cast his nets; the incredible manna he pulled out of the lake is the prefiguration of the spiritual manna promised to him when he would become a fisher of men. But who does not see that, in order to be fruitful, action must be accompanied by detachment? When Peter gets impatient and annoyed, Jesus tells him to wait and trust in the inspiration from above. He does not tell him that he will save himself by conquering the world.[22]

Some readers may be surprised that our study is so full of reservations and criticism. Let us make our position clear: We do not deny that Teilhard was an authentic scientist and an outstanding mystic. There are pages in *The Divine Milieu* or

[20] The Holy Father observed this and testified to it after his trip to India.

[21] Albert Schweitzer, *Christianity and the Religions of the World* (London: Allen and Unwin, 1951), pp. 46-47.

[22] "I wonder if today mankind is not really in the process of cleavage between those who believe and those who disbelieve in the future of the universe. And I feel more decidedly than ever that I must line up with the former, for the conquest of the world." Letter by Teilhard de Chardin dated June 4, 1935, quoted in Cuénot, *Teilhard de Chardin: A Biographical Study*, p. 145.

in *Comment je crois* which one cannot read without being deeply moved; this one for instance, on our position with respect to matter, would have met with Louis Lavelle's approval:

"Above all, matter is not just the weight that drags us down, the mire that sucks us in, the bramble that bars our way. In itself, and anterior to our position and our choice, it is simply the slope on which we can go up as well as down, the medium that can uphold just as well as give way, the wind that can overthrow or lift up. Of its nature, and as a result of original sin, it is true that it represents a perpetual aspiration towards failure. But by nature too, and as a result of the Incarnation, it contains the spur or the allurement to be our accomplice towards heightened being, and this counterbalances and even dominates the *fomes peccati*."[23]

In spite of his tendency toward pantheism which he made no secret, most of all in spite of many hasty and ambiguous formulas which could not but give rise to perilous interpretations, Teilhard would not have been open to criticism had he not thought it possible to cross "on the same level" the interval separating his scientific conclusions, which were bound to be partial,[24] and his mystical experiences. These

[23] Cf. the sequel to this text, which is also very beautiful: "The full truth of our situation is that, here below, and by virtue of our immersion in the universe, we are each one of us placed within its layers, or on its slopes, at a specific point defined by the present moment in the history of the world, the locality of our birth, and our individual vocation. And *from that starting point*, variously situated at different levels, the task assigned to us is to climb towards the light, passing through, so as to attain God, *a given series of created things* which are not exactly obstacles but rather foot-holds, intermediaries to be made use of, nourishment to be taken, sap to be purified, and elements to be associated with us and borne along with us." *The Divine Milieu* (New York: Harper & Row, 1960), pp. 83–84.

[24] Partial since they do not embrace the sciences of life; cf. M. Vernet, *La Grande Illusion de Teilhard de Chardin* (Gedalge, 1964), and also Alexis Carrel, *Man, the Unknown*.

experiences guide him, and not the knowledge of a world which—as he himself will admit—often frustrates our need for intelligibility. For faith alone, and not science, makes it possible for us to overcome the doubts imposed upon our intelligence by the too obvious reality of evil. The optimism of the Greeks stumbled against the problem of "monsters." How then, in this twentieth century, can we accept without an act of trust and love which science cannot arouse the concentration-camp world of today in which the worst instincts are unleashed: the world of *Dirty Hands* and *State of Sieze?*

Mankind is now threatened with a fall back to animality or, what is even worse, with subordination to a world of machines and robots which would alienate us beyond repair. We are not being pessimistic when we refuse to exclude the possibility of such a fall, of such an enslavement to the apprentice-sorcerer overcome by his own inventions. The Ultra-human, to which we cannot find access on our own, has its antipode in an Infra-human, which is threatening us on all sides. Baudelaire saw two simultaneous postulations in the soul. Analysis of our daydreams reveals them both: an endless staircase descends toward the abyss where we find the unhealthy Unconscious of the underground man;[25] a road becomes narrower and steeper as it climbs to the peaks where the soul rises when its "wing" is restored to it.[26] But in this life we have only artificial wings, built by our techniques with a view to conquest and not to love, and as we rise we are scratched by thorns and stumble on the stones of the road; an exhausting progress which we would have to abandon if we did not get help and assistance. In the beautiful tale by Ibn Sina, the companions of the imprisoned bird come to invite it to look

---

[25] Cf. the liminal poetry of *Chers Esclavages*, of the poet Marcello Fabri, which we have studied in a collective work written as a tribute to him.

[26] This is, as we know, the Pythagorean theme that is taken up once more in Ibn Sina Avicenna's *Tale of the Bird.*

upwards: The above, in spite of what Teilhard may say, does
not coincide with the ahead. It is in vain that we would go forward, in this time of which Alain-Fournier said that it is the
principal cause of our "imprisonments;" we would never meet
God. It is true that this God walks by our side, weary and
sometimes discouraged at our indifference; but, as long as in
our actions we seek only the lucrative and the useful, as long
as we are concerned only with our success in this world, we
will not see him. The love of action which Teilhard admired
in the Western man is not necessarily inserted in being; on
the contrary it often pulls him away from it. No one realized
this better than he did at times: Did he not see in respiration,
in the diastole-systole alternation of detachment and attachment, the very rhythm of our Christian life?

"Thus, in the general rhythm of Christian life, development
and renunciation, attachment and detachment, are not mutually exclusive. On the contrary, they harmonize, like breathing
in and out in the movement of our lungs. They are two phases
of the soul's breath, or two components of the impulse by
which the Christian life uses things as a springboard from
which to transcend them."[27]

But this rhythm, whose first phase would be, according to
Teilhard, to "take possession of the world in order to be"—
the danger being that we may see as an end that which can
in any case be only a means—this rhythm is disturbed by the
very excess of the tensions we must experience. The task of
man was always to overcome these tensions and to harmonize
them. But now he suddenly feels obliged to assume dimensions that are not his: those of the "cosmic man." Teilhard
was not the only one to notice this sudden metamorphosis
which is still only in its initial stages, and we cannot foresee
what biological and psychical transformations it will bring

[27] The Divine Milieu, pp. 73–74.

about. During his solitary meditations in Austria, Alphonse de Chateaubriant also discovered the "cosmic man":

"Everyone feels," he wrote on February 6, 1942, "that yesterday's man has created a universe for which he himself has to be transformed and become something completely different, precisely like this man for whom Nietzsche, with his genial intuition of the future, found the perfect name of 'cosmic man.' Now the cosmic man is the man of all earths, the man of the whole Earth, a man who feels closely related to the air in the sky, the man of intercontinental voyages and of innumerable transmutations, the man of the planet, and not just the man of a little village.

"This cosmic man is certainly the man who is already, in the radiant dawn of the future, taking shape in us, who 'outlines his appearance in us,'—as the vine-growers would say of the bud that is about to emerge through the bark and break forth in leaf—though we are still far from seeing rise in our enlarged frame the luminous consciousness of this planetary man."[28]

These texts—and many others that can be read in this work —allow us to measure the ground that has been covered since the fifteenth century. The Renaissance man, it is true, saw in himself the image of the universe, but a reduced, a shrunken image; he is but a microcosm in which the exact proportions of the Great Body are reflected. The measurements applied to Him were inscribed in a limited and stable world in which Space and Time remained distinct. Only a few innovators— Leonardo da Vinci, Paracelsus, Campanella—scrutinized the future and predicted strange transformations. They saw a man

[28] Alphonse de Chateaubriant goes on—and here again, despite a somewhat different emphasis, we are not far from Teilhard's conclusions—"True Christianity is cosmic; it is even so cosmic as to contain and embrace all cosmisms. By not being cosmic we are not Christian." *Cahiers,* 7th ed. (Paris: Grasset, 1955), p. 209.

291

that was unsatisfied with his planetary isolation. They dreamt of an even more ambitious science which would transform the world instead of inviting us to contemplate it.

The cosmic man of tomorrow will have to enlarge his consciousness to the point of embracing all the vast universe. This universe is no longer present in him in its stationary totality; it travels and expands in a Space-Time continuum in which the speed of light is the only impassable limit. To rise to this immensity, to surpass oneself incessantly so as to be able to live in this unlimited world and dominate it, to adopt its very rhythm and to seek in an elusive "forward" the point of supreme unity, to solve one enigma after the other up to the greatest of all, the enigma he has become to himself, how could he not be overcome by such an effort? It is this whole he must carry in himself to its highest power: his tortured body, his uselessly lucid thought; his imagination, which must orient, in terms of a more and more distant future, a present that has been emancipated from its too heavy past, and especially his will which he must stretch to the utmost so that it can cross without faltering the desert in which anguish and fear are lying in wait for him.

It is true that the images we cast ahead of us are always the same—on the plane of "values": the sage, the hero, the genius, and the saint, on the plane of the "existential" or pseudo-values that mark out our existence: the prestigious leader who combines prophetic or demiurgic intuition with the calm resolve of an inflexible will,[29] and, below him, that man whom Max Scheler calls the "pioneer of civilization"; he too blazes a trail and prepares for the future, while on the lowest rung of the ladder, the art lover knows how to extract from the instant its greatest delights. But these types who lead or

[29] Campanella distinguishes, and rightly so, several kinds of inspiration, ranging from prophetic inspiration that comes from God to that of the Devil, who went so far as to tempt Christ.

encourage us, are they the same as those who earned the admiration of our fathers by their respect for moderation and for the rhythm of numbers.[30] It is in the midst of lack of measure that the man of the cosmos, the man of the "passage," must introduce proportion. One has only to think of the present condition of the saint, compelled to live among men and to be exposed to all temptations instead of being able to withdraw in the serenity of contemplative life!

What temptations, but also what uncertainties! Those which assailed the Curé d'Ambricourt are not the least formidable ones! When confronted with certain calls, certain incitements, we sometimes wonder whether, like the Saint Anthony of Jerome Bosch, we are not progressing the wrong way around and confusing heaven and earth, so that the hell of *No Exit* is above us, in the glare of a vast fire, instead of the apotheosis of twilight. The Superman in whom the will to power stretches to a paroxysm and whom some would want us to imitate, is he not dragging us toward abysses that are illuminated by deceptive lights? Do we not, in our constant drive forward, risk an endless fall, as, in the fresco by Signorelli in the dome of Orvieto, this Francesca da Rimini followed in her fall by her fascinated lover?

True, if this is the case, rather than try to surpass himself by yielding to the spirit of domination that hides his own passions from him, man would have to strive toward his fulfillment; trying to surmount his tensions rather than to surmount himself, he would have to aim at acquiring this new equilibrium which is constantly endangered by his ambition. If he did not succeed he would then be placed before Nietzsche's tragic dilemma:

Alas! my brothers . . . either . . . or.

[30] Cf. Saint Augustine, *D. Musica.*

Either you will follow a dream of false greatness and will
be lost.

Or you will save yourself by recognizing your limits, by
acknowledging that that which surpasses you is not yourself
but the God who is calling you and toward whom you must
confidently go.

Index

295

DATE DUE